Henry Kissinger

HENRY KISSINGER

Perceptions of International Politics

HARVEY STARR

THE UNIVERSITY PRESS OF KENTUCKY

Scholarly publisher for the Commonwealth,
serving Bellarmine College, Berea College, Centre
College of Kentucky, Eastern Kentucky University,
The Filson Club, Georgetown College, Kentucky
Historical Society, Kentucky State University,
Morehead State University, Murray State University,
Northern Kentucky University, Transylvania University,
University of Kentucky, University of Louisville,
and Western Kentucky University.

Editorial and Sales Offices: Lexington, Kentucky 40506-0024

Library of Congress Cataloging in Publication Data

Starr, Harvey.
  Henry Kissinger: perceptions of international politics.

  Includes index.
  1. Kissinger, Henry, 1923–   . 2. United States—
Foreign Relations—1945–   . 3. World politics—
1945–   . I. Title.
E840.8.K58S73 1983   327.73   83-16747
ISBN 0–8131–1500–0

To JOHN V. GILLESPIE
in recognition of
his support for this project

Contents

Contents

Illustrations

Tables

Acknowledgments

A number of acknowledgments must be made to the individuals and institutions without whose support this research would not have been possible. Special thanks and appreciation are owed to John V. Gillespie, whose unflagging interest in this project was instrumental to its pursuit. This book is dedicated to his memory.

The Center for International Policy Studies at Indiana University, under Grant 750-0514 from the Ford Foundation, provided support for this research through a Faculty Research Seed Grant and a Supplementary Research Grant. A number of other typing and reproduction services have also been afforded to me by the center. Additional monetary support was provided by Indiana University through a Summer Faculty Fellowship. I would also like to thank Professor Edward E. Azar, then at the University of North Carolina at Chapel Hill, and now at the University of Maryland, for generously providing events data from the Conflict and Peace Data Bank (COPDAB). The Indiana University Department of Political Science Data Laboratory, under Director Ronald Weber, also provided assistance in data preparation, keypunching, and programming. Finally, in offering me a Leverhulme Fellowship, the Department of Politics of the University of Aberdeen, Scotland, provided me with a congenial setting for drafting major portions of the original manuscript.

I would also like to acknowledge my great debt to Professor Ole R. Holsti, who afforded me invaluable guidance at a number of points during the course of this research. Numerous colleagues at Indiana University and elsewhere provided comments on earlier drafts and presentations, copies of their own papers on various aspects of this work, and encouragement. To begin to name all these people would be to risk omitting some. You all know who you are, and have my heartfelt thanks. In the end, it was the help of William Jerome Crouch, editor of the

University Press of Kentucky, and of a set of anonymous reviewers, that made the final version of this book possible.

Finally, I am grateful to a group of research assistants whose hard work and enthusiasm would be difficult to surpass. They are Constance H. Cole, Margot Meeks, Martin Sampson, Gregory Sanjian, and most especially Paul Hagner. This book is a product of a research process nourished by the above individuals and institutions.

PART I

Henry Kissinger: Biographical and Psychological Study

1

The Study of Henry Kissinger: Why and How

In his Harvard senior thesis, "The Meaning of History," Henry Kissinger observed that, "Everybody is a product of an age, a nation, and environment. But beyond that, he constitutes what is essentially unapproachable by analysis, the form of the form, the creative essence of history, the moral personality."[1] However, the personalities of foreign-policy decision makers are *not* "essentially unapproachable by analysis." Although the decision maker is, indeed, difficult to study, there are ways one can approach understanding the individual and can "gain access" to his personality as revealed in his thoughts, ideas, and beliefs. This book is an application of these approaches to the study of one particular policymaker, Henry Kissinger.

To begin, I use and merge biographical and psychobiographical studies of Henry Kissinger. Through the use of secondary sources, such as the biographies by Marvin and Bernard Kalb, David Landau, Ralph Blumenfeld, Dana Ward, and Bruce Mazlish, a chronology of the important events of Kissinger's life and other psychobiographical traces may be identified. In addition, the large body of Kissinger's professional, pre–public office, academic writings also contains clues to the nature of the subsequent foreign-policy decision maker. These academic works can be studied through the use of an operational code framework that identifies their author's political "belief system." My operational-code analysis also draws heavily from works that were concerned with Kissinger's writings, especially those of Stephen Graubard, Peter Dickson, John Stoessinger, and Mazlish, and the work of Stephen Walker.

My initial goal is not only to set out Kissinger's belief system as delineated by operational-code analysis, but also to examine how the belief system derives from the individual's personality as it was formed in childhood, adolescence, and young manhood.[2] This goal is directly relevant to the first half of the general, integrative theme of this work, which is a description of 1) Henry Kissinger's belief system and 2) a specific aspect of that belief system—his images of opponents. Subsidiary themes addressed in various sections of the book include the developmental background for that belief system, how images of the opponent relate to behavior, and the methodological problems associated with the understanding of these topics.

Just as Kissinger the child/adolescent/young man and Kissinger the academic left "traces" that could be analyzed, so did Kissinger the policymaker. As a policymaker, Kissinger made numerous public statements and performed numerous public acts that could be studied. To identify Kissinger's images of contemporary opponents, I apply formal content analysis (evaluative assertion analysis) to the public statements of Kissinger the foreign-policy decision maker. This analysis focuses as well upon U.S. foreign policy during Kissinger's policy-making tenure, in order to reveal the relationship between his belief system and the nation's eventual foreign policy.

KISSINGER AS SUBJECT: FOREIGN-POLICY ACTOR

Henry Kissinger was the key presidential adviser on foreign policy under two presidents; therefore, a study of Kissinger is necessarily a study of American foreign policy. In this book, the emphasis is upon the Nixon-Kissinger foreign policy as it concerned the triangular or triadic framework of American, Soviet, and Chinese relations. These relations are studied using Kissinger's images of the Soviet Union and the People's Republic of China, as well as events data that describe each state's behavior toward the other two. The Nixon-Kissinger years were dramatic: they encompass the Chinese-American breakthrough and the growing era of U.S. détente with the Soviet Union. The eventual extrication of the U.S. from the trauma of Indochina, U.S. policy in the Middle East after the fourth war within twenty-five years, and the eventual cooling down of détente during the Ford presidency were also based upon policies developed by the Nixon-Kissinger team.

In this era of dramatic American policy (from the "Nixon Doctrine" through the opening with China, to "shuttle diplomacy"), Henry Kissinger was undoubtedly the primary foreign-policy adviser to President Nixon. As Stephen Walker points out, Kissinger emerged as the "star" of the Nixon Administration because of Nixon's strong emphasis on foreign policy and Nixon's own lack of charisma. In contrast to Nixon,

Kissinger was "amenable to popularization and, just as importantly, to humanization."[3]

Henry Kissinger is one of the major foreign-policy phenomena of our times. His background, style of behavior, foreign-policy positions, relationships with Presidents Nixon and Ford, and preeminence in American foreign policy for eight years, have fascinated the man in the street, journalists, and academics alike. In 1972, Kissinger was ranked fourth in the Gallup Poll's "Most Admired Man Index." The next year Kissinger was *first*. Never before had a secretary of state, or any presidential adviser, even made the list—and Kissinger topped it in 1973. In May of that year, 78% of Americans were able to identify Kissinger, a recognition factor matched only by presidents, presidential candidates, and major sports and entertainment figures.[4]

Much commentary has been devoted to the relative influences of Kissinger and Nixon on U.S. foreign policy. From earlier statements, as well as Kissinger's memoirs, it is clear that Nixon and Kissinger both understood the formal hierarchy of authority, and they had similar views of the world and how international relations should be shaped in that world. In 1973, Henry Brandon observed, "But one only needs to examine the prolific writings of the former Harvard professor to realize how much Mr. Nixon's views happened to coincide with Kissinger's and to what extent these two in fact saw the world from a similar vantage point."[5] Albert Eldridge notes in greater detail the intellectual similarities between Nixon and Kissinger:

In fact the "operational codes" of both men were highly congruent. Both men held a classic realpolitik view of the world; both believed that flexibility and opportunity for manuevering were crucial to the successful outcome of American diplomacy; both shared the conviction that centralized authority was a prerequisite for flexibility; both men were critical of *ad hoc* styles of decision making. In Kissinger, Nixon would find an elitist who was distrustful of bureaucracies. It is no wonder their thinking on the reorganization of the NSC coincided.[6]

Along with a similarity of views came the development of Kissinger's central position within the foreign-policy process. In brief, as National Security adviser, Kissinger controlled the apparatus of the National Security Council and its staff. Kissinger became the conduit and the screen for the great bulk of information about foreign policy and foreign-policy alternatives that moved from the bureaucracy upward to the president. The many "bureaucratic politics" battles that occurred in the Nixon administration are vividly described by Kissinger time and again in his memoirs.[7] Kissinger eventually dominated these struggles, as Graham Allison has suggested, through his personal relations with the President and his position within the formal policy-making process.[8] As National Security adviser, Kissinger became chairman of the five major interagency committees that supervised foreign policy: the Washington Special Actions Group (WSAG), which dealt with crises; the Defense Programs Review Committee; the Viet Nam Special Studies Group; the Forty Committee, which supervised covert intelligence operations; and the Verification Panel, which dealt with the SALT negotiations. In addition, Kissinger headed the Senior Review Group, which dealt with all issues sent up by any of the interdepartmental groups created to handle foreign policy.

Kissinger's memoirs make it clear that although Kissinger and Nixon both recognized the hierarchy of power and responsibility between the two men, Kissinger was provided wide latitude in the foreign-policy arena:

> By the end of 1970 I had worked with Nixon for nearly two years; we had talked at length almost every day; we had gone through all crises in closest cooperation. He tended more and more to delegate the tactical management of foreign policy to me. During the first year or so I would submit for Nixon's approval an outline of what I proposed to say to Dobrynin or the North Vietnamese, for instance, before every meeting. He rarely changed it, though he rarely failed to add tough-sounding exhortations. By the end of 1970 Nixon no longer required these memoranda. He would approve the strategy, usually orally; he would almost never intervene in its day-to-day implementation.[9]

Given Kissinger's central role during a dynamic and fascinating era of American foreign policy, it is not surprising that so many pages have been devoted to him. With all of this attention, however, few writers have employed systematic methods for collecting and analyzing data about Henry Kissinger. Fewer still have undertaken studies using quantitative data.[10]

STUDY OF HENRY KISSINGER: WHY

Much of the impetus for this book has stemmed from the desire to make comparisons—between decision makers, eras of American foreign policy, images of America's adversaries, and influences on the making of foreign policy. Many of the comparisons sought are related to more general issues extant in the contemporary study of foreign policy. Others derive from an interest in individuals: What impact can an individual have? Do individuals make a difference? What factors might account for the ways in which individuals make decisions and behave?[11]

The data on Kissinger's perceptions of the Soviet Union permit a number of comparisons with the perceptions of another influential secretary of state, John Foster Dulles. Ole R. Holsti used evaluative assertion analysis to study the manner in which Dulles perceived the Soviet Union. Holsti's research was concerned with how high-level decision makers viewed other states, especially "enemies." His analyses studied the openness of those images, how resistant they were to new information, changes in parts of one's belief system, and similar questions. Modeling the present study after Holsti's makes possible a comparison between Kissinger and Dulles that also allows comparative statements about U.S. foreign policy under different leaderships, in different historical eras.[12] Such statements as, "Kissinger was an improvement on John Foster Dulles,"[13] can also be partially tested in terms of belief systems, openness of image, image of the Soviet Union, and belief system–behavior relationships.

A major issue in the study of foreign policy, and particularly in the comparative study of foreign policy conducted by those scholars who follow the intellectual lead of James N. Rosenau, is the comparative impact, i.e., "the relative potency," of different variables on foreign policy process and output. In his seminal article on "pre-theories" of foreign policy, Rosenau outlines five types of factors that could influence foreign policy: idiosyncratic, role, governmental, societal, and systemic factors.[14] Rosenau further notes that it is up to the comparative study of foreign policy to delineate and to assess the relative potencies of the variables that affect foreign policy. Another issue raised in the literature is the relative impact of idiosyncratic and role influences, since it is clear that both role and idiosyncratic factors influence decision making. Again, research testing the potency of these variables is limited.[15]

The current study is designed not only to provide evidence concerning existing types of idiosyncratic influences, but also to be a partial test of the idiosyncratic–role issue. By comparing Kissinger's operational code to his words and actions while a foreign-policy decision maker, it is possible to assess the influence of his official role upon his previous idiosyncratic orientations. Employing a more rigorous methodology, I also compare the images of the Soviet Union and China that Kissinger held before and after assuming the post of secretary of state, in order to discover what effect, if any, his official change in role had on his perceptions. Similarly, I examine what effect the change in presidents, from Nixon to Ford, had on Kissinger's images. The change in presidents may also be viewed as an informal change of role for Kissinger within the U.S. governmental structure.

Finally, several explicit methodological purposes motivated this project. Because of its earlier influence on substantive issues, Holsti's study of Dulles was used as a model for the Kissinger study. However, because Holsti's work was an important study that employed content analysis, another goal was to replicate as closely as possible Holsti's methodology. This effort permits closer comparison of substantive results and allows at least a partial assessment of the utility (validity and reliability) of evaluative assertion analysis. The concern with content-analysis methodology may be justified on the grounds that it is one of the few methods now available for gaining access to the perceptual, cognitive, and decision-making processes of foreign-policy decision makers.

In his discussion of the comparative study of foreign policy, Pat McGowan rightly points out that, "We have omitted replication as a basic scientific activity. . . . Only through this painstaking process can we build a body of cumulative knowledge in foreign policy studies, yet most of our research is original and unreplicated."[16] The present study permits some assessment of the use of content analysis as a research tool. A full discussion of how this is done, and why Kissinger is a good subject for a replication of Holsti's methods, is given in Part II of this book.

Further methodological concerns of this project include an investigation of the patterns and results that emerge from different sources of public statements (e.g., prepared speeches compared to press conferences). This analysis helps us to see which sources, if any, depart most from the overall patterns and may be the most questionable in terms of the conceptual assumptions necessary for accepting content analysis as a research tool. Similarly, analyses are presented that indicate the impact, if any, that changes in Kissinger's "audience" had on his evaluation of the Soviet Union and China in his public statements. Both analyses are useful for the evaluation of content analysis as a research tool.[17]

STUDY OF HENRY KISSINGER: HOW

In this book, the approach to the study of Henry Kissinger is psychological and cognitive. Its overarching theme is the individual foreign-policy decision maker and his images of the world, and the elements of this approach, evaluative assertion analysis, operational-code analyses, and psychobiographical or psychohistorical analyses, are all psychological approaches to the study of decision making and the individuals involved.[18] As opposed to "unitary actor" approaches (such as Allison's "Rational Actor" Model I), or organizationally oriented approaches (such as Allison's Model II, "Organizational Process"),[19] psychological approaches deal with the individual and how the individual sees or perceives the world. A large, and growing, body of literature has been devoted to the description and analysis of cognitive constraints on "rationality"—concerning the way psychological factors affect how individuals see the world and process incoming information about that world.[20] As Donald Kinder and Janet Weiss have observed, "For a generation, the social science literature on decision making has been divided into two camps: work premised on rational models of choice and work designed to discredit such models," and "there is by now considerable evidence to suggest that people are incapable of carrying out the mental operations required (by the assumptions of the rational models)."[21]

If one wishes to answer the "why" of decision making, to understand which alternatives were seen and which were chosen, then perceptions are crucial. If decision making is considered to be purposeful behavior related to intentions, then one must ask the "in order to" question: that is, as Rudolph Rummel has argued, if one wishes to explain behavior by investigating intentions—to investigate behavior by asking, "X did Z *in order to* achieve W"—then perceptions of the problem, alternatives, and consequences are important, as is the need for approaches to study these perceptions.[22]

Alexander George has summarized eight basic tenets of cognitive psychology that usefully synthesize, from an enormous body of literature, the basic assumptions and dynamics of cognitive studies:[23]

1. The mind can be fruitfully viewed as an information-processing system.

2. In order to function, every individual acquires, during the course of his development, a set of beliefs and personal constructs about the physical and social environment (the belief system). These beliefs provide him with a relatively coherent way of organizing and making sense of what would otherwise be a confusing and overwhelming array of signals and cues picked up from the environment by his senses.

3. These beliefs and constructs necessarily simplify and structure the external world.

4. Much of an individual's behavior is shaped by the particular ways

in which he perceives, evaluates, and interprets incoming information about events in his environment.

5. Information-processing is selective and subject to bias; the individual's existing beliefs and his "attention-set" at any given time are active agents in determining *what he attends to* and *how he evaluates it.*

6. There is considerable variation among individuals in the richness-complexity as well as the validity of their beliefs and constructs regarding any given portion of the environment.

7. While such beliefs can change, what is noteworthy is that they tend to be relatively stable. They are not easily subject to disconfirmation and to change in response to new information that seems to challenge them.

8. Notwithstanding the preceding tenet, individuals are capable of perceiving the utility of discrepant information and adopting an attitude of openmindedness with regard to new information.

As George's summary indicates, there are important cognitive factors involved in belief and action that can and should be studied through psychological techniques. These techniques are based on the assumption that, despite problems of direct access, decision makers leave many "public traces" in their speeches and other public statements, votes, other behavior, and biographical data. These traces can be studied through observation, interviews, questionnaires, biography, simulation, laboratory experiments, and various forms of content analysis.[24] Ole Holsti's review of the diverse theories and methods used in the psychological and cognitive study of decision making is presented in Table 1.[25]

Holsti has also summarized arguments for and against the utility of cognitive approaches. He has identified the conditions and circumstances under which cognitive studies will prove useful.[26] These are conditions under which gaining access to the decision maker and understanding the individual's images of the world will be an important part of explaining individual (and state) foreign-policy behavior. The conditions are:

1. Nonroutine situations that require more than the mere application of standard operating procedures and decision rules.

2. Decisions made at the pinnacle of the government hierarchy by leaders who are relatively free from organizational and other (role) constraints.

3. Long-range policy planning, a task that involves considerable uncertainty, and in which conceptions of "what is," "what is important," "what is likely," "what is desirable," and "what is related to what" are likely to be at the core of the political process.

4. A highly ambiguous situation that is open to a variety of interpretations.

5. Unanticipated events in which initial reactions are likely to reflect cognitive "sets.'

6. Circumstances in which complex cognitive tasks may be significantly affected by the stresses that impinge on high-level decision makers.

7. Circumstances of information overload in which decision makers are forced to use strategies to cope with the problem.

Note that these conditions, which are not exhaustive, reflect both whether individuals count and whether the characteristics of individuals make a difference. Individual factors, such as belief systems (and the cognitive approaches to their study), will be important where there is a lack of constraint on the individual (role, historical, or organizational constraint), and where ambiguity forces the individual to fall back on his or her images of the world. This last point (illustrated by condition 6) supports the view that cognitive influences can be seen as intervening variables between the decision maker and the decision maker's environment (and thus the decision maker's response to that environment).[27]

Much attention has also been devoted to one major form of intervention or mediation, "screening." This activity is implicitly presented in condition 7. The George study cited earlier treats the process of screening at great length, noting the different ways in which information can be screened. Individuals are continually faced with a vast, ongoing wave of incoming stimuli, both "signals" and "noise." Psychological screens are used to handle this overload—to throw out, ignore, file, or change incoming information that is let through. Decision makers, especially high-level foreign-policy decision makers, are constantly under conditions of information overload, and thus need both psychological and organizational screening mechanisms, which cut down on incoming information and permit action on at least some issues. (But the "real world" will also be distorted in some way. This distortion is not limited to what afflicts psychotics, but will also happen in "normal" individuals trying to decide and act.) Therefore, it is argued that the study of belief systems, as screens, is useful for understanding the choices and actions of decision makers in general, including those in the foreign-policy arena.[28]

This view of the relevance of cognitive studies is also a response to several of the critiques of psychological or cognitive approaches to the study of foreign policy.[29] These critiques begin by arguing for theoretical and analytic parsimony in research: they claim that more of the variance

Table 1. Some "cognitive process" approaches to decision making

Decision Maker as	Stage of Decision Making	Theoretical Literature	Illustrative Constructs and Concepts
Believer	Sources of belief system	Political socialization	First independent political success
		Personality & politics	Mind Set
	Content of belief system	Political philosophy	Image
			Operational code
		Ideology	World view
			Decisional premises
	Structure of belief system	Cognitive psychology	Cognitive balance/ congruity
			Cognitive complexity
			Cognitive rigidity/ dogmatism
			Cognitive "maps"/style
Perceiver	Identification of a problem	Psychology of perception	Definition of situation
			Perception/misperception
		Cognitive psychology	Cognitive "set"
			Selective perception
			Focus on attention
			Stereotyping
Information Processor	Obtain information	Cognitive consistency theories	Search capacity
			Selective exposure
	Production of solutions	Theories of attitude change	Psycho-logic
			Tolerance of ambiguity
	Evaluation of solutions	Information theory	
		Communication theory	Strategies for coping with discrepant information (various)
			Information overload
			Information processing capacity
			Satisficing/maximizing
			Tolerance of inconsistency

Table 1.   Continued

Decision Maker as	Stage of Decision Making	Theoretical Literature	Illustrative Constructs and Concepts
Decision Maker/ Strategist	Selection of a strategy	Game theory	Utility
			Risk taking
		Decision theory	Decision rules
		Deterrence theory	Manipulation of images
			Ends-means links
			Bounded rationality
Learner	Subsequent learning and revisions (post-decision)	Learning theory	Feedback
		Cognitive dissonance theory	"Lessons of history"

Source: Adapted from Ole R. Holsti, "Foreign Policy Decision Makers Viewed Psychologically: 'Cognitive Process' Approaches," in James N. Rosenau ed., *In Search of Global Patterns* (New York: Free Press, 1976), p. 131.

in foreign policy can be explained at other levels of analysis, such as the international system, or the domestic setting, where capabilities and ideology can be used to explain behavior. These levels of analysis reflect the assumption that either the individual is not important, or individual differences do not matter. In the same vein, a bureaucratic politics critique argues that the organizational context contrains the individual, as does the political give-and-take of "governmental politics," and thus it is more important to explain the constraining context.

These critiques argue that other factors can better explain behavior, and that cognitive approaches must do better in linking beliefs and images to behavior. Research like that reported in this book, or Holsti's work on Dulles, or Robert Jervis's wide-ranging analysis of international relations, attempts to develop such links. Jervis presents the cognitive analyst's position:

Perceptions of the world and other actors diverge from reality in patterns that we can detect and for reasons that we can understand. We can find both misperceptions that are common to diverse kinds of people and important differences in perceptions that can be explained without delving too deeply into individuals' psyches. This knowledge can be used not only to explain specific decisions but also to account for patterns of interaction and to improve our general understanding of international relations.[30]

The present work on Henry Kissinger draws heavily upon the assumptions and reasoning presented by Jervis and by Alexander George. In many ways, a cognitive and psychological approach is fitting for an analysis of Kissinger.[31] While Kissinger often insisted that it was foolish to try to understand him using psychological techniques, he himself has always used them. His U.S. Army career introduced him to psychological warfare activities, which he pursued for a number of years. Stephen Graubard's analysis of Kissinger's academic works includes a discussion of *A World Restored,* which highlights Kissinger's concern with knowing and understanding how one's opponents perceived an issue or situation: "States, for Kissinger, were real entities. Their leaders were no less real. The question of the quality of political leadership was therefore absolutely crucial for him. It would determine how a problem was perceived and acted on."[32] Stanley Hoffmann similarly comments on Kissinger's emphasis on the study of leaders. Hoffmann's interpretation of Kissinger's academic writings includes the view that "History is not primarily the product of deep, irresistible forces; it is a clash of wills and a stage for leaders who are either the carriers of new principles or the creative defenders of past experience."[33]

For Kissinger, part of Metternich's "genius" was in his handling of negotiations with Napoleon: "He had to know Napoleon's mind. . . . For Napoleon to have acted other than he did . . . would have meant that he had ceased to be Napoleon."[34] In his memoirs, Kissinger returns to psychology and negotiation: "I have always believed that the secret of negotiations is meticulous preparation. The negotiator should know not only the technical side of the subject but its nuances. He must above all have a clear conception of his objectives and the routes to reach them. He must study the psychology and purposes of his opposite number and determine whether and how to reconcile them with his own."[35] In fact, psychohistorian Bruce Mazlish has called Kissinger a "psychiatrist *manque,* a psychological historian."[36]

SUMMARY

A close relationship exists between this study and my own evolving interests in the study of international conflict and the foreign-policy process. Much of my past work in these areas has been "macro-analytic," concerned with broad patterns of behavior across states and over time.

In terms of the concepts I have used elsewhere, these past works related to the "opportunities" that decision makers' environments have presented to them in regard to their foreign-policy behavior.[37] The present work has shifted to a closer investigation of the "willingness" of decision makers to take certain paths offered to them by their environment.

Therefore, the concerns of this book are primarily at the micro- or decision-making level of analysis, and they may be classified as descriptive, correlational, and comparative focuses. To fulfill its descriptive purpose, the text includes the description of Henry Kissinger's belief system, how he sees and orders international relations in general, and his images of the Soviet Union and China in particular. With the descriptive data as a basis, the correlational analysis presents hypotheses concerning the relationships among the different dimensions of Kissinger's perceptions of the USSR and China, relationships between perceptions of the Soviet Union and perceptions of China, and relationships between perceptions and behavior. Similarly, the descriptive material is used to develop propositions that guide comparisons of Kissinger's view of the Soviet Union to his view of China, comparisons of Kissinger's perceptions of the Soviet Union to Dulles's perceptions of the Soviet Union, comparisons of Kissinger's belief system to Kissinger's behavior, and a number of methodological comparisons.

2

A Biographical and Psychohistorical Overview

BIOGRAPHY: TWO APPROACHES[1]

Biographical studies are a traditional approach to understanding public officials as individuals and their policies. The typical biography draws a portrait of the individual through history, chronology, and descriptive detail. Usually, data sources are interviews, material written by the subject (especially private documents, such as letters, secret memos, etc.), secondary material about the subject and his times, chronologies of historical events, including journalistic accounts, and sometimes interviews with the subject himself.

Several biographies and analyses of Kissinger include all of the above. They are very useful in setting out, step by step, the *public* record of policy while Kissinger was in office, and in setting out the known facts about Kissinger's life before he became a high-level decision maker. These works describe more fully just who Kissinger, as the subject, is—including his background, his family data, his education, and significant events in his life. Thus, the chronicles of Henry Kissinger include not only a very straightforward account of his life in the biography by Ralph Blumenfeld et al. (1974), which is based on over four hundred interviews, but also a flattering account by Marvin and Bernard Kalb (1974), and a critical one by David Landau (1974).[2] All three of these biographies arrived in print the same year, after Kissinger's clear public emergence as a major foreign-policy figure (in 1971-72) and after he became secretary of state (in September 1973). Since then, most works on Kissinger have concentrated on his foreign-policy style and decisions, although John Stoessinger's (1976)[3] treatment of Kissinger also contains some biographical material.

The more traditional biographical approach, especially in regard to its picture of the pre–decision-making Kissinger, may also be supplemented by the psychobiographical or psychohistorical approach. In this approach, which uses approximately the same types of data sources, the analyst employs psychoanalytic techniques to draw additional inferences about the personality, psychological make-up, and style of the subject and links these influences to the subject's behavior. A lively debate about the utility of analysis from a distance began with the publication of Alexander and Juliet George's study of Woodrow Wilson (1956)[4] and has accompanied each of the new works of Bruce Mazlish, who has written about Nixon, Kissinger, and Jimmy Carter. Mazlish's work on Kissinger (1976) is the main source for the psychobiographical complement to the biographical approach; Mazlish "interprets" Kissinger's life, style, scholarly writings, and policies from the perspective of Kissinger's personality and the early life experiences that shaped it.[5] A second psychobiographical source is Dana Ward's (1975) lengthy article,[6] which opens with the observation that "it is indeed curious that political scientists have been so hostile to psychohistorians who attempt to incorporate personality into their political analysis."

HENRY KISSINGER: A BIOGRAPHICAL SKETCH

While most of the facts about the significant events in Kissinger's life are clear, what is striking to the reviewer of the biographical accounts of Kissinger is a general cloudiness in the accounts of Kissinger's childhood. Despite many interviews (or perhaps because of them), no clear picture of what Kissinger was like as a youth emerges. In many areas of his life—sports, girls, schoolwork, his relationship to his father and his brother, memories of the Nazi period—contradictory recollections abound. Kissinger's own later statements and his memoirs of the first four years in Washington help only slightly in clarification. What follows here, then, is a review of events and elements in Kissinger's life about which there is relative agreement.

Early Years. Heinz Alfred (or Alfred Heinz according to one account) Kissinger was born in the city of Fuerth, on May 27, 1923, the same year as the "beer hall putsch" in Munich. Kissinger was the first child of Louis and Paula Stern Kissinger. Louis was thirty-five years old and Paula twenty-one when they married the year before. Louis was a teacher, a "studienrat" at the Madchen Lyceum. It has been stressed that Louis, the son of a teacher, held a respected and prestigious position. He has been described as serious, cultured, and refined, and was a rather strict disciplinarian. (Mazlish is alone in noting that he also had a sense of humor.) Paula Stern, who was a former student of her husband, has been described as outgoing and lively, and as having a sense of fun. Louis was very religious (more so than Paula), and the Kissinger children were raised in an Orthodox Jewish environment. All reports note that, as a child, Kissinger was also very religious. (That this religious practice subsequently dropped away is attested to by the number of people who, in his later life, were astounded to learn that Kissinger was raised an Orthodox Jew.) Kissinger's brother, Walter Bernhard, was born a year later, in June 1924.[7] By all accounts, the Kissingers were an average, middle-class family.

This relatively stable picture began to change radically in 1930, when the Nazis came to power in Fuerth, three years before they took over the national government. While Fuerth had a tradition of tolerance to Jews—about 3000 Jews lived in Fuerth, whose population was between 64,000 and 80,000 at this time—it was also just outside Nuremberg, a center of Nazi activism. In 1933, Louis Kissinger was fired from his job, as a result of regulations that prohibited Jews from holding government positions. He then took a much less prestigious job at a Jewish vocational school in Nuremberg. In 1935, the Nuremberg Laws were promulgated. In addition to revoking the German citizenship of Jews, the laws included an order expelling all Jewish children from public schools. Kissinger and his brother were therefore expelled from their own school and sent to an all-Jewish secular school. In 1936, Louis Kissinger once more lost his job. At Paula Kissinger's instigation, arrangement, and insistence, the Kissingers fled Germany in August, 1938. Three months later, on the night of November 9-10, Jewish property was destroyed or seized throughout Germany, and thousands of Jews were arrested during what came to be called "Kristallnacht," after the shattering of glass in shops and synagogues throughout the country. It is reported that twelve of Kissinger's relatives were eventually killed by the Nazis (although Kissinger later referred to the loss of thirteen relatives), and that only seventy of Fuerth's 3000 Jews were counted alive in 1945.

New York City. The Kissingers first fled to London, and then to the Washington Heights section of Manhattan. Paula Kissinger had relatives in both cities and had made the arrangements for their trip. Henry Kissinger arrived in New York at age fifteen, while the United States was still trying to fight its way out of the Depression. Louis Kissinger, then age fifty, found himself in a depressed economy where his academic credentials were of no use to him. He took a low-paid clerical job as a bookkeeper. Again, it was Paula Kissinger who became the driving force in the family. She began modestly as a cook, but soon was in much demand and ran a thriving catering business for special occasions.

Henry Kissinger entered George Washington High School in September 1938, part of a great wave of immigrant students. While Kissinger began a process through which he dropped his Orthodoxy,[8] he couldn't (or didn't want to) drop his accent; he was a loner and reportedly shy.[9] At this point he first gave evidence of academic talent, and was a straight-A student (he was especially good at mathematics). After getting a job at Leopold Ascher Co., a shaving brush factory in Manhattan, he switched to night school. He worked there from 1939 to 1943, advancing to delivery boy. Kissinger's high-school grades were good enough to get him into City College of New York (CCNY), where he first enrolled in June 1941, in the night school. In part because of his skill in math, Kissinger's goal was to become an accountant, and in January 1942 he moved down to the CCNY Business School on 23rd Street. Sometime in 1941 or early 1942, Kissinger met Anneliese ("Ann") Fleischer (who eventually became his wife in 1949). While Kissinger's Americanization was progressing—including Yankee baseball and trips to the Catskills—it wasn't until his service in the army that this process accelerated and took hold.

Army Service. In January 1943, Kissinger received his draft notice, and he was inducted in February at the age of nineteen. He was sent to Camp Croft, South Carolina, for basic training. All sources indicate that, far from being a traumatic experience, this first separation from his family was exhilarating to Kissinger—he was on his own and seeing parts of America and types of Americans that were new and exotic to him. On June 19, 1943, Henry Kissinger became a naturalized United States citizen.

In July, Kissinger went to nearby Clemson College to take IQ and aptitude tests. His high-school and CCNY grades had alerted the army to Kissinger's potential for a special college training program it was developing. Kissinger tested into the Army Special Training Program (ASTP) with 3000 other men. Although the ASTP was basically an engineering program at Lafayette College, Kissinger again demonstrated excellent academic skills and ranked at the top of the program. For a number of reasons, however, the army had second thoughts about the ASTP, cancelled the program, and sent its participants back to combat units. In April 1944, Kissinger was returned to the 84th Infantry Division at Camp Claiborne, Louisiana.

At Claiborne, two events were of particular importance. After his performance in the ASTP, the twenty-year-old Kissinger was selected to give lectures to the troops, analyzing current events. Reactions were similar to those Kissinger received at the ASTP when he led discussions with his classmates, which Blumenfeld discusses: "Kissinger was the brainiest of a very intelligent class . . . but it was not mere academic excellence that impressed the group. Learning was exciting to Kissinger and he was able to communicate the excitement to the others. That phenomenon made him noticeable, almost popular. For the first time in his life, Henry had a distinct identity."[10] At Claiborne, Kissinger got his first real taste of teaching and a continuation of the "identity" that he had developed at Lafayette College.

The second event of import at Claiborne was one that would change Kissinger's life—he met Fritz Kraemer. Kraemer, then in his mid-thirties and only a private himself, had come to camp to address the troops about why the United States was at war with the Nazis, and why they should be fighting. Kraemer, a flamboyant character, was to become Kissinger's first "patron." All biographical sources note the simple beginning to their relationship, Kissinger's note to Kraemer after Kraemer's talk: "This is how it should be done. Can I help you somehow?"

As clearly as Kissinger was impressed with Kraemer, after meeting Kissinger, Kraemer was in turn impressed, intellectually and personally. Kraemer worked to get Kissinger assigned as an interpreter to a general when the 84th arrived in Germany. In 1944, Kissinger reversed his itinerary of six years earlier; his unit left New York for Britain in September, and left Britain for the continent in November. With Kraemer's aid, Kissinger was made a driver-interpreter to General Bolling, and was officially assigned to Army Intelligence (G-2) in November. Kissinger's duties as a G-2 agent expanded, and he was known as "Mr. Henry" during a winter of bitter fighting. In January 1945, the 84th moved to Krefeld, a city of 200,000 in North Rhine-Westphalia.

The city was in a shambles and required an authority that could restore order. As the Kalbs note:

Kissinger got the assignment of replacing chaos with order; Kraemer had sold the local U.S. General on Kissinger's "extraordinary intelligence and unparalleled objectivity" not to mention his fluency in German. "I could only marvel," Kraemer has since recalled, "at the way this twenty-one-year old did the job. In just two or three days the government was once again working, in a splendid fashion. Henry had planned things won-

derfully. This was a prodigy . . . Here this little Kissinger had
set up in three days a working municipal government in a large
city where everything had been run by the Nazis just two days
before."[12]

Again, two major points can be drawn from this experience (and one
later in the year)—Kissinger's ability to organize, administer, and create
order out of chaos, and his "unparalleled objectivity" in dealing with
Germans. As this task was completed, Kissinger was promoted to PFC and
then sergeant. As the 84th moved eastward across Germany, he rejoined
it as a full-fledged CIC (Counter-Intelligence Corps) agent. In this role,
Kissinger became a "Nazi hunter." Blumenfeld et al. recount stories of
Kissinger's physical stamina and courage as a CIC agent, both for the
84th and the 970th CIC. Richard Valeriani, reporting on Secretary of
State Kissinger years later, also notes Kissinger's extraordinary stamina
and fitness, characterizing him as being apparently unaffected by jet lag
and mentally alert when both staff and reporters were burned out.[13]

Kissinger repeated the successes of Krefeld when he was promoted
to run the district of Bergstrasse in Hesse, with his headquarters in the
town of Bensheim, only 100 miles west of Fuerth. Kissinger, now a staff
sergeant, was the military governor, with broad powers, including arrest
without questions. While Kissinger again demonstrated administrative
and governing skills (Kraemer: "Kissinger showed human understanding, self-discipline. Unbelievable impartiality . . ."[14]), he also displayed a flair for living with power. There are reports of his taking
German mistresses (which the army forbade, but was more easily done
by CIC agents, who had to deal intimately with German civilians), and
of his requisitioning a large house and a Mercedes for his own use.

In April 1946, Kissinger was transferred to the European Command
Intelligence School at Oberammergau, where he was to train agents in
how to find and root out Nazis, and where he was to teach a number of
courses. Because he was a course instructor for officers, yet himself only
a sergeant, the army released Kissinger, and then re-hired him as a
civilian, at the handsome salary of $10,000 per year. Kissinger stayed
almost a year, leaving Oberammergau in the spring of 1947. Several
strands of future behavior were evident here. First, it was because Kissinger was such an effective instructor that the army went to the trouble
of retaining him as a civilian.[15] Again, in an army setting, Kissinger
demonstrated talent as a teacher, and he was also linking his instruction
to action-oriented students, linking the world of the teacher to that of

the activist. Finally, Kissinger was effective, and at ease, in instructing men who were older than he, who outranked him, and who had more general experience in the areas of instruction. Finally, although this extra year in Europe strained Kissinger's relationship with Ann Fleischer, who expected him to return to New York after his release from the army, Kissinger did not forgo being well paid to stay in Europe and teach at Oberammergau.[16]

Harvard. Fritz Kraemer is the source of many well-known observations about Kissinger. He urged Kissinger to get a college education, but not at CCNY. The Kalbs' version of Kraemer's famous advice is: "A gentleman does not go to a local New York school."[17] Kissinger then applied to a number of schools, and was accepted at Harvard with a Harvard National Scholarship (which he used along with the G.I. Bill). He entered Harvard in the fall of 1947, at the age of twenty-four. At Harvard, Kissinger reverted to the hardworking, serious loner he had been in high school. He married Ann Fleischer in February 1949; he was twenty-five and she was twenty-three. However, his marriage removed him even more from his classmates and whatever could be called a typical undergraduate career. It has been estimated that Jewish students made up only about fifteen percent of the Harvard enrollment at that time, and married students living off campus, only about one percent. Ann Fleischer Kissinger has been described as reserved, introverted, "gentle and dependent,"[18] But, at this point in Kissinger's life, her support, both personal and financial, helped him to carry on his undergraduate and graduate studies.

Kissinger wrote a brilliant undergraduate record, receiving a $1500 teaching fellowship in 1948 and a Detur Scholarship, and graduating Phi Beta Kappa and Summa Cum Laude. He finished Harvard in three years, graduating with his BA in 1950, but it must be remembered (as many biographers do not), that he entered as a sophomore, using credits from his CCNY days.[19] With scholarships, Kissinger went on to receive his Master's degree in the government department in 1952, and his Ph.D. in 1954.

At Harvard, Kissinger met his second patron, William Yandell Elliott, the man who opened up the world of the intellect to Kissinger. Elliott, another flamboyant activist, was a "power" at Harvard who had been a college football star, a Rhodes scholar, and a successful Washington figure at the Office of War Mobilization during World War II. Elliott, a prominent Cold Warrior, was one of the two centers of Harvard's Government Department, the second central figure being Carl Friedrich.[20]

In the Harvard system of the day, it was difficult for students to get faculty tutors of any kind. Only the very best managed to secure a senior adviser tutor, such as Elliott, "the high priest of Harvard's Government Department."[21] (Kissinger originally began with Friedrich and then switched to Elliott. He was one of the few students who was able to remain on good terms with both men.) Kissinger's undergraduate career was closely tied to Elliott. In 1950, he presented Elliott with a 377-page senior honor thesis, "The Meaning of History: Reflections on Spengler, Toynbee and Kant." Two consequences of that thesis may be noted: Elliott urged Kissinger to continue in graduate school, and Harvard placed a 150-page limit on senior theses.

With Elliott's patronage, Kissinger experienced a unique graduate program—one that connected him to individuals and centers of learning and power throughout the world. The cornerstone of this career was the Harvard International Seminar. Elliott, in charge of the Harvard Summer Programs, developed the idea of a seminar composed of people from overseas, who spent part of a summer at Harvard and learned about the United States from a variety of perspectives.[22] Analysts have said that this seminar was part of Elliott's anti-Communism campaign, being a chance for the future leaders of the world to view America's superior system.

In 1951, Elliott had the Harvard International Seminar established and had Kissinger named its executive director. The seminar was funded by Ford Foundation money, by Rockefeller money (through the Asia Foundation), and by other sources, including a number of CIA fronts. As described in a seminar report, the program was designed, "for persons between the ages of 26 and 45 who are on the verge of reaching positions of leadership in their own countries."[23] These persons included journalists, media people, administrators, educators, and politicians, originally from Western Europe. In 1953, the first Asians took part in the program; Africans were included in 1957, and Latin Americans began taking part in 1959.

The seminar ran from 1952 to 1969, with over six hundred "future leaders" participating. As many have noted, Kissinger created an unprecedented and unmatched set of worldwide contacts through the seminar. He was responsible for selecting the seminar members and bringing them to the United States, and he guided the seminar through the summer's six-week, all-expenses-paid program. Seminar participants included Japan's future minister of trade (Nakasone, in 1953), the future President of France (Giscard d'Estaing, in 1954), a future foreign minister of Israel (Allon, in 1957), a future Belgian prime minister (Tindemans, in 1962), a future Norwegian foreign minister (Frydenlund, in

1968), and a future leader of Britain's Labour Party (Michael Foot, in 1960). The seminar gave Kissinger access to a network of foreign elites and future policymakers. Through Elliott's intervention, Kissinger also was able to establish a network of intellectual contacts. In early 1952, with money from a Rockefeller Brothers Foundation grant, Kissinger founded a journal, *Confluence: An International Forum.* As the journal's editor, Kissinger was able to contact and interact with some of the greatest American and European intellectuals of the day. (*Confluence* ran through the Summer 1958 issue.) As at Oberammergau, with the seminar and the journal, Kissinger was able to deal with and affect people of greater age, experience, and status on an equal basis.

Kissinger flourished in other ways during his graduate-student years. In 1948, while still an undergraduate, he had been appointed a Lieutenant in the U.S. Army Reserve, Military Intelligence (a position he held until 1959, when he resigned). After receiving his BA, he became a consultant, at $100 a day, to the army's Operations Research Office. In 1951, the Army sent Kissinger to South Korea to study the effect of the army's occupation on the Korean population. By the time Kissinger received his MA in 1952, he was a consultant to the Psychological Strategy Board of the Joint Chiefs of Staff, and he regularly traveled to Washington.[24]

Kissinger also worked on his dissertation under Elliott, finishing it in 1954. Published in 1957 under the title *A World Restored: Metternich, Castlereagh, and the Problems of Peace, 1812-1822,* the work was ostensibly about the interaction of the statesman and the international system in a period that Kissinger thought bore important similarities to the one in which he was writing. As many have noted, and as is developed in the next chapter, the dissertation was a highly personal work that presented Kissinger's general view of international relations, taking off from the more general personal statement about man and history that he gave in his senior thesis. The dissertation won a Sumner Prize for distinguished scholarly achievement.

New York and Rockefeller. In 1954, Harvard handed Kissinger his first major career reversal. After earning his Ph.D., Kissinger (and Elliott) had expected that Harvard would offer him a tenure-line assistant professor promotion (from instructor). It did not. However, Kissinger turned down offers from both the University of Chicago and the University of Pennsylvania to stay on as an instructor at Harvard. Instead of going to Chicago, he went to New York and the Council of Foreign Relations.

Kissinger first came to the attention of people on the Council in their search for a new managing editor for *Foreign Affairs*. Although Kissinger did not get the job, he impressed a number of people involved in that search. In 1954, under Gordon Dean, former chairman of the Atomic Energy Commission, the Council set up a discussion group on nuclear weapons and foreign policy. This group was to explore the broad questions of strategic weapons and United States policy, especially toward the Soviet Union. The group needed a rapporteur, and in March 1955 Kissinger formally accepted the Council's offer to act in that capacity. Kissinger's cause had been supported not only by Elliot, but also by McGeorge Bundy and Arthur Schlesinger, Jr.

Kissinger moved to New York, and into the Eastern foreign-policy establishment. Again, Kissinger was involved with a group of high-powered individuals who were far beyond him in rank and experience,[25] and yet who insisted that he write the report he wanted, in the way he wanted, and in turn Kissinger was not shy about lecturing these gentlemen about international relations and foreign policy. The result of the group's meetings was Kissinger's own interpretation of the issues, *Nuclear Weapons and Foreign Policy*, which was published in 1957, won the Woodrow Wilson Prize, and spent fourteen weeks on the best-seller list.

Nuclear Weapons and Foreign Policy made Kissinger a celebrity in academic and policy circles, and also led to the publication of his dissertation later in 1957. One of the book's biggest fans was then Vice-President Richard Nixon. As Mazlish observes, Kissinger's connection with the Council and *Nuclear Weapons* "marked the successful integration of Kissinger's scholarly abilities and political interests, the union of mind and action."[26]

Through his work with the Council, Kissinger was invited to a conference on arms control at Quantico, in December 1955. The conference had been arranged by Nelson Rockefeller, at that time Eisenhower's Special Assistant for International Affairs. Kissinger, already known to David Rockefeller, who was on the Council's study group on nuclear weapons and foreign policy, first met Nelson at this meeting, and caught his attention.

In the spring of 1956, Nelson Rockefeller began the Special Studies Project, a Rockefeller Brothers Fund study of the major problems that would be facing the U.S. domestically and in foreign policy. According to the Kalbs, Rockefeller was impressed by the congruency of Kissinger's views with his own, and asked him to become the director of the Special Studies Project. In the eighteen months of the Project's existence, Kissinger met with and coordinated the work of a large number of prominent Americans, including Chester Bowles, Lucius Clay, John Gardner, Charles Percy, Dean Rusk, and David Sarnoff.[27] But of greater importance than the further expansion of the Kissinger network of prominent connections during this period was Kissinger's becoming a trusted friend to his third and clearly most powerful patron. Kissinger was now firmly connected to the Rockefeller establishment and the Rockefeller money. The final Special Studies Project report was released in January 1958, after Kissinger had returned to Harvard, but Kissinger continued to be an adviser and consultant to Rockefeller.[28]

Harvard and Washington. In the summer of 1957, at the age of thirty-four, Kissinger returned to Harvard. He was now appointed as a lecturer in the government department in a tenure-track position. His promotion to associate professor came in 1959 (he skipped assistant professor), and he was promoted to full professor, with tenure, in 1962.

This was a period of both success and frustration for Kissinger. A new Center for International Affairs had been planned in 1957, and opened in 1958, under the directorship of Robert Bowie. On a suggestion from Bundy, Bowie offered Kissinger the position of associate director. For a number of reasons (depending on whose side of the story one believes), Bowie and Kissinger's relations were, at best, acrimonious. Bowie was not in the mold of a Kissinger patron, and Kissinger was not about to be anyone's "associate" director. Observers agree that this was a major failure in Kissinger's career. However, other areas of Kissinger's life were compensating for the debacle at the Center. In 1958, the U.S. Chamber of Commerce named Kissinger one of America's Ten Outstanding Young Men. Also, Kissinger had become the director of his own enterprise, the Defense Studies Program. As he did in the Harvard Summer Seminars, which he continued to direct, Kissinger used the Program's Defense Policy Seminar to expand his network of connections, in this case by inviting big-name officials from the State and Defense Departments up to Cambridge. During this period Kissinger also became involved in the Pugwash movement and participated in a series of high-powered Harvard-MIT seminars on arms control and nuclear strategy.

It was also at this point that Kissinger's performance in the classrooms of Harvard seemed to improve dramatically (we already have the evidence from the army that Kissinger was an excellent instructor). Biographical sources agree that Kissinger now was "regarded as a first-rate, stimulating teacher,"[29] and that "students would no doubt give him an 'A' as a teacher."[30] Even Landau notes, "Kissinger was a superb teacher, one who was deeply interested in his subject matter and able to impart it in an interesting, often electric manner."[31] On the home front, Kissinger's first child, Elizabeth, was born in March 1959; son David followed in August 1961.

The world of policy making also opened up to Kissinger to a degree far beyond anything previously possible. With John Kennedy's victory in 1960, a flood of academics went from Cambridge to the nation's capital. With the aid of Arthur Schlesinger Jr. and McGeorge Bundy, Kissinger was introduced to Kennedy and was named a consultant to the National Security Council and the Arms Control and Disarmament Agency. He also became a RAND consultant.

From this promising beginning, Kissinger experienced his second major failure since his return to Harvard. Kissinger's advice was ignored, then *he* was ignored, and finally "fired" by Bundy. Kissinger disagreed with much of the Kennedy foreign policy, which he considered too conciliatory and too inconsistent. The Berlin Wall was a major point of disagreement. Intertwined with this disagreement was Kissinger's status as an outsider in Camelot—his style and personality didn't fit with the Kennedy people, making his advice even less likely to be well received. In a theme developed by Mazlish (see the subtitle of his book), Landau notes that Kissinger "was never assimilated by the culture and society that made up America; in taste and style, he would always be distinctly European." Kissinger was "too German," his thinking "was firmly rooted in the European tradition of a sharing of power among the great nation-states," and thus, "he was less arrogantly America-centered than the hard-nosed, pragmatic fix-it men who trampled on America's allies and believed that, by themselves, they could mastermind the world."[32]

Kissinger's final, and crucial, mistake was an attempt to end-run Kennedy's National Security adviser, McGeorge Bundy, in order to present his own ideas to the President. Not only did Bundy prevent Kissinger's gaining access to the President, but Kissinger's failure led to his leaving the National Security Council job in February 1962. He stayed on with ACDA until 1967, and RAND until 1968.

From 1962 to 1965, Kissinger was at Harvard full time, only taking some time off during 1964 to serve as a Rockefeller aide during the Governor's unsuccessful run for the Republican presidential nomination. During this period Kissinger wrote a number of articles and a book, *The Troubled Partnership,* which were critiques of the Kennedy administration's foreign policy, just as *The Necessity for Choice,* published in 1961, was a major critique of the Eisenhower administration.[33]

In the period immediately after he left the National Security Council, the strains on Kissinger's marriage became insupportable. In 1963, Kissinger moved out of his home, and the couple was divorced in the summer of 1964. During Rockefeller's 1964 campaign, Kissinger met Nancy Maginnes (ten years his junior), who was then a volunteer on Rockefeller's convention staff and who later became his wife.

Vietnam: The Introduction. Kissinger's re-entry to Washington came in 1965, when Henry Cabot Lodge was appointed ambassador to South Vietnam. In part through his connection with George Lodge, the ambassador's son, Kissinger was asked to become a consultant to the State Department on Vietnam. Kissinger made his first visit to Vietnam in October 1965. According to the Kalbs, his analysis of the situation received high marks both in Washington and at RAND. It is acknowledged that Kissinger was in no way an Asian expert. He did, however, read extensively on Vietnam before his trip, and he consulted with Paul Mus at Yale. Mus, a Frenchman, had extensive experience in Indochina, and was an expert on Vietnam who had known Ho Chi Minh and other Vietnamese leaders for over twenty years.

Kissinger returned to Vietnam for a second visit in October 1966. In the period June–October 1967, Kissinger played a fairly substantial role as a go-between in the exchange of high-level secret messages between Washington and Hanoi. Although this bargaining effort eventually failed, Kissinger, who spent a good deal of time in Paris, got some direct experience in dealing with the North Vietnamese. The Kalbs note: "According to some on the Washington end . . . Kissinger, for a newcomer to the business, had turned in a surprisingly professional performance."[34]

After this initial exposure to Vietnam, Kissinger spent most of 1968 working on Rockefeller's second presidential campaign. The story of his work with Rockefeller and the process by which President-elect Nixon extended the offer of the position of National Security adviser to Kissinger is well told elsewhere (see the Kalbs or Kissinger's *White House Years*). In late November 1968, with the aid of his third and last patron, Nelson Rockefeller, Kissinger was asked to join the Nixon White House as the president's assistant for National Security affairs. At the age of forty-five, Kissinger had made his way to the upper reaches of the American foreign-policy machine—and was soon to be its undisputed master.[35]

A PSYCHOHISTORICAL OVERVIEW

The general thesis of proponents of a psychohistorical approach is that personality is important in affecting and shaping performance, while not in any sense determining it. James Barber, in his study of presidential character, breaks personality into character, style, and world view.[36] While Kissinger's world view is investigated in the next chapter, the remainder of this chapter is devoted to observations about his character and style, based on a psychohistorical review of his biography. The observations touch on the three different (if overlapping) tasks of "psychodiagnosis" discussed by Fred Greenstein.[37] The tasks are the presentation of a subject's characteristics ("more readily observable traits," and regular patterns of perception and action); the "overall juxtaposition of character traits in the individual," or dynamic analysis of personality traits; and the developmental analysis of the genesis of an individual's adult personality and behavioral patterns.[38]

Greenstein also summarizes the most common criticisms of the psychobiographical approach, along with strategies for offsetting its weaknesses. The five common difficulties with psychobiographies that Greenstein outlines are:

1. They tend to see adult character as immutably fixed by early childhood experience.

2. They are preoccupied with inner conflict arising out of sexuality as a singular source of character formation.

3. They equate character with pathological tendencies and unconscious forces, and in general underplay character-related sources of strength and conscious adaptive capacities.

4. They underplay situational determinants of behavior.

5. They make diagnoses, often on the basis of fragmentary data, without explicating standards of evidence and inference.[39]

Greenstein advises the psychobiographer to be explicit in forming hypotheses and to clearly distinguish between observation and interpretation. Edwin Weinstein et al., in their critique of the Georges' work on Wilson, stress that, "Above all, the psychobiographer should immerse himself in the primary biographical sources, not least of all for the reason that the criteria for clinical evidence may be quite different from those for historical work."[40] Mazlish and Ward have a mixed record in terms of both critiques and correctives, but, in conjunction with the various biographical material they examined and the number of interviews they conducted, a good deal of confidence may be placed in their work.

The Boy, The Father, and the Nazis. While Mazlish and especially Ward discuss the Kissinger family structure and the dynamics of family relationships in general, they both (along with other biographers) focus mainly on the life-disrupting impact of Nazism on the Kissinger household. In fact, all of the major biographies discuss the effects that his father's loss of job and status, the various acts of persecution against Jews, the forced flight from their home and native land, and the ultimate destruction of many relatives and friends had on Kissinger. A general theme in both biographical and psychobiographical analyses is that his early experiences forged Kissinger's basic philosophic belief that the world is constantly on the edge of chaos, that order and chaos are in constant struggle.

Ward's main argument is that Kissinger exhibits a "dysmutual," or depressive, personality. This, Ward argues, accounts for Kissinger's need for love and praise and for the relationship between this need and his insecurity and arrogance. It also accounts for his fascination with risk, which he strives to avoid. Ward notes that scholars have "pointed to the tendency for such individuals to view the world as one in which chaos is the predominant characteristic." Thus, Ward continues, "We must assume that the conditions of Kissinger's early life in Germany are the social root of what will be shown to be a depressive personality."[41] (This analysis of Kissinger is developed in the section on character below.)

Mazlish simply notes that Kissinger drew many lessons from his childhood: "He came to feel deeply the 'tragic' sense of life . . .; he became convinced that 'goodwill' was not enough. . . . The lesson that young Henry drew was that one needed somehow to acquire power."[42] The conclusion that observers draw is that Kissinger's overwhelming concern and passion for order, stability, and balance are derived from his firsthand experience with the tragedy of upheaval and from the desire to prevent it from recurring. Stanley Hoffmann summarizes this argument:

> These experiences have to have an effect. But the lessons one derives are not predictable. I think he came out of it with a kind of burning need for order . . . this whole emphasis on *structures* of peace and world order. People in these experiences have a real memory of chaos, of violence and brutality, like the whole world is collapsing under them. Kissinger's whole search has been to impose a stable world order, a moderate order which would not humiliate anybody.[43]

The evidence supporting this conclusion, derived from the operational code found in Kissinger's academic writings, seems undeniable. Yet, in his early years of celebrity, Kissinger constantly denied that the Nazi experience had any lasting effect on his behavior. He was, in general, averse to discussing his childhood. Blumenfeld et al., Landau,

Mazlish, and Ward all cite the same quote from a November 1971 interview with the *New York Times:* "That part of my childhood was not a key to anything. I was not consciously unhappy. I was not acutely aware of what was going on."[44]

While biographers attempt to find incidents indicating that the effect on Kissinger was greater than he was willing to admit, the post-policy-making Kissinger has readily discussed the effect of that part of his life. Ten days before leaving office, in a speech to the presidents of American Jewish organizations, he admitted, "I have never forgotten that thirteen members of my family died in concentration camps, nor could I ever fail to remember what it was like to live in Nazi Germany as a member of a persecuted minority."[45]

In *White House Years,* Kissinger comes closest to noting the trauma of his youth:

> The principles of America's honor and America's responsibility were not empty phrases to me. I felt them powerfully. I had been born in Germany in the Bavarian town of Fuerth, six months before Hitler's attempted beerhall putsch in Bavaria's capital, Munich. Hitler came to power when I was nine years old. Nuremberg, of which Fuerth was a neighbor with the same physical and psychological relationship as Brooklyn has to New York, was known for its Nazi support, massive Nazi Party rallies, and notorious racial laws. Until I emigrated to America, my family and I endured progressive ostracism and discrimination. My father lost the teaching job for which he had worked all his life; the friends of my parents' youth shunned them. I was forced to attend a segregated school. Every walk in the street turned into an adventure, for my German contemporaries were free to beat up Jewish children without interference by the police. . . . Unlike most of my contemporaries I had experienced the fragility of the fabric of modern society. I had seen the likely outcome of the dissolution of all social bonds, and the undermining of all basic values in extremism, despair, and brutality.[46]

An earlier interview response, presented by Mazlish, begins to uncover the dynamics and major effects of the Nazi experience:

> I think the deepest impact it (the rise of National Socialism) made on me was that twice, once in 1933 when the Nazis came to power, then in 1938 [sic] when I came to the United States,

all the things that had seemed secure and stable collapsed and many of the people that one had considered the steady examples suddenly were thrown into enormous turmoil themselves and into fantastic insecurities.[47]

The "steady example" who was central to Kissinger was his father. Blumenfeld et al. quote Fritz Kraemer: "Imagine what it means when your father, who is your authority, the father you admire, is suddenly transformed into a frightened little mouse."[48]

Both Mazlish and Ward come to the conclusion that the Nazi experience led Kissinger to his search for strong individuals. The experience of watching his father's life come apart, without a struggle, is seen as leading directly to the men that Kissinger would later see as "heroes," and the men that Kissinger would choose as patrons. While experiencing Americanization in the army, Kissinger also met Kraemer, who would provide him with "a new model . . ., emancipating him from his bourgeois Jewish parents and community."[49] While Kissinger's father was shy and was perceived as weak, Kraemer was arrogant and exuded strength and power. After this analysis, Mazlish notes that observers have seen Kissinger's own mixture of shyness and arrogance.[50]

Kraemer set the mold for Kissinger's subsequent patrons, who were all strong individuals who would not simply accept the world. Ward points out the similarities between Kraemer and Elliott—that they were both men of action, and both preached action. In addition, they were elitists, aristocrats who lived in past worlds.[51] Kraemer served as a link between Kissinger's old world and his new one—a "German Oasis" as Ward terms it. Elliott, as Kissinger's Harvard mentor, introduced him to the world of ideas linked to action. And, in Rockefeller, "we see a man whose personal style is a toned down version of Kraemer and Elliott but whose intellectual maxims fall into the same sort of willingness to confront the forces of history."[52] Mazlish points out that Kissinger's patrons fit a basic mold: "Renaissance types, men of seigneurial presence." In Rockefeller, Kissinger found his final and "quintessential patron: a renaissance man who was also a Prince."[53]

From Kissinger's experience as a child who watched his father's world crumble, there developed the image of the patron, which generalized into an image of the hero. Kissinger's heroes of the modern age included De Gaulle and Chou En-lai, who were men of action, "who have faced adversity and won—men who have stood alone and passed the test."[54] From the hero there developed an even more generalized picture of the "statesman" (discussed in the next chapter), and Kissinger's operational-code beliefs on the place of the individual in history and on optimism and pessimism. Men of action, of daring and vision, could stand against history, and stand alone if need be. Kissinger's eulogy of Nelson Rockefeller, given at Rockefeller's funeral on February 2, 1979, exemplifies this view: "One had to work with Nelson Rockefeller to sense his dauntless strength, his pragmatic genius, his unquenchable optimism. Obstacles were to be overcome; problems were opportunities. He could never imagine that a wrong could not be righted or that an honorable aspiration was beyond reach."[55]

The Army and "Success." The abrupt termination of childhood in Germany by a traumatic exodus contains clues to aspects of Kissinger's character. Having fled Germany at age fifteen, he arrived in the United States needing to relearn social mores that one could usually expect to take for granted. Ward discussed Kissinger's "prolonged adolescence" due to this disruption in his life. Even in high school, Kissinger did not have the opportunity to begin to mold his own style.

James David Barber observes that an individual's character has its main development in childhood. (This is argued in Kissinger's case under the discussion of character.) Barber further notes that world view is shaped in adolescence (as is discussed above and is developed further in the next chapter). Finally, style has its main development in early adulthood. Borrowing from Erik Erikson, Barber argues that, in early adulthood, an individual moves into "responsible action" for the first time, and must develop a style to handle this process:

> In most biographical accounts this period stands out in stark clarity—the time of emergence, the time the young man found himself. I call it his first independent political success. It was then he moved beyond the detailed guidance of the family; then his self-esteem was dramatically boosted; then he came forth as a person to be reckoned with by other people. The *way* he did that is profoundly important to him. Typically he grasps that style and hangs onto it.[56]

In Kissinger's biography, his experience in the army clearly stands out as a young man's "first independent political success." Accounts tell of his exhilaration upon leaving his family and upon seeing new and exotic parts of the United States. It was also here that he gained confidence in his intellectual abilities, in his ability to teach others, to take command of a situation, and most important, to take chaos and turn it into order. This latter was not just an intellectual exercise, but an exercise in policy in the real world. As is developed in the next chapter, this experience profoundly affected Kissinger's operational-code views of the activist and optimism, his instrumental beliefs about tackling the world, and his philosophic beliefs about what the world looks like. As Mazlish observes, "The army had given Kissinger his first recognition as someone special. . . . He did well in the fusion of his intellectual abilities and the military needs, a theme to be encountered throughout the rest of his life."[57]

Observers have commented on the varied experiences Kissinger had in the army and their effects on him. Ward notes that, in the army, Kissinger became an "actor" rather than "an object of history"; as a result of his positions as agent and administrator, he was able to prove his worth to himself and to others.[58] While the influence of the ASTP experience and of the teaching experience at the camps before he left for Europe cannot be underestimated, we must focus on the "activist" roles Kissinger filled in Germany. Garry Wills states that these experiences marked Kissinger deeply, that at Krefeld and Bergstrasse Kissinger learned about power and how to use it.[59] Writing about another aspect of Kissinger's career, Albert Eldridge focuses on one of the major lessons that Kissinger learned in Germany—that " 'authority' gives the individual some self-assurance, a sense of self-confidence, and an inward security."[60]

Like Kissinger's view of his father and his subsequent development of a concept of the patron/hero, Kissinger's army experiences reinforced his admiration of the activist and his view that the right individual at the right time could grasp the situation and affect the events of history. This view was extended to his notion of the statesman. Thus, his activist experiences in the army reinforced his view that one could be optimistic, that actions could count, and finally, that actions could count if the individual could marry intellect and action. The individual had to understand history and its forces in order to recognize the opportunities of history when they appeared, and in order to know how best to take advantage of those opportunities. He also had to be willing to act, to grasp the moment when it presented itself.

Style: The Opponent, The Negotiator, and the Educator. Three specific aspects of Henry Kissinger's "style" as policymaker may be reviewed in light of Kissinger's biography and the psychobiographical analysis of that biography.[61] From his childhood and the events of his adolescence come Kissinger's overriding concern about chaos, his passion for order and structure, and his willingness to constrain behavior and to act within accepted limits. These concerns are directly related to Kissinger's rejection of his father and his search for patrons (later developing into the intellectual concept of the statesman). These biographical factors are also related to an important aspect of style—personal relations. They are important in understanding how Kissinger relates to, and deals with, superiors, subordinates, and opponents.

Both Mazlish and Ward (Mazlish to a greater extent) discuss Kissinger's use of projection in relationships of dependence. His denial of the father role-model led Kissinger to patrons on whom he became extremely dependent. Kissinger's abusive and condescending treatment of subordinates—graduate students, secretaries, and his first wife, Ann—are legendary. His behavior is seen by Ward as pure projection: Kissinger's aversion to powerlessness and dependence. Mazlish notes that Kissinger, "whose career was so dependent on patrons, could not tolerate emotionally those who were dependent on him. . . . Thus, his dislike of dependency in others mirrored his feelings about himself."[62]

Lloyd Etheredge, in a study of American foreign-policy decision makers, developed a typology of individual "orientations" to the international political system. Using individuals from the 1898-1968 period (and thus not including Kissinger in the original analysis), he developed four categories based on High and Low Dominance and Introversion and Extroversion.[63] The High Dominance category is related to reshaping the immediate environment and is especially drawn from dominance over subordinates. In a personal communication, Etheredge confirmed that Kissinger would be classified under High Dominance. Kissinger's dominance is certainly widely recorded, from observations of the working press to those who actually had to endure it. Valeriani notes that Kissinger "was not a great man to many who worked under him; he was an administrative terror who bullied and abused his staff."[64] In a January 1977 interview, one State Department official said that Kissinger was "utterly contemptuous of subordinates." The same official noted that Kissinger was the "perfect German bureaucrat," a demon to subordinates but obsequious to Nixon.[65]

This picture of a "bully" (a description commonly applied to Kissinger) fits with Ward's analysis of Kissinger as a dysmutual personality, characterized by insecurity and arrogance, and also coincidentally, with what Etheredge has called the "narcissistic personality disorder politician."[66] Any such analysis, however, must return to the concept of projection as a defense mechanism against dependence. Kissinger, who was developing operational-code images about the hero-activist who could control his destiny, could not also admit to the role and effect that continued dependency had in his own, successful, career. Kissinger projected his negative feelings about his own dependency on his patrons onto those who would become, or try to become, dependent on him.

Kissinger's search for strong figures also took the form of the "strong opponent."[67] Rather than being unwilling to deal with a strong, and therefore possibly threatening, opponent, Kissinger was fascinated by and learned to deal with such a person. Mazlish comes to the same conclusion from a different perspective: He includes much discussion of Kissinger's "identification with the aggressor" as his way of dealing with the Nazi experience—"By empathy and identification, Kissinger was able to forgive as well as to forget the past."[68] The strong opponent concept describes another defense mechanism against the past, and it may also account for much of Kissinger's "Germanness" and lack of Jewishness. Biographers often recount the astonishment with which Washington observers in the early seventies (after Kissinger achieved celebrity) reacted to the fact of Kissinger's Orthodox Jewish upbringing. Only the Teutonic flavor of Kissinger had come through. Much of this same identification with the opponent or aggressor had been displayed at Krefeld and Bergstrasse, with Kissinger's remarkably effective administration, conducted objectively and apparently without rancor (as noted by Kraemer). Discussing this performance, Mazlish notes: "His behavior at this point forms the first thread of a pattern that persists in all of his diplomatic action. He was able to enter into the other person's view, in a sense to identify himself with his opponent, and thus to seek accommodation rather than pursue animosities."[69]

This is extraordinarily important for understanding Kissinger's negotiating style and techniques, and his success in negotiation in general, and with opponents in particular. Kissinger's life experiences created the framework for a desire to meet and to deal with the opponent, especially the strong opponent. It led Kissinger to a mechanism by which he wanted to understand and to identify with the opponent, in part to avoid the discomfort of recognizing how powerless opponents had made his father, his family, and himself during his childhood, and in part to help avoid the expression of the rage that this powerlessness must have engendered. As is developed later in our discussion of negotiation, this identification with the opponent may also be a means of protecting others from the pain of powerlessness and of mitigating the process of conflict that brings about such pain. Here, Kissinger's biography gives clues to his style and personality traits that are vital to his later performance as a decision maker and negotiator. Especially important is the fact that these traits moved Kissinger away from the classic defense-mechanism response of "the image of the enemy" discussed earlier. This made him a very different person from John Foster Dulles, for example (see chapter 6).[70]

Kissinger's negotiating style reflects his identification and empathy with the opponent, and although some observers have characterized his style as somehow dishonest or highly manipulative, it must be seen in light of this identification and empathy. One State Department official described the style as "conspiratorial"—Kissinger would give his negotiating partner the feeling that it was them against the world. Kissinger would convey that he understood the opponent's position and that it was not that much different from his own, and thus together they could somehow outwit the other parties. In an insightful observation, the official described it as a process of "cooptation." Mazlish presents a similar analysis: "He [Kissinger] appears also to have the remarkable capacity of giving the hearer the impression that they share a common view, and that both Kissinger and his interlocutor are smarter and more intelligent than the 'others.' "[71]

How is this achieved? In broad strokes, Mazlish says: "Kissinger's unique genius in persuading others seems to lie in his ability to convince them that he understands and sympathizes with their point of view. This ability, I believe, is based mainly on Kissinger's basic trait of identifying with his opponent."[72] More specifically, Kissinger tries to put the other party at ease, often by using humor, but humor that takes the form of putting down other parties to the conflict. This style has led to the reports of Kissinger's "duplicity," such as Matti Golan's accounts of Middle East negotiations. In addition, if possible, Kissinger would try to put the other party at ease by telling him what that person would like to hear. Mazlish concludes that Kissinger would do this, but, in fact, would not blatantly lie.[73] Valeriani supports this conclusion by noting that Kissinger might shade or exaggerate the truth, emphasizing different things to different people.[74]

In his memoirs, Kissinger gives this version of his style: "My normal approach to negotiations was to conduct them in a bantering tone to put my opposite number at ease, to avoid turning every issue into a test of will, and to emphasize the turn toward firmness when a line had to be drawn."[75] This fits with Mazlish's analysis, written years earlier. It also fits with the observations made by Valeriani, who notes Kissinger's use of wit and humor "to charm, to disarm, and to relieve tension. . . . His banter inspired banter in others and usually led to a more relaxed atmosphere in the private, formal discussions or negotiations."[76] Valeriani illustrates this style, including the use of humor as a means to pull the parties together (i.e., to use it against third parties): "Assad [of Syria] was also fascinated by Kissinger's accounts—often humorous—of his meetings with the Israelis. . . . Kissinger's use of humor apparently encouraged Assad to respond in kind."[77]

Another part of his style is Kissinger's penchant for secrecy. While his concern with secrecy stems from a number of sources (such as a desire to maintain control, exercise power, etc.), secrecy in negotiations was also a way of showing his negotiating partner that he trusted him.[78] For example, a number of explanations can be given for Kissinger's and Nixon's use of *only* Chinese interpreters in their trips to China. One possible explanation is their desire to indicate the trust that they had in their Chinese hosts.[79]

Kissinger's style, then, was based on creating a relaxed and comfortable atmosphere, and on letting the other parties (especially an adversary) know that Kissinger understood their position and problems, and would work with them in good faith. However, one other important aspect of his style was Kissinger's role as "educator." Both Mazlish and Ward note that Kissinger did not wholly throw off the model of his father: He retained the dedication to teaching, but he needed to add activism to the teacher's intellectual style. In the army, Kissinger had discovered that teaching could give him an identity and even popularity while at the same time he was discovering the heroic activism of Fritz Kraemer.

Characteristically, Kissinger combined the two strands in developing the intellectual concept of the statesman that is central to his operational code. The statesman not only must negotiate with, and thus educate, the opponent, but also must use education to overcome the domestic constraints of public and governmental opinion. The statesman must see himself as an educator. Kissinger's success as a teacher, first in the army and later at Harvard, and his success in linking intellectual and activist pursuits (also in the army and later at the Council for Foreign Affairs and with Rockefeller), presaged his use of this technique as a policymaker. Many observers have noted that Kissinger ran meetings or negotiations as he did his Harvard seminar—whether in the education of a possible opponent, such as Syria's Assad, or in teaching American political leaders about "the reality" of the international arena.[80]

Kissinger's view of the statesman as educator is presented in a number of places in *White House Years*. Especially in regard to Vietnam, one sees his concern with trying to make the Nixon administration's critics understand what the administration was trying to do. The educator role helped Kissinger keep a good relationship with the press (as opposed to his relationship with subordinates). Valeriani notes that, "in dealing with the traveling press, he was more open in talking about the directions of American foreign policy than any other official in recent times. . . . The openness of his discussions with the press astonished [the] foreign diplomats who occasionally sat in on them."[81] Kissinger was fond of lecturing, and his press briefings often took that form (as well as the occasional give-and-take of a seminar). Kissinger's extensive use of "backgrounders" and "deep backgrounders," especially while he was still National Security adviser, was in part due to his desire to inform and to help the press understand what was going on within the political constraints working on him.

It must be made clear that the idea of the educator was not the same as the idea of the "academic." Kissinger's lack of commitment to academia is apparent in almost every biographical account, by both friend and critic. Analyses of his career have pointed out that Kissinger had always been preparing for public service, and that academic pursuits were simply not enough for his activist drive. One observer has noted that Kissinger never became a member of the American Political Science Association. His scorn for academic politics and the goals of traditional academia is well known and noted by biographers.

Kissinger's activism and the drive for public service that led him to separate the educator from the academic are so evident that Vincent Davis sees Kissinger as a case study in "running for non-elective office."[82] Davis describes the three types of tacticians who engage in this effort—the networker, the expert, and the manipulator. He states that Kissinger became all three to achieve office. For our discussion, Davis's "expert" type is illustrative of the difference between educator and academic. However, it is important to keep in mind the influence of the conception of the educator on Kissinger's style of interaction with foreign leaders, the press, and American political figures.

Character. Overall assessments of how Henry Kissinger "orients himself towards life," in Barber's words, may be a useful way to review Kissinger's personality and psychobiography in general. Ward's view is that Kissinger is a depressive, or dysmutual, personality. He notes that this is a "diagnostic category for a broad range of behavior," including: extreme ambition; excessive work; overall drive for supremacy; insatiability in love, sex, friendship, glory, status, or possessions; tactlessness, particularly toward friends; and an attitude of being on the defensive.[83]

Much of this description could fit in with one of Barber's four basic character patterns, the "active-negative," who engages in "relatively intense effort and [who reaps] relatively low emotional reward for that effort. The activity has a compulsive quality, as if the man were trying to make up for something or to escape from anxiety into hard work."[84] Barber concludes that Nixon is an active-negative also, a conclusion supported by descriptions of Nixon given in *White House Years*.[85] Perhaps one reason that Nixon and Kissinger could get along was a shared basic character; nevertheless, Kissinger's descriptions may be used as another example of projection.

As noted, many of the characteristics of the depressive personality also show up in Etheredge's "narcissistic personality disorder syndrome" —an ideal personality type describing individuals who engage in "hardball politics." Etheredge describes the type as follows:

> The key internal feature of the narcissistic personality disorder politician (NP) is the simultaneous existence of two different and unintegrated conceptions of the self. In the foreground of the mind is a depleted insecure self. Here is a sense of low self-esteem and of self-doubt, a strong propensity to feel inadequate, insecure, and ashamed, continuing worry about social acceptability, discomfort with intimacy, fear of genuineness, candor and self-revelation, insecurity and apprehension about (vaguely defined) impending disaster. But in the background, and above, there exists a different relatively split-off sector of the mind, a "grandiose self." An unintegrated heir to early childhood feelings and dreams of omnipotence. This sector includes fantasies and drives for grandiose accomplishment, total recognition and administration, complete dominance of events of the world, and a complete self-confidence.[86]

These characteristics are similar to those Ward discusses and to other analyses that have been used to describe Kissinger's personality, such as "Machiavellianism."[87] One very striking point Etheredge makes about the NP, which is also central to the "high Mach" (highly Machiavellian person), is the need to have "a feeling of directorship in the unfolding social and political drama of his times."[88] This fits with Kissinger's activism, and his views of the hero/patron and the statesman. It might also be noted that high Machs also lie more plausibly, prefer face-to-face interaction, enjoy manipulating others, and prefer utility over morality. Each of these attributes appears to accurately describe Kissinger.

As noted above, it should be remembered that a depressive personality can range from well integrated to psychotic. Mazlish, for example, disagrees with Ward's characterization of Kissinger, preferring to call Kissinger a "conditional optimist," a characterization that also emerges in the operational-code analysis of Kissinger's belief system. Mazlish's list of Kissinger's traits is a mixed bag, with positive and negative aspects, including: distrust of good will, intense desire for stability, ability to identify with opponents, the wish to assimilate, keen intellect, hard work, "heaviness," tendencies toward megalomania and paranoia, and arrogance.[89]

These characteristics, in addition to the relevant characteristics of the NP and the highly Machiavellian personality, are important for understanding Kissinger's style, and much of his success as a high-level decision maker. Given Kissinger's background in the army and the jobs he was assigned to and which he successfully carried out, it is important to highlight the fact that Machiavellianism is not simply a negative description or characterization. Richard Christie and F. L. Geis note that high Machs should be recommended for positions in which "they are sent on what amounts to detached service in which there is freedom to wheel and deal for both their own and (their) organization's benefit."[90] This description clearly fits Kissinger's army assignments and his later tasks as a high-level decision maker. As noted in the first chapter, after initial discussion of foreign-policy content with Nixon, Kissinger began the process whereby he increasingly became an independent actor in the implementation of that policy. This process apparently reached completion under Ford.

In summary, Kissinger's biography enables us to make psychobiographical observations about his personality, style, and character, and to direct these observations toward an understanding of central features of his belief system, as well as an understanding of a variety of the behaviors he exhibited as a high-level policymaker.

FROM PSYCHOBIOGRAPHY TO THE OPERATIONAL CODE

In the introduction to his study of Kissinger, Mazlish makes an important observation about Kissinger's personality and character: "Perhaps his major characteristic is his ability to change and grow."[91] Similarly, Valeriani uses a quote from Bill Moyers as the beginning of his book: "Henry Kissinger is still learning, he is still open."[92] Certainly, if there were one theme that could tie together the approaches to Kissinger outlined in this chapter and that could bridge the psychobiographical and operational-code analyses, it would be his ability to change and to be open. This ability is directly related to the construction of Kissinger's belief system and to his use of a set of categories by which he regularly re-evaluated world leaders and states. Rather than freezing an opponent into the image of the enemy—in contrast to Dulles—Kissinger let his experiences lead him to an empathy and identification with opponents that permitted him to be flexible in dealing with them.

And, although Kissinger's fundamental drive was for security and order, the same experiences that created this need also were responsible for the flexibility and moderation in his style and character. The basis for this conclusion is the psychobiographical analysis, which provides us with an understanding of the core aspects of Kissinger's belief system. Kissinger's fear of chaos, based on his view of a world in permanent conflict, was translated into a quest for order, but an order that could be achieved only by a hero/statesman who behaved flexibly (and was moderate and limited in his demands—a point developed in chapter 3).

Kissinger's life experiences help us understand *Kissinger's* views of order and how to achieve it, and why, for instance, he did not develop a "belligerent personality," as delineated by Saul Friedlander and Raymond Cohen.[93] (In this delineation, a belligerent personality, characterized by intransigence, pugnacity, and unwillingness to compromise, is the product of three recurrent factors: a rebellious attitude toward authority, the dominating exercise of authority, and verbal aggressiveness. While Dulles could be included in this group, a review of Kissinger's personality shows that he could not.)

However, Kissinger's fundamental need for security and order raises the question of how this goal was to be achieved. The need was planted in childhood, and some alternatives to satisfying the need were substantially discarded (e.g., regarding his father as a role model, except for the important teaching component). In young adulthood came the patron models, who helped to form Kissinger's need for order into a Machiavellianism based on activism (as well as on Kissinger's own empathy for and identification with opponents). From the patron model, which became the hero/statesman, evolved Kissinger's power motive.[94]

Kissinger's power motive was tied to his need for activism, coupled with his need to acquire a role from which that activism could have an effect. Even so, it does not seem proper to apply the term "ambitious" to Kissinger. He evidenced little ambition in his pre-army days, when his objective was to be an accountant. It was only through the Kissinger-patron interaction that his patron/hero/statesman notion crystalized, containing, as it did, the need for activism. Note also that it was the

Kissinger–patron interaction with Kraemer that made sure that Kissinger did not return to CCNY, and with Elliott that directed Kissinger's academic career.

Kissinger's drive for activism was tempered by the teacher in him and by the statesman's need to have a knowledge and understanding of history that would enable him to grasp the correct moment for action. In the army, Kissinger successfully combined the teacher with the activism, as he would by becoming a Harvard faculty member (in a way that a Chicago or Pennsylvania academic could not). Finally, his entire postgraduate career was designed to combine the teacher-activist and eventually to achieve a role through which he could become the statesman.

It is appropriate, then, to develop next Kissinger's concept of the statesman and the other elements of his belief system. Now that his motives and personality have been discussed as a general context, origins and development of his belief system can be better understood. The appropriateness of deriving the operational-code analysis from Kissinger's academic writings, as is done next, is supported by Mazlish's conception of the flexibility in Kissinger's character, and the intellectual level is exactly the place Mazlish feels useful analysis can be made: "It is ultimately on the intellectual level, the level of Kissinger's conceptualization, that one must seek to evaluate him most comprehensively."[95] How the biographical and psychobiographical factors affected Kissinger the policymaker can be understood only by examining the intervening stage of Kissinger the intellectual. The intellectual concepts that Kissinger developed to orient himself toward the world were then employed in guiding Kissinger the policymaker through the political arenas of Washington and of international relations.

3

Kissinger's Operational Code

Over the years, political observers have referred to the "mysterious" Kissinger—characterizing him as inexplicable, unpredictable, and full of surprises.[1] During Kissinger's tenure in Washington, others indicated concern about his personal style, personality, or "way of thinking" about international politics. These views are usually based upon a caricature of Kissinger's complex personality and his equally complex belief system and conceptual framework. Kissinger was not really that mysterious. In addition to the access to Kissinger gained through review of his biography and a psychohistorical overview of those biographical facts, for an academic like Kissinger there is a large body of scholarly, pre-office writings that also contains clues to the foreign-policy decision maker to come. The present chapter, on the operational-code approach to analysis, taps these professional writings.[2]

The mystery of Kissinger may be unravelled first as one looks at his life experiences and psychoanalytic development, which form the basis for concepts developed by Kissinger the academic. Furthermore, while more attention has been paid to Kissinger's academic work in recent years, it is still possible to agree with the spirit of Stephen Graubard's observation: "It is curious that all attention has been given to what Kissinger has done since he joined the Nixon Administration, and that so few have thought to inquire as to what he proposed before he went to Washington."[3] In this chapter, an operational-code approach to Kissinger's pre-office thoughts and proposals provides vital clues to the belief system that Kissinger carried with him when he entered office.

USE OF THE OPERATIONAL CODE AND ACCESS

Decision makers, like all other human beings, can act only in terms of their image of the world. Every individual is subject to a variety of psychological processes that affect perception and behavior. As a result of these processes, an individual possesses a belief system, which is composed of images, which are the products of past experiences, values, attitudes, and personality factors. At any time, the images that an individual holds of the world filter that individual's perceptions of the world around him. Therefore, perception, the process by which an individual selects and evaluates, is influenced by the images that the individual already holds. The images may be open or closed, and affect how much, the type of, and in what form new information is taken in and processed. This process is important in a decision maker's selection of a problem, in his identification of the alternatives for solving that problem, and ultimately in his choice of a plan of action to meet that problem.

An individual's images make up his total "belief system," and are affected by the other images in that belief system. Milton Rokeach defines the belief system as "a representation of all the beliefs, sets, explanations, or hypotheses, conscious and unconscious, that a person at a given time accepts as true of the world he lives in."[4] More simply, Giovanni Sartori defines a political belief system as "the set of beliefs according to which individuals navigate and orient themselves in the sea of politics."[5] Ole Holsti asserts that, "The belief system is composed of a more or less integrated set of images which make up the entire relevant universe for the individual. They encompass past, present and future expectations of future reality."[6] Holsti also notes several important functions that the belief system performs for the individual:

> orienting the individual to his total environment, defining it for him, and identifying for him its salient characteristics; acting as a filter to select relevant information from the irrelevant in any given situation; organizing perceptions into a coherent guide for behavior; establishing goals and ordering preferences.[7]

In an enumeration of strategies by which individuals might cope with cognitive complexity, Holsti and Alexander George list reliance on operational-code beliefs.[8] Thus, in a situation of complexity, the individual may fall back on an established belief system. This is one obvious effect that individual factors will have on a decision-making situation. Robert Jervis summarizes the relationship between the belief system and operational code as:

> *expectations or perceptual sets represent standing estimates of what the world is like and, therefore, of what the person is likely to be confronted with.* In everyday life, in the interpretation of other states' behavior, and in the scientific laboratory, expecta-

tions create predispositions that lead actors to notice certain things and to neglect others, to immediately and often unconsciously draw certain inferences from what is noticed, and to find it difficult to consider alternatives. Furthermore, as we will discuss below, this way of perceiving is rational . . . understanding the general predispositions held by decision-makers is an important step in explaining their specific perceptions. We therefore need to learn about both the predispositions that are frequently held by whole classes of decision-makers and about how the general predispositions held by an individual decision-maker relate to each other. Operational code studies can help accomplish the latter task.[9]

The operational-code approach was originally developed by Nathan Leites in order to derive an operational code of the Soviet leadership.[10] A number of years later, Alexander George sought to counter what he saw as a neglect of the operational-code approach. In his modification of Leites's approach, George suggested ten questions that would form the operational-code framework and would act as a guide to research.[11] Five were "philosophical" questions (about an individual's philosophic beliefs and attitudes), and five were "instrumental" questions (about the best ways to reach one's goals, and to interact with others):

Philosophical Questions

1. What is the "essential" nature of political life? Is the political universe essentially one of harmony or conflict? What is the fundamental character of one's political opponents?

2. What are the prospects for the eventual realization of one's fundamental political values and aspirations? Can one be optimistic or pessimistic on this score?

3. Is the political future predictable? In what sense and to what extent?

4. How much "control" or "mastery" can one have over historical development? What is one's role in "moving" and "shaping" history in the desired direction?

5. What is the role of "chance" in human affairs and in historical developments?

Instrumental Questions

1. What is the best approach for selecting goals or objectives for political action?

2. How are the goals of action pursued most effectively?

3. How are the risks of political action calculated, controlled and accepted?

4. What is the best "timing" of action to advance one's interest?

5. What is the utility and role of different means for advancing one's interests?

More recently, Holsti has taken George's original ten questions and broken them down into a much more extensive set of subsidiary questions (not included in the present study).[12]

The operational-code approach, taken as George's ten questions, may be seen as a set of independent variables that can be used to explain foreign policy. In this view, the belief system (composed of images of what has been and what should be) acts upon incoming information, so that variance in the belief system helps explain both the individual's perceptions of reality and the decisions made. In this sense the belief system acts as a mediator in a stimulus-response process. How the individual responds to the incoming stimuli depends upon how much and which parts of that information are taken in, and the subsequent interpretation of the information. Before the individual can respond, the stimuli have to go through the "screens" of the individual's belief system. Thus, just as personality, style, and character development predispose an individual to respond to situations in certain ways, an individual's belief system predisposes him to see the world in certain ways, and the development of the belief system is based on the same life experiences reviewed in the biographical and psychobiographical analyses.

In regard to the operational-code approach, Holsti has asked, "Does it help us to understand how political actors perceive, diagnose, prescribe, and make choices in specific situations?"[13] In partial answer to this question, we can say, as does George, that an operational-code analysis helps us to narrow the range from which we think choices will be made. This is a form of negative prediction, which means that the analysis may permit us to exclude the policy alternatives that are least likely to gain the support. Holsti notes that the results of his study of John Foster Dulles support this view of the utility of the operational-code approach. In summarizing his operational-code study of Dean Acheson, David McLellan concurs, noting that, "There appears to be a suggestive correspondence between what we presume to know about foreign policy decisions and outcomes during the Truman period and the distinctive features of Acheson's operational code which sets it off from the Byrnes and Marshall eras which preceded it and from the Dulles era which followed."[14] Stephen Walker's studies of Kissinger's operational code (strongly supported by data in Kissinger's memoirs) also indicate powerful links between the operational code and Kissinger's behavior toward the Soviet Union, in the Arab-Israeli conflict, and in the Vietnam war.[15]

George's questions have been employed in many studies, and their utility has been demonstrated many ways. They provide the analyst with signposts upon which to hang data and commentary as he moves through the writings of the individual being studied. The approach has been useful as a means for isolating relevant aspects of decision-makers' belief systems, and then, given the use of the same guide, for comparing individuals. In short, this method of gaining access to foreign-policy decision makers has been applied with relative success to a number of individuals, including Dulles, Acheson, Dean Rusk, J. William Fulbright, and Frank Church, and foreign leaders, such as Lester Pearson, Willy Brandt, and Mao Tse-Tung.[16]

The operational-code questions can, without a doubt, be applied to the writings of Henry Kissinger. In many ways, Kissinger is an ideal subject for an operational-code study. In a study of Frank Church, Loch Johnson reclassifies George's ten questions into categories that even more clearly apply to Kissinger's writings in international relations. Instead of dividing them into philosophical and instrumental questions, Johnson divides them into questions on "the nature of politics and political conflict" and "shaping historical development."[17] Peter Dickson goes so far as to say that he would "attempt to demonstrate that Kissinger's complex personality and behavior cannot be fairly evaluated unless one appreciates the longstanding importance he has attached to man's perpetual quest for meaning in history."[18] (In fact, Kissinger's attention to history and its meaning provide clear answers to both the philosophical questions and the instrumental ones that derive from them.)

Kissinger fits a number of other criteria for a good operational-code subject. As an academic, Kissinger wrote extensively on international politics, including works on European diplomatic history, international relations in general, and contemporary international problems, such as nuclear weapons policy and strategy, alliance politics, and American foreign policy. Having written or edited six books and almost fifty articles before 1969, Kissinger provides the analyst with a good data base. Furthermore, the academic works satisfy several prerequisites for a useful operational-code study.[19] First, Kissinger's academic writings are broad, in that they cover a range of topics wide enough to reveal an operational code. Second, secondary sources, discussions with acquaintances, and content-analysis research reveal that these writings can be considered honest, in that they appear to reflect Kissinger's real beliefs. For instance, in discussing Kissinger's senior honors thesis, "The Meaning of History," Graubard observes, "Much of what he learned at Harvard was incorporated into a thesis that pretended to deal with selected philosophies of history since the 18th century; it was, in fact, a kind of personal testament."[20]

Finally, Kissinger's writings reflect an important continuity, in that Kissinger's philosophy and political style appear to be essentially the same during his period as a decision maker as they were when he produced his academic works. Continuity is an important criterion for using an operational-code approach, and it is especially well met in the case of Kissinger. Bruce Mazlish notes that Kissinger "turned scholarship into projective biography."[21] That is, in his writings on international relations, Kissinger stated clearly what he would do as a policymaker under certain circumstances. As Walker and others have noted, a distinctive characteristic of Kissinger's writing is the tendency to generalize and to hypothesize lessons and conclusions from the analysis of historical cases.[22] Through these generalizations, Kissinger outlined his operational code and provided a guide to his future behavior. From this we can identify the continuity in Kissinger's thought as reflected in his academic works. When Kissinger was asked, in 1976, how Professor Kissinger of Harvard was appraised by Secretary of State Kissinger, he replied: "I have tried—with what success historians will have to judge—to have an overriding concept. It can be found in innumerable, maybe pedantic, speeches I have given over the years."[23] In 1975, when he was asked if he had changed his basic conception of international politics over the past twenty years, his reply was consistent (if somewhat facetious): "I think it is possible—at least I leave open the theoretical possibility—that I might have changed my mind on something in my life, but don't press me too hard."[24]

Many examples of the continuity of his philosophy and style can be found in Kissinger's academic works and in his subsequent statements as a policymaker. One of the basic points about world order that Kissinger makes in his Ph.D. thesis, published as *A World Restored: Castlereagh, Metternich and the Restoration of Peace, 1812-1822,* is about the nature of peace: "Whenever peace—conceived as the avoidance of war—has been the primary objective of a power or a group of powers, the international system has been at the mercy of the most ruthless member of the international community. Whenever the international order has acknowledged that certain principles could not be compromised even for the sake of peace, stability based on equilibrium of force was at least conceivable."[25] He echoed this belief in 1974, at hearings before the Senate Foreign Relations Committee: "If peace is pursued to the exclusion of any other goal, other values will be compromised and perhaps lost."[26]

Other sections and passages from *A World Restored* have been echoed many times in Kissinger's statements as a decision maker. As John Stoessinger and Stephen Walker have pointed out, Kissinger was virtually quoting from several passages in Chapter 8 of his dissertation when he explained the Indochina peace agreement to a news conference on January 24, 1973: "It was always clear that a lasting peace could come about only if neither side sought to achieve everything it wanted; indeed that stability depended on the relative satisfaction and therefore the relative dissatisfaction of all the parties concerned."[27] In a January 1978 interview with Walter Laqueur, Kissinger repeated the point first developed in his Ph.D. thesis: "Absolute security for one side must mean absolute insecurity for all other sides. . . . The structural problem of foreign policy is therefore to try to guarantee the relative security and therefore the insecurity of all the parties."[28] This theme is also central to Kissinger's operational-code beliefs of limits and constraint, and his conception of "legitimate" and "revolutionary" states. As in many other instances, the continuity of his thinking extends from his academic works to the policy-making years and on to the post-policy-making period.

Examples of continuity are not limited to Kissinger's dissertation. In a 1956 article in *Foreign Affairs,* he discussed the relationship between Kant and contemporary international politics:

> In his whimsical essay "Perpetual Peace" written in 1795, the German philosopher Kant predicted that world peace could be attained in one of two ways: by a moral consensus which he identified with a republican form of government, or by a cycle of wars of ever-increasing violence which would reduce the major powers to impotence.[29]

Kissinger applied this point to the impact of nuclear weapons, and quoted Eisenhower's observation that "there is no alternative to peace." Then, in his first speech as secretary of state, at the United Nations on September 24, 1973, he said:

> Two centuries ago, the philosopher Kant predicted that perpetual peace would come about eventually—either as the creation

of man's moral aspirations or as the consequence of physical necessity. What seemed utopian then looms as tomorrow's reality; soon there will be no alternative.[30]

The continuity of both these themes is demonstrated in a single passage from *White House Years*. Writing about the era of international politics in which he was soon to become a major participant, Kissinger reflects:

> In the late eighteenth century the philosopher Immanuel Kant in his essay "Perpetual Peace," had written that world peace was inevitable; it would come about either because all nations shared the same sense of justice or because a cycle of wars of ever-increasing violence would teach men the futility of conflict.... But the root dilemma of our time is that if the quest for peace turns into the *sole* objective of policy, the fear of war becomes a weapon in the hands of the most ruthless.[31]

Stoessinger, a fellow graduate student with Kissinger at Harvard in the early 1950s and a friend since, provides a useful summary concerning continuity: "His diplomacy as Secretary of State is deeply rooted in the insights of the young doctoral student at Harvard a quarter century ago. It is, in fact, a virtual transplant from the world of thought into the world of power.... We are witness here to a unique experiment in the application of scholarship to statesmanship, of history to statecraft."[32]

Finally, it is important to note that, in looking at Kissinger's writings to develop an operational-code overview of his belief system, we are not looking at specific judgments, views, or interpretations of specific events, objects, or people—but at the more general set of images that shaped his perception of, interpretation of, and possible behavior toward specific events or individuals. The analyses presented are of necessity more summary than detail, and omit most of the various illustrative passages from Kissinger's writings or the lengthy analysis by other scholars that led to the conclusions presented.[33]

THE FIRST PHILOSOPHICAL QUESTION:
THE ESSENTIAL NATURE OF POLITICAL LIFE

Legitimacy and Order. The first philosophical question concerns Kissinger's view of the essential nature of political life, including his views on conflict and harmony and the character of opponents. Here we can begin to delineate ideas that are central to Kissinger's entire operational code.

Most of the ideas were first developed in Kissinger's dissertation, but they run throughout his works, especially in a later article on Bismarck, the "white revolutionary."[34] Furthermore, Kissinger was twenty-seven years old when he completed his *undergraduate* honors thesis, one of Harvard's "veteran" students. His undergraduate and Ph.D. theses, then, were the work of a mature man, not the thoughts of an inexperienced youngster.

In *A World Restored,* Kissinger expands a conception of political life introduced in "The Meaning of History": his writing is shaped by a view of life that pits the forces of chaos against the forces of order. (Kissinger's personal background provided him with an experience of, and understanding of, the tragedy of upheaval, and this experience fostered his passion, some say obsession, for stability, balance, and order.) This view was developed at length in his honors and doctoral theses, and can be summarized by a sentence from a 1968 article: "The greatest need of the contemporary international system is an agreed concept of order . . . without it, stability will prove elusive."[35]

Translated into international political terms, Kissinger's view saw stability as "a generally accepted legitimacy," an international agreement "about the nature of workable arrangements and about the *permissible* [emphasis added] aims and methods of foreign policy."[36] On the basis of this view of stability, Kissinger created in *A World Restored,* a typology for international political life that he has applied ever since. Two types of international orders, two types of states, were conceived: the legitimate and the revolutionary. The legitimate state used diplomacy for achieving limited objectives; it accepted the international context as legitimate and agreed to negotiate its differences within the rules and constraints of that context. The revolutionary state was ideological, and in pursuit of its consequently unlimited objectives, did not accept as axiomatic the survival of other states. The revolutionary state challenged the existing order—it was revisionist in its quest for its desired order, which was usually one in which its victory was total and its security absolute. As noted above, for Kissinger this outcome was impossible: if one state were to have absolute security, the others must be insecure. The revolutionary state thus ignored the need for limits that was another cornerstone of Kissinger's view of legitimacy and stability.[37]

The two types of states were crucial to Kissinger's conception of the need for stability and order. While war could occur under a legitimate order, it would be limited; the survival of states would not be threatened, and diplomacy and negotiation could continue.[38] A revolutionary state welcomed war and used war to change the existing order. As Stoessinger summarizes: "The attainment of a stable international order thus depended on the creation of a system of legitimate states and on the elimination from such a system of the revolutionary state. Peace became a kind of bonus that history awarded to those statemen who were able to create a stable international equilibrium of states that recognized each other's right to a permanent existence."[39]

This philosophical principle is extremely important to Kissinger's instrumental principles, particularly with regard to the role and use of negotiations. In a stable, legitimate order, states accept the rules of the international game. The revolutionary state, however, means to change the rules. It does not negotiate in good faith, as the legitimate state does, but rather for propaganda and psychologically manipulative ends. In an example from his White House years, Kissinger recalls his first round of talks with Le Duc Tho: "I grew to understand that Le Duc Tho considered negotiations as another battle. . . . He was there to wear me down. As the representative of truth, he had no category for compromise."[40]

The Statesman. The two basic types of states also reflect the nature of the men who lead those states. As states represent different responses to the problem of international order, so do their leaders. Kissinger categorized leaders as conquerors, prophets, or statesmen. Napoleon was a conqueror, and Czar Alexander a prophet—but both "were revolutionaries, because both strove to identify the organization of Europe with their will."[41]

The prophet is also viewed as a revolutionary because of the ideologically timeless aspect of his leadership. The prophet's vision is used as the standard for order, truth, and reality. In contrast, Kissinger developed the concept of the statesman, represented by Castlereagh and Metternich. Statesmen "live in time"—they recognize the limits and the possibilities of the present; they conduct themselves on the basis of the recognition of limits, which include the survival of the states in the system. Statesmen employ diplomacy and negotiation to recreate and restore international order. In *A World Restored,* the statesman is characterized:

> Statesmanship was the science of the interests of states, and subject to laws entirely analogous to the laws of the physical world. The statesman was a philosopher who understood these maxims, who performed his tasks. . . . The test of a statesman, then, is his ability to recognize the real relationship of forces and to make this knowledge serve his ends. . . . His instrument is

diplomacy, the art of relating states to each other by agreement rather than the exercise of force, by the representation of a ground of action which reconciles particular aspirations with a general consensus . . .; diplomacy depends upon persuasion and not imposition.[42]

This view of the statesman relates directly to Kissinger's style in dealing with the opponent: moderation and restraint, and the desire not to impose one's own interests on others. Both style and operational-code beliefs derive from the same biographical experiences.

Another interesting juxtaposition of psychohistorical and operational-code analysis is afforded by a look at Kissinger's relationship to Richard Nixon—the man and the statesman. The Nixon case is useful in that it demonstrates that Kissinger's behavior and style are consistent with psychological and intellectual components of Kissinger's make-up that have been identified in psychohistorical and operational-code studies. Critics have often pointed to Kissinger's duplicity in disparaging Nixon the person, and yet working for Nixon the president, and even lauding various aspects of Nixon's foreign-policy performance, but the key point is that Kissinger, for all his criticism of Nixon's personal style and personality, also saw Richard Nixon as a statesman, and approved of his behavior in that role.

In *White House Years,* Kissinger gives Nixon high marks for his courage, purposes, and principle in creating, carrying out, and sticking to his foreign policy. Examples abound: In Moscow, during the 1972 summit, while faced with powerful bureaucratic pressure from all sides, Nixon agreed to let Kissinger carry on the SALT discussions on the basis of the unequal number of launch vehicles. A conversation was held while Nixon was having his back treated: "Lying naked on the rubbing table, Nixon made one of the more courageous decisions of his Presidency. . . . Nixon took a heroic position from a decidedly unheroic posture." In discussing the last stages of the Indochina agreements, Kissinger similarly observes that "maddening as Nixon's conduct could be in calm times, it verged on the heroic when really critical issues were at stake." Much of this was due to another strength of the statesman that Kissinger saw in Nixon: "No political leader I have met understood the dynamics of negotiations better than Nixon."[43]

Of course, in large measure, Nixon was being praised for holding the "correct" principles—those that Kissinger believed the statesman should hold, and that Kissinger himself possessed. For example, as noted, Kissinger held that peace at *any* price is an invitation to disaster. In a meeting between Nixon and Prime Minister Heath in December 1971 in which they reviewed the world situation, Nixon repeated, "Part of our reason for conducting our Vietnam withdrawal so slowly is to give some message that we are not prepared to pay *any* price for ending a war; we must now ask ourselves what we are willing to pay to avert war. If we are not, we have tough days head."[44]

Similarly, Kissinger praises Nixon for understanding geopolitical structures and balance, of balancing interests, goals, and the capabilities of competing states:

> It was a hard lesson to convey to a people who rarely read about the balance of power without seeing the adjective "outdated" precede it. It was not one of the least ironies of the period that it was a flawed man, so ungenerous in some of his human impulses, who took the initiative in leading America toward a concept of peace compatible with its new realities and the awful perils of the nuclear age, and that the foreign leaders who best understood this were the two grizzled veterans of the Long March, Mao and Chou, who openly expressed their preference for Richard Nixon over the wayward representatives of American liberalism. . . . For sovereign nations, predictability is more crucial than spasmodic brilliance or idiosyncratic moralistic rhetoric. They must gear their actions to the performance of others over extended periods of time; their domestic survival and international security alike may depend upon it. And it was on this level of shared geopolitical interest transcending philosophies and history that the former Red-baiter and the crusaders for world revolution found each other.[45]

As both Ward and Mazlish point out, as the years passed, Kissinger also sought out men whose intellectual positions fit with his own. Ward comments that Kissinger "would commit himself to the ideas of Nixon, a man for whom he has no personal respect."[46] Mazlish notes that the relationship between the two men was formal and intellectual, that they never became friends. Mazlish contends that, in his relationship with Nixon, Kissinger supported Mazlish's proposition that Kissinger had a unique ability to fit with different kinds of men.[47] Ward echoes this idea: "Perhaps because of his growing confidence in his own ability and his own ideas, Kissinger became able and willing to accept the challenge of trying to put his ideas into action even if the man who would make the final decision was not a man who Kissinger particularly admired."[48]

Nixon the individual, however, held little charm for Kissinger. He was not typical of the patrons who had figured so conspicuously in

Kissinger's personal and professional development. The patrons were renaissance types and great gentlemen, and Nixon was not of that mold, as is apparent from other interviews, and from numerous passages in *White House Years*. Kissinger uses phrases like "this lonely, tortured and insecure man" (p. 1086); a "vulnerable and austere" personality, "eager for acceptance but incapable of the act of grace" that could have brought him such acceptance (p. 933); "shy" and "ill at ease with strangers" (p. 760). Nixon is often portrayed as petty (as in the case of forbidding any channel of communication with China being opened through Canada, due to his thorough dislike of Trudeau [p. 736]), overly concerned with image and public relations (p. 734), and a paranoid—pursued by the "same liberal conspiracy that had sought to destroy him ever since the Alger Hiss case" (p. 299).

An interesting aspect of this relationship is a certain parallel with criticisms that have been made of Kissinger's own personality. David Landau, in particular, describes the paranoia Kissinger exhibited while a faculty member at Harvard. Ward's description of Kissinger as a dysmutual, or depressive, personality mirrors many of the observations that Kissinger made of Nixon. Our earlier discussion of Kissinger's personality and his use of projection provides an understanding of Kissinger that is consistent with his observations of the personal Nixon. The focus on Nixon's "active-negative" characteristics in Kissinger's memoirs is a consistent example. Kissinger's writings and his operational code illuminate his concept of the statesman and the prominent, positive place it holds in his belief system. Kissinger's apparently contradictory views of Nixon are thus neither petty nor inconsistent. Rather, they derive from his background and a longstanding intellectual concept.

The Essential Nature of Politics: Overview and Comparison. In viewing conflict and harmony, and the nature of international opponents, Kissinger had created a set of analytic boxes. He saw the clash between legitimate and revolutionary states and leaders as the central element of international politics, and a tragic one. The legitimate state was justified in using force against the revolutionary one in order to ensure its survival, and the survival of order over chaos. The key to Kissinger's view of order may well be revealed in his response to the question of how he would choose between the statesman who pursued unjust ends and the revolutionary who had justice on his side. Kissinger is reported to have replied with the words of Goethe: "If I had to choose between justice and disorder, on the one hand, and injustice and order, on the other, I would always choose the latter."[49] Dickson attributes Kissinger's concern with this "fundamental dilemma of life"—the tension between morality and historical experience—to Kant, who, Dickson argues, was the primary influence on Kissinger's philosophy of history and his view of man.[50]

In his "projective biography," Kissinger the decision maker acted the part of the statesman, pursuing stability and defending the status quo. Rightly or wrongly, he labeled other states as revolutionary or legitimate, and behaved accordingly. Thus, Kissinger's overall design for a stable international order, which he began to construct in 1968 while writing foreign-policy papers for Nelson Rockefeller, was based on his conviction that the Soviet Union and the People's Republic of China were no longer revolutionary states.[51] Stanley Hoffmann asserts that Kissinger came to the conclusion that the Soviet Union and China were no longer revolutionary states through his analysis of their perceived needs and self-interest. The change in weapons technology and the mutual balance of terror, as well as the Sino-Soviet split, brought about the primacy of prudence over ideology, Kissinger concluded.[52] Hoffmann's assertion may be supported by the following sequence. Kissinger clearly identified the Soviet Union as revolutionary in *Nuclear Weapons and Foreign Policy* (1957). The changeover began in *The Necessity for Choice* (1961), where Kissinger was developing a number of his ideas on arms control. He saw the Soviet Union as being willing to enter into arms-control agreements through the self-interest of survival. The changeover became more explicit in *The Troubled Partnership* (1965), where he wrote of both the necessity of nuclear survival and of the Sino-Soviet split. The final step came in early 1968, when Kissinger was writing Rockefeller's foreign-policy papers during Rockefeller's unsuccessful bid for the Republican presidential nomination. Graubard chronicles how Rockefeller's public statements called for new "understandings being reached with the Soviet Union and Communist China."[53]

Also rightly or wrongly, Kissinger labeled situations as those that threatened international order or stability and those that did not, and acted accordingly. His difference from Dulles on this point is striking. Townsend Hoopes points out that by 1949-50, when Dulles wrote *War or Peace,* Dulles's view of the Soviet Union had become grounded in morality. Dulles said that, "Soviet Communism starts with an atheistic, Godless premise. Everything flows from that premise."[54] Kissinger, on the other hand, derived his images of the enemy from sources very different from Dulles's morality. As we have seen, empathy and identification with the opponent made Kissinger far more flexible and willing to deal with an opponent—understanding and successfully dealing with an opponent were an exhilarating challenge. Also, as we have seen from Kissinger's citation of Goethe, morality held little appeal for him as a guide to behavior. Behavior was to be structured by the belief-system categories he had developed for viewing international politics. Whereas Dulles's image could become closed on the basis of moral judgments, Kissinger's perception remained open, evaluating and re-evaluating incoming information about states, leaders, and situations in terms of his categories. While the analytic boxes remained constant, Kissinger's images of states and leaders could, and did, change on the basis of new information about them.

These views of the essential nature of political life underlie Kissinger's beliefs concerning the remaining philosophical and instrumental questions. Kissinger's views on the first question also form a basis for comparisons between his general approach to politics and the approach of other leaders whose operational codes have been studied. For example, Holsti delineated Dulles's beliefs on man's nature as being:

1. Man's selfish and emotional nature is the primary source of individual motivation and social dynamics.

2. Conflict is the basic form of human interaction.

3. Social cohesion depends upon the existence of external enemies.

4. Leadership goes to those who have mastered the dangerous art of arousing in their followers a high degree of emotional energy.[55]

Kissinger's view of the essence of leadership and the nature of state behavior is less general than Dulles's, and provides leeway for dealing differently with different kinds of states and leaders. For Kissinger, while the search for order and stability amid chaos is constant, the search may be much less fraught with conflict within a system of legitimate states led by statesmen. While Kissinger believed in limits and constraint, and subscribed to a view that states could not win absolute victories or gain absolute security, Dulles believed that "The cold war is fundamentally a moral rather than a political conflict," and "Cold War politics are a zero-sum game."[56] Kissinger's contrary view—that international politics was not a zero-sum game—is also reflected in his instrumental values concerning the use of force and diplomacy. Dulles's "spiritual determinism," on the other hand, leads him to a zero-sum view, and therefore into a classic "image of the enemy" for the Soviet Union. Once this image was formed, it was locked in.

In terms of operational-code analyses, it is interesting also to compare Dulles to his predecessor Dean Acheson, who dealt with the Soviet Union in some of the most tense periods of the cold war. Acheson's views on the "nature of politics" are much closer to those of Kissinger. On politics in general, Acheson's beliefs were "Politics is man's struggle to maintain a manageable social universe," and "The substance of politics is relative and contingent." Acheson too was concerned with order, but not order based upon absolute moral tenets. Similarly, his views on leadership are closer to those of Kissinger: "To govern is to make knowledge the basis of action," and "Policy in a democratic society must rest upon popular knowledge and understanding."[57] The last belief is close to Kissinger's view that a leader is constrained by domestic consensus and cannot move too far in advance of the consensus.

Compared to the moral rigidity that overlay Dulles's "realist" beliefs, Acheson's beliefs were a "pragmatic, strategic, non-ideological view of the universe, one in which the opponent is viewed as a threat but with whom one can coexist without the ultimate folly of war."[58] The Acheson and Kissinger beliefs reflect the realism that George Kennan represented in his writings and actions in the late 1940s and early 1950s. Kennan's call to recognize, and to act in, only a limited set of "vital" areas and to retain flexibility in viewing the changing constellation of opponents, allies, and opportunities is apparent in the Acheson and Kissinger operational codes.[59] Dulles's addition of a restrictive cold-war morality was the feature that led Kennan to criticize Dulles's policy as too general, too rigid, and too determined, justifying itself with an unlimited moral ideology. In Kissinger's terms, we can say that Dulles was demonstrating characteristics of the prophet. For example, in *The Necessity for Choice,* Kissinger was highly critical of Dulles's unwillingness to negotiate with the Soviets. At other points Kissinger also criticized the "undifferentiated globalism" of the Dulles policy, and its "confusion about our purposes." While Kissinger observed that the Truman period had produced substantial accomplishments, the Eisenhower period was seen as dismal.[60]

In pursuing Kennan's criticisms of Dulles, Kissinger was also rejecting the classic psychological image of the enemy as an omniscient and omnipotent actor who left nothing to chance and who pursued a coherent grand strategy.[61] This attitude carried into the White House years. In his memoirs, Kissinger describes an analysis of Soviet policy that he sent to Nixon: "It began by rejecting the proposition that Soviet policy necessarily followed a master plan." The document continued: "It is always tempting to arrange diverse Soviet moves into a grand design. The more esoteric brands of Kremlinology often purport to see each and every move as part of a carefully orchestrated score in which events inexorably move to the grand finale. Experience has shown that this has rarely been the case."[62]

OTHER PHILOSOPHICAL QUESTIONS

Optimism and Pessimism. The second philosophical question is concerned with optimism or pessimism, and the third is concerned with the predictability of the future. Beginning with the third question, Kissinger's views are that predictability would be enhanced under a legitimate order where statesmen dominate, and would decrease in a revolutionary order. Because statesmen are oriented toward the status quo, and toward reducing risks with more incremental behavior, prediction is easier in a system dominated by statesmen. As is reflected in both his senior honors thesis and his Ph.D. dissertation, Kissinger believed that the present resembles the past, while, of course, never repeating it exactly. The statesman's goal, then, is to uncover the correct and relevant similarities and differences, and then to act accordingly. This task is made more manageable by the more slowly paced and less radical change that occurs within a legitimate international order.

In response to the second philosophical question, there will be less predictability within a revolutionary order, and therefore one must make a more pessimistic assessment for the prospects of political success within a revolutionary order.[63] On the basis of his central dichotomy, Kissinger's views on optimism and pessimism are a clear dualism. Kissinger's assessments are pessimistic if seen through the prism of a revolutionary order, as in his undergraduate thesis, where he says, "The generation of Buchenwald and Siberian labor camps cannot talk with the same optimism as its fathers."[64] Kissinger's assessment of the world is far more optimistic, however, if the more stable and predictable legitimate international order prevails. Thus, Kissinger's optimism and pessimism are related to the type of order he perceived to be in existence or in the ascendancy.

The dualism of optimism and pessimism is exhibited elsewhere as well. Observers who paint Kissinger as a pessimist point out Kissinger's affinity to the pessimistic outlook Spengler presented in *The Decline of the West.* Stoessinger, for example, quotes the concluding passage of *A World Restored,* where Kissinger observes "life involves suffering and transitoriness."[65] (However, Kissinger never totally accepts Spengler's view, since he also believed in the ability of individuals, at least some individuals, to affect the world and their own destiny.) Kissinger's early writings—"The Meaning of History" and *A World Restored*—coming after his youth in Germany and his rapid rise to positions of authority and power in the U.S. Army during World War II, reflect the dualism between hope and despair. Kissinger the historian and thinker tended to be pessimistic when reviewing man's historical drama. Kissinger the *activist* (or when writing about how a policymaker should behave), whether in the army or as foreign-policy decision maker, was an individual to whom struggle against history was crucial, and thus was an optimist. In a 1974 interview, Kissinger observed, "As a historian one has to live with a sense of the inevitability of tragedy. As a statesman, one has to act on the assumption that problems must be solved."[66] The next year, at a U.N. Day concert, Kissinger expressed the optimistic view: "The great orchestra and great music we are about to hear should recall to us that man is not a creature of circumstance or of despair. Man is driven and ennobled by his dreams."[67]

Mazlish, too, presents the optimism/pessimism dualism as being oriented toward activism and will. He notes that, "At the core of Kissinger's commitment to activism, both psychologically and intellectually, is his despair over the ability of 'good will' by itself to effect anything in the real world."[68] Kissinger saw that the good will of his father and men like him meant little in the real world. Instead, he took to heart the lessons that Fritz Kraemer taught him. Kraemer's widely quoted imagery pits good will against reality: "A man does not know the world until he has been out alone on the docks of Marseilles, hungry and with only one suit, being stalked by another man who wants that suit. Then being reasonable or good doesn't matter. Then a man has to stand up for himself or die."[69] Good will is not enough, but "will" is crucial: will creates its own reality.[70]

Dickson particularly picks up on this theme. Drawing upon "The Meaning of History" as his main source, Dickson clearly illustrates the alternation between optimism and pessimism in Kissinger's thinking. There are references to Spengler's gloomy scenarios of Western materialism, and also to Kissinger's use of the optimistic aspects of Kant's philosophy. As Dickson notes: "The idea of man as *noumenon,* as a personality endowed with a transcendental sense of freedom, exerted a powerful hold on Kissinger." The dualism of Kissinger's optimism and pessimism has been described by Dickson as a "lapsed Kantianism": "He is Kantian in so far as he continues to affirm the existence of human freedom. . . . His emphatic rejection of teleology, however, indicates his inability to share Kant's 'rational faith' that there is purpose and perhaps progress in human history."[71]

But Kissinger did see hopeful signs. Again reflecting the dual perspective, Stoessinger notes that, although shaken by the Cuban missile crisis, Kissinger also perceived its positive consequences. Out of pessimism came optimism. Stoessinger observed: "He had always believed that America, unlike Europe, was rather innocent of tragedy and therefore incapable of truly understanding that states, like men, could die . . . What heartened Kissinger was that both superpowers apparently had learned a lesson. The narrowness of their escape had left a mark."[72]

Albert Eldridge closes his analysis of Kissinger with a summary of Kissinger's orientation toward optimism and pessimism:

> Kissinger's perception of the world and the problems that confront it *are* pessimistic. One reason is that he sees the world and its problems as posing an almost unsurmountable obstacle to the realization of his goals. Kissinger values security. Yet the world he sees is filled with conflict and aggression. Kissinger values stability and harmony. Yet the world he perceives was filled with tension, anxiety, a lack of accommodation and unbridled competition. Kissinger has faith in the long range utility of personal knowledge, creativity and boldness. Yet he confronts a society that does not always put a premium on these attributes. . . . If there has been pessimism in Kissinger's statements there has been optimism as well. Kissinger believes that knowledge, intelligence, determination, flexibility and creativity eventually can lead to solutions. He affirms a belief that man has some control over his environment. Indeed it is in the challenge of the obstacles that his hope lies.[73]

Control and Chance. Kissinger's optimism—as reflected in the sincere belief that he could bring about peace in Vietnam and the Middle East, reverse over two decades of antagonistic relations with China, solve the riddles of Cyprus and Rhodesia, and link the Soviet Union more firmly with his conception of the legitimate world order—is closely related to the fourth and fifth philosophical questions, which are concerned with control or mastery of history and with the role of chance in human affairs, respectively.

Most of Kissinger's explicit thoughts on these two questions are presented in "The Meaning of History." His conclusion is that the successful statesman must realize that he has only a modest control over history, to which he must adjust with care. Yet the statesman must reject determinism or fatalism, and consciously understand that, while he must accept uncertainty and tragedy, he must also recognize his ability to affect history. In *The Necessity for Choice,* Kissinger says simply, "We can still shape our future."[74] In "The Meaning of History," Kissinger expresses himself in more detail:

> History is the past and the past is the most inexorable necessity with which we live. We know the past only as a phenomena. Even our own actions in retrospect lose the inner experience

that accompanied them. . . . The past is dead and ruled by necessity but freedom governs the future. . . . The experience of freedom enables us to raise beyond the suffering of the past and the frustrations of history. In this spirituality resides humanity's essence, the unique which each man imparts to the necessity for his life, the self-transcendence which gives peace. . . . Respect for the forces of history does not mean blind submission to history.[75]

Kissinger understood the importance of accident or chance in history, also. In writing on America's European policies, he noted that, "Opportunities cannot be hoarded; once past they are usually irretrievable."[76] In *Necessity for Choice,* Kissinger similarly criticized the West for "failing to act in the face of the historical imperative."[77] Together, these views summarize his beliefs on control or mastery in history. The basic ideas presented in "The Meaning of History" are complemented by his evaluation of two statesmen—Castlereagh and Metternich—in *A World Restored.*

A major theme in *A World Restored* (and to which he returned in his 1966 article "Domestic Structure and Foreign Policy") is the domestic and international constraints under which the statesman has to operate. These constraints are summarized by Kissinger:

The statesman is inevitably confronted by the inertia of his material, by the fact that other powers are not factors to be manipulated but forces to be reconciled; that the requirements of security differ with the geographic location and the domestic structure of the powers. . . . The acid test of a policy . . . is its ability to obtain domestic support. This has two aspects: the problem of legitimizing a policy within the governmental apparatus, which is a problem of bureaucratic rationality; and that of harmonizing it with the national experience, which is a problem of historical development.[78]

The point here, however, is that, in discussing the domestic and international constraints on the statesman and the various shortcomings of both Castlereagh and Metternich, Kissinger made it clear that he believed that certain statesmen, in history's fateful moments, *could* influence history through acts of vision and courage. The statesmen first had to recognize such moments. Second, they had to overcome the constraints of domestic opinion and governmental bureaucracy—and in this the statesman had to take on the role of educator for both the mass and the governmental elite.[79] Thus, a leader who "understands" the world (as Kissinger, with his explicit and strongly held concept of world order, was), at a crucial time in history (such as a time of emerging Soviet parity with the United States, and a new era of American "introversion"),[80] could, through the exercise of will and skillful personal diplomacy, affect history.

Kissinger's view was that the lonely, and heroic leader (as reflected in his famous "cowboy" statement to journalist Oriana Fallaci), could be effective only if not encumbered by the webs and weight of bureaucracy. This view was in accord with both his academic writings and his personality and style, (e.g., the "low affiliation" motive noted in chapter 2). Both Nixon and Kissinger were, to varying degrees, loners, and Kissinger's view of the bureaucracy fit perfectly with Nixon's desire to tame the bureaucratic system and turn it into his own "commissar"-style system. The Kalbs summarize the point, made by many other observers, that "In Kissinger, Nixon found an enthusiastic disciple, equally elitist in orientation, equally distrustful of the bureaucracy."[81] All descriptions of "Henry's Wonderful Machine" (to use the Kalbs' phrase) point out the mutual delight of both men in creating a national security system that could be controlled from the White House and that would circumvent and ignore the State Department. Kissinger sketches an identical picture in reporting the meeting at which Nixon offered him the job of National Security adviser: "The President-elect repeated essentially the same arguments he had made two days earlier, emphasizing more strongly his view of the incompetence of the CIA and the untrustworthiness of the State Department. The position of security adviser was therefore crucial to him and his plan to run foreign policy from the White House."[82]

Kissinger's antipathy to bureaucratic constraints on the statesman and diplomacy go back to his discussion of the statesman in *A World Restored.* The theme of the bureaucracy's quest for "safety" and conservatism, which first appeared in *A World Restored,* reappeared in *Nuclear Weapons and Foreign Policy* and subsequent writings. As Mazlish and Stoessinger, among others, have noted, Kissinger's experiences with the Kennedy and Johnson administrations only served to reinforce his views on bureaucratic constraints. The best summary of these views is to be found in "Domestic Structure and Foreign Policy," published in 1966, and repeated and elaborated to varying degrees in "The Policymaker and the Intellectual" (1959), and "Bureaucracy and Policy Making: The Effect of Insiders and Outsiders on the Policy Process" (1968).[83]

Observations from "Domestic Structure and Foreign Policy" illustrate the position Kissinger took into government in 1969:

The vast bureaucratic mechanisms that emerge develop a momentum and a vested interest of their own. . . . There is a trend toward autarky. . . . The purpose of the bureaucracy is to devise a standard operating procedure which can cope effectively with most problems. . . . Bureaucracy becomes an obstacle when what it defines as routine does not address the most significant range of issues or when its prescribed mode of action proves irrelevant to the problem. . . . When this occurs, the bureaucracy absorbs the energies of top executives. . . . Serving the machine becomes a more absorbing occupation than defining its purpose.[84]

Indeed, the Kissinger-Nixon style followed the blueprint Kissinger set out in "Domestic Structure and Foreign Policy." Kissinger predicted that the executive would be forced into "extra-bureaucratic" mechanisms in order to avoid the problems of the administrative machine: "Faced with an administrative machine which is both elaborate and fragmented, the executive is forced into essentially lateral means of control. . . . All of this drives the executive in the direction of extra-bureaucratic means of decision. The practice of relying on special emissaries or personal envoys is an example; their status outside the bureaucracy frees them from some of its restraints."[85] Kissinger, in another example of projective biography, became just such a special emissary, and relied on lateral means of control.

Nixon not only got his special extra-bureaucratic emissary, but also set up elaborate communications procedures by which to end-run the State Department. Some of the most fascinating material in *White House Years* is found in Kissinger's description of the various "backchannels" developed to conduct foreign relations without using the State Department or without its knowledge: "As time went by, the President, or I on his behalf, in order to avoid these endless confrontations, came to deal increasingly with key foreign leaders through channels that directly linked the White House Situation Room to the field without going through the State Department—the so-called backchannels. This process started on the day after Inauguration" (p. 29).

The establishment of the backchannel, how it circumvented the State Department, and the dual process of carrying out foreign-policy negotiations in public (State Department) and private tracks all come to play a central role in the Nixon-Kissinger foreign policy. The effort was enormous, but the purpose was a foreign policy of statesman unconstrained by the bureaucratic politics, leaks, and the time-consuming nature of working through the State Department.

It is possible that Kissinger reflected too well those men whom he analyzed in his delineation of the statesman. In *A World Restored,* Kissinger described Metternich as "a mediocre strategist but a great tactician." Conversely, George Ball made the observation, quoted by Stoessinger, that Kissinger's "step-by-step approach was the work of a tactician when the times called for a strategist."[86] Similarly, Stanley Hoffmann criticizes Kissinger's excessive pragmatism, a trait that Kissinger had previously assailed in works like "Domestic Structure and Foreign Policy."[87]

KISSINGER'S OPERATIONAL CODE: INSTRUMENTAL QUESTIONS

Negotiation, Limits, Force. In addition to being an academic concerned with philosophical and historical questions, Kissinger was also an activist, concerned with the ways in which a statesman could overcome domestic and international constraints. As Stoessinger notes: "To conceive was not enough. A statesman was more than a philosopher. He had to implement his vision and execute his policies."[88] Therefore, Kissinger's instrumental values are also closely linked to his earlier life experiences. In the army, Kissinger learned that to have any impact, "visions" indeed had to be carried through in the real world. At this point, then, all of the necessary ingredients for answering the first two instrumental questions, which concern the manner in which goals are selected and pursued most effectively, have been introduced—the statesman and his mode of behavior, the domestic and international constraints that provide the context for the statesman's diplomacy, and the goals that the statesman will pursue (a legitimate, stable, world order).[89]

The statesman recognizes the constraint of the international environment—the need to coexist with other states, each wishing for security and survival, and each espousing different perceptions and conceptions of justice.[90] The statesman also recognizes the constraints of the historical situation as it exists, including the domestic influences of elite and public opinion and the bureaucracy. Within these constraints, the statesman, unlike the prophet or the conqueror, must not try to impose one state's idea of order or justice on the international system. *Negotiation,* especially with opponents, is the primary tool of the statesman, and the only tool that can be used for the creation of an accepted, common legitimacy in the system. Goals are selected that are in accordance with the creation or continuance of a stable international system. The tools used are those that are acceptable to the legitimacy of the system— such as negotiation. Force is used only to defend those principles that are part of the legitimate international order. War, as noted, may be used to defeat a revolutionary state, to ensure the survival of the system members, to maintain stability, and to redress the international balance.

Kissinger developed these ideas in *A World Restored* and in later works, particularly that on Bismarck. In a 1978 interview, Kissinger's further comments on Bismarck reinforce and summarize these instrumental beliefs, introduced a quarter of a century earlier:

> I studied Bismarck and developed a great admiration for him. I think he is the first modern statesman in this sense: that he attempted to conduct foreign policy on the basis of an assessment of the balance of forces, unrestrained by the clichés of a previous period. . . . What is more important is that he understood that power can be used only as an instrument in the political consequences you draw from it—if you respect the right to existence of other states with whom, over an historic period, you have to coexist.[91]

In this statement Kissinger declares explicitly another belief central to the pursuit of goals—self-limitation. The idea of limits is both derived from, and central to, Kissinger's concept of the legitimate state, with the statesman at its helm. Just as the concepts of legitimacy and the statesman evolved from Kissinger's earlier experiences, so does the notion of limits. Order, respect for others' survival, and stability all require self-limitation of the sort lacking in the revolutionary state and its leaders (e.g., lacking in Hitler and Nazi Germany).

To pursue what Dickson calls the "doctrine of limits," as in the quote about Bismarck above, in *A World Restored* Kissinger praises Metternich and Castlereagh when they recognized the limits of their power and chose diplomacy over force. Earlier, in "The Meaning of History," he wrote that, "Freedom derives not merely from an inward state but from an experience that has to come from the recognition of limits. This acceptance is tolerance, the knowledge that one must set boundaries to one's striving."[92] In *A World Restored,* Kissinger argues that neither the conqueror nor the prophet understands the moderation of limits—only the statesman does. Order can derive only from a recognition of limits. Limits, as a component of order, have priority over morality or justice. In *The Necessity for Choice,* Kissinger writes of limits in exactly these terms: "to be meaningful, self-restraint must set limits even to the exercise of righteous power."[93] Indeed, in the period before

Nixon's first inauguration, Kissinger outlined a number of principles that were to guide U.S.-Soviet relations. One of these was the principle of restraint: "reasonable relations between the two superpowers could not survive the constant attempt to pursue unilateral advantages and exploit areas of crisis."[94] The principle of restraint was the basis for détente and its implementation—each side would recognize limits to its behavior. "Détente as a policy of peace . . . is rational because it rests on the recognition of the *limits* of power."[95] World order was the goal; restraint was a vital path to that goal (even if it had to be "taught" to the other side). In sum, Mazlish observes: "Kissinger was, and is, obsessed with the notion of 'limits.' It is a major theme, both in his life and his writings."[96]

The use of force in combination with diplomatic negotiations relates more closely to the third instrumental question, regarding the calculation and control of risk in political action. Just as a legitimate order is associated with optimism, negotiation is associated with the least risky means for achieving the statesman's goals. Negotiation is an incremental and deliberate process, a relatively slow process that therefore helps to reduce history's uncertainties. Because of these uncertainties, and the general lack of control over history, the use of force (e.g., by the conqueror) or of charisma (e.g., by the prophet) is far more risky. As Walker says, "Morally, the negotiation process is the most appropriate way to insure that foreign policy is based upon a sense of self limitation, respect for human dignity, and tolerance for the aspirations of others."[97]

As is developed in *Nuclear Weapons and Foreign Policy,* Kissinger saw the risks of the nuclear age as especially grave.[98] If force has to be used, negotiations have to be employed both before and during the use of force, in order to reduce the risks. Bargaining must continue during military confrontation, as negotiation and force could be combined to establish mutually acceptable outcomes. Kissinger outlines four possible outcomes—local military victory by one side, a stalemate, a negotiated settlement, or nuclear devastation if the parties are nuclear powers.[99] The statesman must avoid both nuclear holocaust and complete victory by either side, in order to ensure the principle of state survival and to maintain stability.

Walker's summary is useful:

Kissinger's emphasis upon the role of negotiations prior to and during a military conflict, plus the eschewing of military victory as a political objective, are the two principal ways in which he controls the risks of political action that involves the use of force. At some point in a military conflict Kissinger's objective is to maneuver the opponent into a situation where he must choose among three outcomes to the conflict: military defeat or withdrawal and absolute loss; military stalemate and relative loss; negotiated settlement and a relative gain.[100]

In his memoirs, Kissinger again indicates that these instrumental beliefs, developed and expressed years earlier, guided his behavior. Discussing Vietnam, he notes:

> Nixon and I both sought to end the war as rapidly as possible. But there was a nuance of difference between us over the strategy for doing so. My aim was to weave a complex web that would give us the greatest number of options. Though favoring a strong military reaction, I never wanted to rely on power alone or, for that matter, on negotiation by itself. In my view diplomacy and strategy should support each other. I always favored preceding or at least accompanying a military move with a diplomatic one, even when I rated the chances of success as low.[101]

A View of Détente. Walker, Stoessinger, and Ward demonstrate that Kissinger followed his instrumental beliefs concerning force, negotiation, and risk in his Indochinese settlement policies. Similar policies, including the principle that neither side should be permitted to win a decisive victory, were pursued in the Middle East and Cyprus. Kissinger was apparently also willing to apply some version of this policy in Angola, but was thwarted by Congressional opposition (Castlereagh's problem of a "vision beyond the conception of his domestic structure"?). Détente was pursued as a policy that would ensure the existence of negotiation procedures and possibilities between legitimate powers, powers that should avoid the risk of nuclear destruction.

Observers of Kissinger-era foreign policy, those who have analyzed his pre-office writing as well as his speeches as policymaker, have commented that American policy was centered on the Soviet Union. All other policy issues were considered only as they impinged upon this central relationship. (Support for this assertion is provided in Part II.) Why is this the case in terms particular to Henry Kissinger? The stable world order that is the core of Kissinger's belief system requires that the major opponent in the system be central to one's policy. This is particularly true if that power, along with oneself, has the military capability to destroy the world. But, how was the Soviet Union to be fit into a stable structure of peace? Kissinger's views have always taken two tracks (the "dual policy" he was to follow as a policymaker)—1) increasing the economic, political, and cultural ties of interdependence, to give any state a major stake in the system and thus to impose costs on it should it break the rules of the system; and 2) utilizing a balance of power process, based on the costs that countervailing power would impose on states that broke the "rules" of the system. During his time in office, Kissinger often spoke of entangling the Soviet Union within the "webs" of economic and political relations that existed in the system:

> We have an historic obligation to mankind to engage the Soviet Union in settlements of concrete problems and to push back the shadow of nuclear catastrophe. . . . And we have begun to construct a network of cooperative agreements in a variety of functional areas—economic, scientific, medical, environmental and others—which promise concrete benefits if political conditions permit. . . . It has been our belief that, with patience, a pattern of restraints and a network of vested interests can develop which will give coexistence a more hopeful dimension and make both sides conscious of what they would stand to lose by reverting to the politics of pressure, confrontation and crisis.[102]

This logic formed the basis for the Kissinger-Nixon ideas of linkage, where limits were imposed by self-restraint. The restraint came from understanding that lack of restraint would impose costs in other areas, "because in an interdependent world the actions of a major power are inevitably related and have consequences beyond the issue or region immediately concerned."[103] Restraint would not come from simply demonstrating one's "good will,"(a lesson Kissinger learned in his youth). In a 1962 article on the Cuban missile crisis, Kissinger questioned the lessons that the Soviets learned from U.S. behavior at Suez, in Lebanon, and in the Bay of Pigs. Kissinger's view, following Kennan's was that GRIT-like acts of good will were not enough. Soviet behavior would best be influenced by demonstrating that costs would be imposed, in the form of the loss of cooperative arrangements or the possibility of the use of military force. Walker's analysis of Kissinger's use of negotiations and force is relevant to this "dual track" policy toward the Soviet Union. In his memoirs, Kissinger presents a strategy similar to the one Walker has extracted from pre-office writings: "In dealing with the Soviets a point is inevitably reached where it is important to make clear brutally that the limits of flexibility have been reached, that the time has come either to settle or to end the negotiation. This is a more complex matter than simply getting 'tough'."[104] To Kissinger, "getting tough" was part of a larger process of positive incentives and negative costs that one used to help an opponent see that his own interest lay in restraint, and to impose restraint if necessary.

Thus, Kissinger's policy toward the Soviet Union was one part détente (the use of positive incentives of mutual benefit, and increasing webs of interdependence), and one part Kennan (firm response to adventurist, expansionist, and de-stabilizing behavior). This dual policy is indicated in numerous discussions of détente in *White House Years*. For example, Kissinger notes, "Our strategy of détente always depended on a firm application of psychological and physical restraints and determined resistance to challenge." Specifically, "All experience teaches that Soviet military moves, which usually begin as tentative, must be resisted early, unequivocally, and in a fashion that gives Soviet leaders a justification for withdrawal." Early in the memoirs, discussing SALT and U.S. defense policy, Kissinger notes, "It was the perennial debate whether Soviet interest in compromise was best elicited by making unilateral American gestures or by presenting the Kremlin with risks and programs they were eager to stop."[105]

That Kissinger as a policymaker used force and risk may have appeared arbitrary to some observers, but Kissinger was willing to become tough and to threaten the use of force when he felt the risk was worth it—in order to defend or preserve those principles he saw necessary to a stable, legitimate international order. Kissinger's willingness to risk a confrontation in Angola is a case in point. Kissinger's view was that the Soviet Union could not be permitted to use its resources to achieve such successes—successes he considered de-stabilizing to international order. Détente had supposedly made such interventions beyond the rules of the game (or at least in Kissinger's view of détente). In challenging those rules, the Soviet Union was challenging a principle of legitimacy. It was, therefore, worth the risk to Kissinger to meet this challenge. However, in his attempts to meet this challenge, Kissinger the statesman, like his nineteenth-century counterparts, was frustrated by political and bureaucratic constraints.

Kissinger's reaction to the challenge of Eurocommunism can also be investigated in terms of his operational-code beliefs. One could argue that the United States and the Soviet Union have had both tacit and more formal agreements (e.g., the Helsinki agreements) not to engage in intervention in the other's European bloc or sphere of influence. An important part of European order, world order, and Soviet-American stability is based upon the limits of non-intervention into each other's spheres. The probability that one of the powers will challenge this order, that this informal rule will be broken, increases if there is a lack of clarity in the European situation. When it is unclear or ambiguous whether a European state is still a "full" block member, whether it is still a full ally, or an area still wholly within a superpower's sphere of influence, then there is greater danger that the rule of non-intervention will be broken.[106] Thus, lack of clarity increases the probability of instability by increasing the chances of intervention. Kissinger saw Eurocommunism as a mechanism of ambiguity, blurring the lines of alliance in the European situation, and thus a potential threat to the stability of the area. The establishment of Communist governments in countries like Portugal, Italy, or France would create ambiguity—the nation would be a NATO member, but with an avowedly Communist government. Each superpower would then have claims to various "interventionary" activities in such countries. The possibility of political and military confrontation in Europe would be enhanced, and the situation would become unstable and dangerous in Kissinger's conception of world order. Therefore, it is not contradictory that, while opening and increasing contacts with the principal Communist powers—Russia and China—Kissinger was also taking a firm position against the possibility of Communist governments in Western Europe.

The last two instrumental questions are concerned with timing and the use of different means for advancing one's goals. The primary issue involved with both of these questions is whether one's opponent is a legitimate or revolutionary actor. The means of interaction—negotiation or force—used, and their order and combination, will depend upon the nature of the opponent. Stoessinger provides an example of timing in this sense when he notes that Kissinger saw Yasir Arafat as a revolutionary who could be coopted into a legitimate world order. Kissinger's means of statecraft would depend on whether he perceived Arafat as crossing the line from revolutionary to statesman.[107]

Drawing from *Nuclear Weapons and Foreign Policy*, Walker provides a summary of the sequence of steps that a stateman will employ to achieve the best timing in the combined use of force and negotiations: "Negotiate throughout the conflict; use threats only to counter threats or the use of force initiated by the opponent; use enough force combined with generous peace terms so that the opponent is faced with an attractive peace settlement vs. the unattractive alternatives of military defeat or the necessity to escalate."[108] In sum, Kissinger's use of such instrumental beliefs in his policies and reactions to Soviet behavior give his dealings a distinctly "Kennan" touch: firm response, with the appropriate capabilities at the appropriate places. His preference for this mode of foreign-policy behavior has also been the basis of Kissinger's various critiques of the Carter administration's foreign policy.

CONCLUSION

The summation of Kissinger's operational code must start with Mazlish's statement that, "The most important overall comment to be made about Kissinger's world view, or ideology, is that it is conservative."[109] Kissinger's philosophical beliefs are conservative in their concern with order, restraint, and the general maintenance of the status quo against the revolutionary (prophet or conqueror). The statesman, while possessing a number of "dynamic" characteristics, reflects the basic conservatism of Kissinger's ideology. Kissinger's instrumental beliefs, in turn, reflect his conservative philosophical beliefs.

The beliefs in Kissinger's operational code derive from a desire for safety and stability that is primarily defensive and reactive. The roots of his conservative goals are found in the uncertainty and trauma of Kissinger's boyhood. Similarly, instrumental beliefs stressing the use of negotiations derive from the complex of factors that make up Kissinger's identification with the opponent. In terms of this identification, negotiations are the most important tool of the statesman, since they help establish a view of a situation that can be shared with one's negotiating partner. They also help to lower the risks inherent in the use of force. The use of force is also closely related to Kissinger's stance toward the use of power, which was conservative—that is, power is used to preserve or protect the stability of legitimate states, and it is to be used in a limited and restrained manner, and always within the statesman's need to pursue negotiation.

Mazlish gives a fitting overview of Kissinger's operational code: "He has formulated this world view in order to restore a world of stability. Right or wrong, its farsighted analysis . . . provides a consistent, coherent perspective that supplies guidance to an operational code . . . and a sense of direction and certainty."[110]

PART II

Images of the Soviet Union and China: A Content-Analytic Study

4

Introduction: Operational Code and Content Analysis

OPERATIONAL CODE AND CONTENT ANALYSIS

Part I brings together biographical, perceptual, intellectual, and policy-making analyses of Henry Kissinger—the youth, the adult, the academic, and the foreign-policy decision maker. Part II focuses specifically on the last of these stages. Henry Kissinger the foreign-policy decision maker is investigated in depth and in a more focused manner than was possible for the broad descriptions of policy positions that were presented in conjunction with his operational code.

The original empirical research reported in Part II describes and analyzes the images of the Soviet Union and China that Kissinger held while he was a high-level decision maker. The description and analysis employ a formal and rigorous method of content analysis: evaluative assertion analysis. Besides being more formal than the analysis used for the operational code, evaluative assertion analysis moves on to the policy-making stage of Kissinger's career, looking not at his academic writings but at a different set of "traces"—the public statements made by Kissinger as a foreign-policy decision maker.

The relationship between Parts I and II, between the less formal operational-code analysis and the more formal evaluative assertion analysis, may be viewed in two ways. First, Part I is a comment on the life, personality, style, and operational code of Henry Kissinger, using mostly secondary sources. Part II, instead of looking at Kissinger's full operational code or belief system (as related to and derived from psychobiographical factors), concentrates on one major aspect of the belief system: Kissinger's "image of the opponent." This image is seen by some as a "master belief." Using this master belief as a focus, we can highlight many areas of Kissinger's belief system, but the important point is that the empirical research in Part II should be viewed as one empirical test of the accuracy and validity of the observations and conclusions drawn in Part I. This test is performed by looking at one portion of Kissinger's belief system at a different stage of his career and using a different data base for the analyses.

The method of this research is related to the second basic way in which Parts I and II are connected. If one's primary interests are the comparative study of foreign policy, foreign-policy decision making, and/or the place of individual factors in the study of international relations and foreign policy, then the broad context of Part I, consisting of an overview of Kissinger's personality, style, and belief system, is needed before one can embark on the formal content analysis presented in Part II. This connection is necessary because, although formal content analysis, such as evaluative assertion analysis, is a means of access to foreign-policy decision makers, it, like many formal and quantitative methodologies, requires application by researchers firmly grounded in a preliminary substantive knowledge of the research topic. Without such preliminary understanding, it is easy to draw spurious conclusions from the quantitative data, or, more importantly, to ask the wrong questions and therefore to design the research improperly.

Therefore, the material in Part I, especially as it aids in understanding and setting out Kissinger's operational code, is necessary to inform the content analysis of Kissinger's images of the opponent. Furthermore, the Soviet Union is not just any opponent, but an international actor central to this statesman's overriding concern with stability and order in the contemporary international system. Having gained a clear understanding of Kissinger's beliefs concerning opponents in general, and this opponent in particular, we can be certain that Kissinger is not concerned with Communism per se (e.g., in the rigid, morality-based images of someone like Dulles), and that Kissinger perceives the Soviet Union as a legitimate state, which, although dangerous to the stability of the international order, can be treated in ways that ameliorate and constrain its danger. Understanding Kissinger's instrumental beliefs about risk, force, and the use of negotiations is central to understanding his conception of détente and his attitudes toward the Soviet Union over time (as well as the way in which he manipulated both the cooperative and coercive instruments of foreign policy).

While the evaluative assertion analysis in Part II is used to test these conclusions—through comparisons of Kissinger and Dulles, comparison of his images of the Soviet Union to his images of China, and analyses of the interaction of Soviet and Chinese images and behavior—the operational-code analyses are also required in order to ensure that the content analysis was designed and executed properly (for example, see the coding rules set out in chapter 5).

Therefore, not only does Part II supplement Part I, but also Part I may be seen as the necessary background or context within which to place the content analysis of Part II. This study, then, is structured to check the validity of both of these major techniques for gaining access to decision makers. The operational code, drawn from an earlier life period, is used to guide the content analysis, to generate hypotheses, and to understand how the belief system might affect later images, bring about closure of images, or function in the operation of defense mechanisms to protect those images. The content analysis, based on a later life stage, uses the hypotheses of the operational-code results to look at specific images in Kissinger's belief system. General congruence or agreement will give us greater faith in both methods.

It should be clear, then, that Part II undertakes a very different task from Part I, even though they are closely tied together. Part II, in looking at Kissinger's images of two states, tests the work of Part I, tests cognitive methods for gaining access to decision makers, and reveals very specific aspects of Kissinger the policymaker and of American foreign policy. But the tasks set out in Part II are not possible without Part I as the necessary context.

DESIGN: HOLSTI AND DULLES

Part II consists of the research design and content analyses derived from that design, which is substantially similar to the design employed by Ole Holsti in his study of John Foster Dulles.[1] As noted in chapter 1, a purpose of the present study is to add to the literature concerning individual factors in the making of foreign policy, and Holsti's research on Dulles was a classic, pioneering study in this area. Another purpose of the present study is to replicate the form of Holsti's study of Dulles in a similar study of Henry Kissinger.

Briefly, Holsti employed content analysis to study Dulles's belief system, particularly the way in which Dulles perceived the "enemy"—the Soviet Union. The notion of the enemy, some "them" out there different from "us," is a powerful psychological concept, and is central to the study of individuals who must guide their nations through the "anarchic" international system.[2] Holsti was concerned with the "cognitive dynamics associated with images of the enemy."[3] (Rudolph Rummel has noted that "one perceives others in terms of how and in which ways they differ from oneself. In particular, we perceive intentions toward us, their power compared to ours, and their value differences from us."[4]) Holsti was interested in discovering whether there were cognitive processes that would tend to sustain and reinforce images of the enemy, how these images did or did not change, and, if they did change, in what directions. We look at similar questions in chapter 6, which undertakes a contrast of Kissinger and Dulles, guided by the operational-code differences outlined in chapter 3.

In using Kissinger as a subject for an evaluative assertion analysis that is to parallel the study of Dulles, one discovers that in many ways (including governmental role, governmental structure, and individual style) the two men evince striking parallels. These parallels are useful in viewing the Kissinger study as a replication of Holsti's study. On the other hand, there appear to be major personality, intellectual, and stylistic differences that suggest contrasts between Kissinger's and Dulles's views of the Soviet Union, and the rigidity of those views. As Townsend Hoopes observes, there are "striking similarities in the characters and performances of the two Secretaries, but equally striking differences."[5]

Holsti selected Dulles for his study because Dulles "was acknowledged as the central figure in foreign policy formulation. . . . His forceful personality, combined with an almost absolute reliance upon his own abilities served to increase his influence."[6] Holsti also cites Richard Rovere's observations about Dulles: "He made military commitments without consulting military officials, and economic commitments without consulting Treasury officials. He bypassed American embassies, and he only occasionally availed himself of the services of the experts in his own department."[7]

Kissinger's position in the foreign-policy process and his attitude toward control (especially of the bureaucracy) were similar. Both men clearly saw the president as the ultimate foreign-policy authority, and Garry Wills draws a compelling picture of Dulles applying the flesh to the foreign-policy skeleton constructed by Eisenhower.[8] Similarly, with regard to Kissinger and Nixon, Henry Brandon writes: "One high official who has attended many meetings with both present believes that the working relationship between them is comparable to one between an architect and a contractor. The decisions about the basic design were the President's but Kissinger had great freedom on how to build the house."[9] Brandon reports Kissinger's observation that, "Often I don't know whether I am the actor or the director."[10] Hoopes notes that Dulles and Kissinger both possessed strong intellects and forceful personalities, with the tendency to act and to act alone. Both men believed in personal diplomacy and felt comfortable manipulating the political and military elements of diplomacy while neglecting international economic matters. Both secretaries clearly dominated the operational and public-relations aspects of foreign policy.[11]

Another reason that Holsti chose Dulles for study was Dulles's apparently "well-defined belief system, which is set forth not only in his official pronouncements, but also in numerous theoretical writings."[12] Kissinger also developed a body of academic (theoretical) writing on international relations, and, as Dulles did, he provided voluminous documentary material during his years as secretary of state (and somewhat less during his early years as National Security adviser).

The operational-code comparisons between Dulles and Kissinger are summarized by Hoopes, who draws capsule sketches of the two secretaries that indicate the contrasts between Dulles and Kissinger.

> In part because of his commitment to the Wilsonian ideal of universal freedom and democracy, Mr. Dulles was committed to sustaining an indefinite American crusade against Godless Communism; and because his ideological convictions ruled out any possibility of genuine compromise with the other side, his negotiations with the Soviet Union and China were not seriously directed toward a settlement. . . . Though no less tough-minded in specific adversary situations, Mr. Kissinger is a serious seeker of practical compromise in negotiations with the Communist powers and less concerned about the resulting ideological patterns. These differences show up not only in policy but in style.[13]

The content-analysis findings, presented primarily in chapter 6, delineate a number of differences in the images of the Soviet Union held by Dulles and Kissinger. These differences, discovered through the content analysis of public statements made while the subjects were decision makers, are clearly traceable to differences in operational codes developed in pre-policy maker writings.

The analytic chapters in Part II are a series of comparisons: chapter 6 compares Kissinger's images of the Soviet Union with those of Dulles; chapter 7 compares Kissinger's images of the Soviet Union with his images of the People's Republic of China; chapter 8 compares the images to the actual foreign-policy behavior of the United States, the Soviet Union, and China; and chapter 9 makes a comparison of Kissinger's images before and after he became secretary of state, and a comparison of the images he held under Nixon with those he held during the Ford presidency.

5

Research Design

RESEARCH QUESTIONS AND CONCERNS

The content analysis of Henry Kissinger's images of the Soviet Union and China is designed to address issues involved in the study of foreign policy and international relations. The issues raise the questions of whether individuals make a difference and how they might do so, and under what conditions. These questions involve access to decision makers, the study of perceptions, images, and belief systems, and related concerns.

In the simplest terms, Kissinger's images have been examined for how open or closed they might be, how they relate to previous beliefs, and how they relate to U.S., Soviet, and Chinese foreign-policy behavior. This examination reflects the research questions originally asked by Holsti in his study of John Foster Dulles:

1. To determine the effect of his [Dulles's] belief system upon his perceptions and interpretation of information concerning the Soviet Union and its foreign policy.

2. To determine the effect of events upon his belief system itself.[1]

Holsti translated these concerns into three general hypotheses:

1. That information concerning the Soviet Union tended to be perceived and interpreted in a manner consistent with his belief system.

2. That information not consistent with his image of the Soviet Union tended to be ignored, to be re-interpreted so as to be more consistent with his belief system, or to be questioned as to its truth or relevance.

3. That information supporting and re-enforcing his image of the Soviet Union was most readily accepted and acted upon.[2]

In this study, the first research question is basically descriptive—What were Kissinger's images of the Soviet Union and China during his policy-making years? Once that question is addressed, the comparisons discussed above can be made. How open or closed Kissinger's images are is examined in relation to changes in these images across time, and through a comparison to Dulles's images of the Soviet Union. In addition, events data are employed in an examination of how Kissinger's images reflect superpower foreign-policy behavior, and vice versa.

This chapter is devoted to the design issues raised by these substantive concerns. A brief discussion of content analysis and evaluative assertion analysis provides an introduction to the procedures by which Kissinger's public words were converted into images, or evaluations, of the Soviet Union and China. The data sources for the study are then presented, along with some preliminary data analysis. The hypotheses derived from the research concerns noted above as well as the operational-code and psychohistorical analyses are set out in the succeeding chapters.

CONTENT ANALYSIS

As discussed earlier, the operational-code approach is one of a variety of means of gaining access to decision makers through their use of words and symbols.[3] Another, more rigorous and quantitative content-analysis methodology is now introduced.

As sociologists, anthropologists, and cyberneticists have argued, communication is the cement that holds all groups and organizations together.[4] Content analysis is based on the study of communication. As David Bell notes, we "think with words and we see the world through them."[5] Content analysis was developed to investigate phenomena in which the content of communication serves as the basis of *inference*. It is a process whereby the content of messages is transformed into data that can be analyzed and compared. Bernard Berelson has defined content analysis as "a research technique for the objective, systematic and quantitative description of the manifest content of communication."[6] Holsti reviews a variety of definitions of content analysis, but concludes that there is agreement that content analysis requires "objectivity, system and generality."[7] Holsti also observes that content analysis is appropriate, and may prove useful when the subjects of study are not directly accessible, and the researcher's data are limited to documentary evidence. Also, content analysis has the advantage of being "unobtrusive" or "nonreactive."[8] In sum, content analysis may be especially useful for subjects who are inaccessible, where there is a large base of documentary evidence, and where *words* are an important facet of interaction. The study of foreign-policy decision making closely conforms to these criteria/assumptions.

The study of foreign policy is also an area in which some of the basic criticisms of content analysis may be refuted. Paul Anderson has summarized two major criticisms: "The first perspective suggests that because verbal behavior is not systematically related to the actual beliefs or intentions of the decision makers it is generally irrelevant in understanding foreign policy behavior. The second perspective discounts verbal behavior as mere background noise, which, while part of the setting of inter-state interaction is irrelevant to the process of international politics."[9] But, as Anderson and others have pointed out, the great bulk of foreign policy is words: "the vast majority of foreign policy behaviors are verbal."[10] In particular, both of the critiques ignore a vital aspect of foreign policy: "Statements and postures define precedents which act as constraints on what counts as an acceptable alternative in foreign policy decision making. Public statements, justifications, and actions define precedents because of the central role of expectations in international politics. . . . Consistency in word and deed is one of the primary devices open to decision makers to establish and sustain desired expectations."[11] In his memoirs, Kissinger makes the same point much more succinctly —"Hidden motives may be the stuff of memoirs. The actual expression of views is what influences policy."[12]

Anderson's point also puts the debate on "representational" vs "instrumental" models of communication in perspective. Holsti summarizes the contrast: "The representational model assumes that verbal expressions are valid indicators of the communicator's beliefs, motivations, and the like, whereas the instrumental view begins with the premise that words may be chosen to have an impact on the target of communication."[13] It seems useful to follow Holsti in treating the representational model as a tentative, working hypothesis, but also to design research that tests the instrumental view. Although we are engaged in linking the content analysis of Kissinger's public words to psychohistorical and operational-code analyses, the representational-instrumental debate loses importance if we keep in mind Anderson's point that words are important symbolic acts, producing precedent and constraint and indicating consistency or changes in policies and positions.

Whatever view one takes of content analysis, it can be used to describe the attributes or content of messages. Content analysis may also be used for three basic types of comparison. Holsti notes that if an analyst wishes to use content analysis to compare the content of documents from the same source, then the content can be compared over time, to delineate secular trends. In addition, an analyst may wish to compare the content of messages from a single source across different situations, in

Figure 1. The use of content analysis
to compare the content of communications

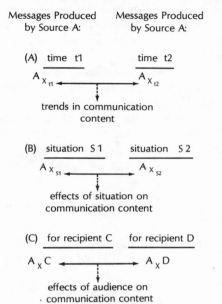

Messages Produced
by Source A:

Messages Produced
by Source A:

(A) time t1

time t2

$A_{X_{t1}}$ ←——————————→ $A_{X_{t2}}$

trends in communication
content

(B) situation S 1

situation S 2

$A_{X_{S1}}$ ←——————————→ $A_{X_{S2}}$

effects of situation on
communication content

(C) for recipient C

for recipient D

$A_X C$ ←——————————→ $A_X D$

effects of audience on
· communication content

Source: Derived from Figures 2.2, 2.3, and 2.4 of Holsti,
Content Analysis, 27-29.

which events data (e.g., a change in status—becoming secretary of state
—or change of presidents) represent the differing situations (Figure 1
Part B). Finally, "The proposition that the character of audiences affects
the content and style of communication has been tested in a number of
content analysis studies. In this case the research design calls for comparison of messages produced by a single source across different audiences."[14] (As applied to Henry Kissinger in this text, all of the
comparisons noted involve Kissinger's perceptions of two specific "attitude objects"—the Soviet Union and China.)

In Holsti's study of Dulles, the specific object of study was Dulles's
perceptions of the Soviet Union. Holsti selected evaluative assertion
analysis as the form of content analysis particularly suited for the objectives of his research,[15] since evaluative assertion analysis specifically
seeks to measure "beliefs, attitudes, and, possibly, expectancies about
objects (other actors, nations, etc.) of political relevance."[16] As Holsti
has noted, evaluative assertion analysis is probably most useful when the

researcher is interested in only a limited number of politically relevant attitude objects. Such a research design makes possible the coding of many documents, more quickly than is possible in less focused applications of evaluative assertion analysis, because this design has greater specificity in the first stage of the analysis—identifying and isolating attitude objects.[17]

The purpose of evaluative assertion analysis, according to the developers, is to "extract from a message the evaluations being made of significant concepts."[18] The first stage is the delineation of the significant concept, or objects. In the present study, all of Kissinger's references to the Soviet Union and China had to be identified and isolated. The second stage of evaluative assertion analysis calls for the translation of every sentence in which such references are found into one of two common forms:

    1. attitude object/ verb/ common-meaning evaluator
        (AO)   (c)   (cm)

    2. attitude object/ verb/ second attitude object
        (AO)   (c) (AO_2)

Osgood et al. refer to the verb as the connector (c) between the attitude object (AO) and the common-meaning evaluator (cm), which is an adjective, adverb, or modifying phrase that signifies an evaluation of the attitude object. The evaluation may also be made by connecting the attitude object to another noun or attitude object (AO_2) that indicates how the person producing the message feels about the AO.[19]

After the translation of the text of the message into the above forms, numerical values ranging from +3.00 to –3.00 are assigned to the verbs and to the evaluators. A verb is either associative (+) or dissociative (–) and a cm evaluator is either favorable (+) or unfavorable (–). The intensity of each is indicated in increasing order by the values of 1, 2, and 3.[20]

The final step is the computation of the evaluation values. Holsti employed a three-step formula. For each statement, the value of the verb is multiplied by the value of the evaluator. For any document (or any other unit of aggregation), the products of these multiplications are then summed. The total of the product column is then divided by three times the number of statements involved, in order to keep the final evaluation in the +3.00 to –3.00 range.[21]

For example, if a document has five evaluative statements, the document's total evaluation score would be computed as shown on the following page:

statement	verb value	evaluator value	product
1.	+3	+3	9
2.	+3	-3	-9
3.	+2	-3	-6
4.	+1	-2	-2
5.	-1	-3	3
			$\overline{-5}$

$$\text{evaluation} = -5/5(3) = -5/15 = -.333$$

Therefore, the evaluation for the document as a whole is $-.333$, slightly negative (the substantive meaning depending upon the scale used for evaluation—see note 20).

Although in this study there are only two attitude objects—the Soviet Union and China—Kissinger's evaluative assertions about them are placed into four different categories, which follow from those developed and used by Holsti in his published analyses of Dulles. The four categories are:

1. *Friendship-hostility*—used to assess Kissinger's perceptions of how hostile or friendly Soviet or Chinese foreign policy is toward the United States.

2. *Strength-weakness*—used to assess Kissinger's perceptions of Soviet or Chinese capabilities.

3. *Satisfaction-frustration*—used to assess Kissinger's perceptions of the *success* of Soviet or Chinese policy.

4. *Good-bad*—used to assess Kissinger's perceptions of the Soviet Union or China in terms of a *general evaluation,* based on his values as they are delineated by his belief system.[22]

An important modification of Holsti's procedures should be noted. In this study, we have *reversed* Holsti's scale on the hostility dimension. Holsti had coded hostility as (+), and friendship as (-). However, it appeared that to be more logically consistent with the semantic differential approach, a reversal was in order. Thus, in the present study, hostility is coded (-), to go with the minus codings for bad, weak, and failure, and frienship is coded (+), to go with the plus codings for good, strong, and successful. All our analyses that make comparisons to Holsti's study will have already taken this change into account (for example, comparison of the direction of correlations).

Thus, the public words of Henry Kissinger were subjected to evaluative assertion analysis in order to extract the evaluations of the Soviet Union and China that Kissinger made in his various public statements.

This is a "representational" form of content analysis, which decribes what the message says per se, and not what the speaker/author may have "really intended" (as the "instrumental" form would do). The sources of these public words are discussed next.

DATA: SOURCES, FORMS, AND SOME BASIC INFERENCES

The task of identifying and locating "the complete set of publicly available statements" made by Henry Kissinger during his years as a principal foreign-policy decision maker under Nixon and Ford involved the identification and location of the texts of all of Kissinger's speeches, prepared statements, interviews, testimony in Congressional hearings, press conferences, articles, etc. The complete set of public statements was sought, rather than a sample, because, as Holsti argues, "by using all . . . public statements it is assumed that a significant pattern . . . will appear. Thus, while assertions taken out of context might not reveal . . . personal beliefs accurately, the sum total of . . . statements should present a faithful reproduction of the subject's thinking."[23]

Through a search of many sources, the most important being the *Department of State Bulletin,* 603 public statements of Henry Kissinger were identified and located (see Table 2).[24] The statements were the complete, verbatim transcripts of prepared documents, such as speeches and addresses, toasts, statements upon arrival or departure in the United States or foreign locales, articles, and letters. The documentary material also included a complete set of extemporaneous remarks made in "response" situations, such as press conferences, interviews, and question-and-answer sessions after speeches. Finally, the documents include all Congressional testimony, both prepared statements and responses to questions at hearings.[25]

Kissinger's public statements are not evenly distributed across his eight-year tenure, but are heavily concentrated into 1974, 1975, and 1976, the years that he was secretary of state. As special assistant to the president for National Security affairs, he provided *no* public statements (that could be found) in 1969, only two in 1970, and three in 1971. Although during this time Kissinger provided extensive background and deep background material to reporters, he avoided full statements that could be directly attributed to him. It wasn't until after the dramatic China breakthrough in 1971, and the Chinese trip in early 1972, that Kissinger's visibility rose, and he stood out as an identifiable public figure making public statements.[26]

With only six full years in office as secretary of state, Dulles made

Table 2. Documentary basis for evaluative assertion analysis: Kissinger's public statements

Type of Document	Year							Total
	1970	1971	1972	1973	1974	1975	1976	
Prepared Statements								
Speeches		1	2	12	27	50	40	132
Toasts					21	12	22	55
Arrival/departure				9	63	44	23	139
Articles/letters			1	1	1	3	5	11
								337
Extemporaneous								
Press Conference		2	10	17	43	58	42	172
Q & A						9	14	23
Interviews	1		1	4	4	13	8	31
								226
Congressional Testimony	1		1	1	14	9	14	40
	2	3	15	44	173	198	168	603

Note: Under Nixon (Jan. 1969–Aug. 1974): 148 documents; under Ford (Aug. 1974–Dec. 1976): 455 documents.

434 public statements that Holsti could locate.[27] However, Dulles's statements were much more evenly distributed than Kissinger's:

1953— 64 statements	1957— 70
1954— 86	1958— 70
1955— 73	1959— 8
1956— 63	

Table 3 indicates the number of documents out of the total universe that contained evaluative assertions about either the Soviet Union or China. Of the 603 documents located and read, only 264 (44%) yielded evaluative assertions on the selected attitude objects. It is interesting to note some of the patterns that emerge simply by scrutinizing the documents in which Kissinger *does not* make evaluative assertions about either of the two Communist powers.

In contrast to Dulles, Kissinger did not see a vague, but threatening and insatiable Communist movement advancing everywhere on the globe.[28] In numerous statements relating to intra-American affairs or to specific Latin American areas, Kissinger almost never refers to either

Table 3. Kissinger's public statements with evaluative assertions

Type of Document	Year							Total
	1970	1971	1972	1973	1974	1975	1976	
Prepared								
Speeches		1	2	6	10	19	16	54
Toasts					6	2	4	12
Arrival/departure				2	2	5	1	10
Articles/letters							2	2
								78
Extemporaneous								
Press Conference		2	8	15	26	28	29	108
Q & A						7	14	21
Interviews			1	3	3	14	7	28
								157
Congressional								
Testimony			1	1	9	5	13	29
	0	3	12	27	56	80	86	264

Note: Under Nixon: 74 documents; under Ford: 190 documents.

Communist power directly or even indirectly as the Communist "threat," "danger," "menace," etc. Similarly, in the separate pieces of his Congressional testimony (numerous documents and literally hundreds of pages of text) on foreign aid, there are only one or two, and frequently no references to the Soviet Union or China. Kissinger clearly avoided all the cold-war rhetoric that aid was necessary to "prevent," or to "save" or "rescue" a nation from, imminent or long-term Communist takeover. In fact, his few references to the Soviet Union or China in aid testimony are generally positive observations about the progress of the administration's foreign policy toward them (statements probably intended to soften up the Congressional committee for the aid requests to follow). Finally, the many documents dealing with Western economic issues—currency, trade, energy—have no references to the Soviet Union or China, or to the spectre of external Communist dangers waiting to descend upon Europe. Again, Kissinger could have used references to Soviet Power, hostility, or threats in his statements, but he did not. The alternative of using the possibility of external threats to promote internal unity, or to provide pressure to accept U.S. policy, existed, but Kissinger clearly did not employ that alternative in his public statements.[29] The contrasts between Kissinger and Dulles drawn in the operational-code analysis are partially substantiated by Kissinger's simple, but important, refusal to discuss the Soviet Union and China within certain contexts.

The many documents without evaluative assertions also include numerous documents concerning Indochina, particularly the progress of the peace talks. Kissinger was unwilling to discuss publicly the various roles he wanted the Soviet Union and China to play in the Indochina settlement (see Part IV of *White House Years*). He was also unwilling to use either power as a scapegoat for the lack of progress during certain periods, or to blame either for supporting Hanoi at crucial periods. The very scarcity of references to either the Soviet Union or China in the Indochinese documents highlights the care Kissinger took in his sensitive and delicate diplomatic manuevers, which included all the Vietnamese parties as well as the Soviet Union and China.

This documentary base provided several thousand evaluative assertions. The exact number depends upon the inclusion or exclusion of what have been termed "dual subject" (DS) assertions. That is, the Kissinger documents contain a number of assertions that employ a compound subject or a dual subject, e.g., "the two superpowers have enormous military capability," "the Soviet Union and the United States have agreed on this important issue," or "both of our countries recognize our great power and responsibility to the world." Personal communication with Holsti revealed that Dulles had used very few such sentences. By itself, this is an important observation, since it supports the operational-code analyses contrasting Dulles and Kissinger. Following Holsti's suggestions, two data sets were developed. The main data set, because it most closely resembles the Dulles data, omits the DS assertions, for a total of 2847 assertions. A second data set consists of all assertions, including the DS assertions. This second data set contains a grand total of 3935 evaluative assertions. For a breakdown of these assertions by attitude object and by evaluative category, see Table 4.

All analyses have been performed using both data sets. Because of the "dual" nature of the DS assertions, the evaluations in these assertions are usually (but not always) more positive—more friendly, more successful, stronger, more "good."[30] However, the two data sets are very close in their overall form. Thus, the use of one or both is dictated by the analyses being undertaken, keeping in mind that the non-DS data set is more comparable to the Dulles data.[31]

For Dulles, Holsti identified 3238 assertions. Note that Dulles's assertions parallel Kissinger's in that the greatest number of assertions fall into the hostility category; the next most populous assertion category

Table 4.   Assertions used in the Kissinger evaluative assertion analysis

| Scale/Category | Attitude Object | |
	Soviet Union	China
Capability	681 (591)[a]	55 (54)[a]
General Evaluation	311 (244)	143 (104)
Hostility	2026 (1388)	552 (322)
Success	158 (135)	9 (9)
	3176 (2358)	759 (489)
Total: Soviet Union + China = 3935 (2847)		

[a] Number of assertions, with number *omitting* DS assertions in parentheses.

being capability, followed by general evaluation, and, finally, success (see Table 5).[32] Confidence in the methodology and coding and in the comparisons between Dulles and Kissinger is increased by the finding that the data sets are remarkably comparable. The complete congruence in the ranking of the categories by number of assertions, and the similarity of numbers by category, preclude analytic differences based on widely divergent data sets.

We should also note several preliminary observations regarding Soviet-Chinese comparisons (see Table 4). Clearly, Chinese capability is not as salient a concern for Kissinger as is Soviet power: There is only *one* China capability assertion that has a dual subject, while there are 90 such dual assertions with the Soviet Union. Kissinger obviously sees the superpower duopoly as a central aspect of U.S.-Soviet relations and world order in general.

Another salient aspect of the study of foreign policy that can be discerned from the basic data presented is the issue that arises concerning the attention and information-processing capabilities of individuals and governments. Some analyses indicate that it is difficult for organizations to handle more than one or two problems at a time, e.g., one hypothesis concerning the badly mishandled Skybolt affair with Britain in 1962 proposes that the outcome was due in part to lack of attention by the Americans, given the co-occurrence of the Cuban missile crisis and the Sino-Indian border war.[33] One question, therefore, concerns the overall attention paid to the Soviet Union and China. Various observers of the Nixon-Kissinger/Ford foreign policy have asserted that the main focus and concern of American foreign policy was the Soviet Union. Given Kissinger's operational code, one would also expect that his estimation for the prospects for world order would hinge on U.S.-Soviet relations.

Table 5. Dulles and Kissinger: Assertions about the Soviet Union by category

Category	Dulles	Kissinger
Hostility	1900	2026
Capability	732	681
General Evaluation	316	311
Success	290	158
Total	3238	3176

While this view is discussed in more detail in later chapters, it is sufficient for a working hypothesis concerning salience.

Sorting the Kissinger documents reveals that the Soviet Union is referred to in 246 of the 264 documents (93%), while China is discussed in evaluative terms in only 111 documents (42%). There are 151 instances in which Kissinger's public statement makes reference only to the Soviet Union, with no reference to China, but only 17 instances where the reverse is true. From this *frequency* of reference by document, and from the simple comparison of frequency of assertions (see Table 4), it is obvious that the Soviet Union is by far the more salient attitude object. For either DS assertions or non-DS assertions, Kissinger produced more than four times as many assertions on the Soviet Union as on China. As noted above, Kissinger is also much more concerned with Soviet capabilities and with Soviet success or failure. The centrality of the Soviet Union to American foreign policy, at least vis-à-vis China, is reflected in Kissinger's public statements. Yet, as noted, Kissinger could, and did, deal with many substantive and geographic areas without feeling it necessary to refer to either the Soviet Union or China. Using only these simple data, we still are able to sketch a picture of how Kissinger saw the Soviet Union in broad terms. The Soviet Union is more salient than China, but this salience is not unlimited, and is constrained by certain issues and areas. (The various dimensions of this salience and constraint are developed in the next three chapters.)

6

Perceptions of the Soviet Union:
Kissinger and Dulles

This chapter sets out Kissinger's evaluations, or images, of the Soviet Union. This task is primarily descriptive, indicating the content of the images and presenting their patterns of change over time.

As we have seen, Kissinger's operational code delineated his general views of international relations. This chapter concentrates on Kissinger's general evaluation and hostility evaluation of America's main opponent in the international system, the state most likely to be perceived as the "enemy." How positive or negative were Kissinger's images of the Soviet Union? How "open" or "closed" was he to new information? Did his images change in response to Soviet activity or were they frozen in place? Were psychological processes operating that would tend to keep negative images negative and/or to keep the image closed? Kissinger's operational code strongly predisposes us to anticipate an "open" image. Therefore, it would also indicate that Kissinger's images would be dependent on Soviet behavior, and that his general evaluation and hostility evaluations would reflect Soviet behavior—they would not automatically be positive or negative.

The relationship between Kissinger's belief system and his evaluation of the Soviet Union (his "attributional" behavior) is brought into sharp focus by contrasting it to Dulles's "inherent bad faith" belief system. Comparisons of the two decision makers enable formulation of comparative hypotheses concerning both the content and openness of Kissinger's images of the Soviet Union. Comparison of Kissinger to Dulles, an individual whose operational code has been shown to be very different, highlights Kissinger's own beliefs and images. In addition, the comparisons allow us to contrast idiosyncratic factors across two different eras in American foreign policy (while holding the role factor fairly

constant). Finally, not only are we able to examine the relationship
between the two content-analysis techniques used to gain access to foreign-policy decision makers, but also by looking at two so different
individuals, we are able to evaluate the use and validity of those techniques.

DULLES AND KISSINGER: GENERAL EVALUATION OF
THE SOVIET UNION

As noted, Holsti's study of Dulles explored several basic questions.
Holsti summarizes his interest in the psychological aspects of foreign-
policy decision making, in the study of the belief system and its component images and how those images may change or be reinforced, and in
the more specific image of the enemy, in the opening paragraphs of
"Cognitive Dynamics and Images of the Enemy":

> It is a basic theorem in the social sciences that "if men define
> situations as real, they are real in their consequences." Stated
> somewhat differently, the theorem asserts that an individual
> responds not only to the "objective" characteristics of a situa-
> tion, but also to the meaning the situation has for him; the
> person's subsequent behavior and the results of that behavior
> are determined by the meaning ascribed to the situation. . . .
> This theorem can be applied more specifically to the concept of
> the enemy. Enemies are those who are defined as such, and if
> one acts upon that interpretation, it is more than likely that the
> original definition will be confirmed.[1]

The thrust of Holsti's analyses is that there exist cognitive processes that
support the continuation of images of the enemy. On this basis, he
presents a picture of Dulles's images of the Soviet Union and demonstrates not only that the picture was negative, but also that it resisted
change.

Since Kissinger's belief system stresses the role of the statesman,
with all that that concept entails, including acceptance of the existence
(and continued existence) of the adversary as part of the norms of international behavior, and since Kissinger's view was that the Soviet Union
was no longer a revolutionary state (in the words of a State Department
colleague, Kissinger did not see the Soviet Union as "destructionist"),
Kissinger's non-"image of the enemy" kept his image of the Soviet
Union in perspective.[2] He states in his memoirs: "Communist policy is
often described as diabolically clever, complicated, following well-

thought-out routes toward world domination. This was not my impression."[3] Kissinger's view, expressed in 1978, was of a more haphazard process: "I think they (the Soviets) have a strategy designed to accumulate strength and a conviction that this strength will sooner or later be translatable into some geo-political position; but *they do not have a fixed plan* [emphasis added]. Soviet actions are not the result of a fixed plan, but the result of an accumulation of opportunities."[4] He saw the Soviet Union as a major power, a competitor that would be an active member of the international system for a very long time. Therefore, he saw the Soviet Union as being caught up in the same evolutionary process that the other members of the international system were subject to and whereby they were made subject to the rules and norms of that evolving system.

Given all the Dulles/Kissinger contrasts, one would expect Kissinger's image of the Soviet Union to be the more positive. Kissinger's image might also reflect the evolution from intense and hostile cold war to coexistence and détente. Also, beyond reflecting the differences in historical eras, the images of the two American decision makers might have played a large part in the shaping of those eras, and in impeding or speeding up the direction of relations suggested by the international context of the day. These suppositions may be formulated in a straightforward way as *Hypothesis 1:* Kissinger's general evaluation of the Soviet Union will, in aggregate, be "better" (more positive) than that of Dulles; there will be statistically significant differences between the general evaluation scores of the two decision makers.

While there are confounding factors that could account for discovered differences, and a number of methodological concerns that could qualify the analyses, it is impossible to conceive of these comparisons as one, incomplete evaluation of the methodology employed. On an intuitive level, (basically the notion of "face validity"), there should be certain differences between Kissinger and Dulles. As Ted Gurr has pointed out, face validity "depends partly on what is already known of the subject being studied."[5] On the basis of the biographies, scholarly analysis, and the operational-code analyses, we can expect significant differences between Kissinger and Dulles—at least in regard to general evaluation and hostility perceptions, and in the openness and flexibility of these images. If this study were to indicate no differences, or only minor differences, then it would be fair to question the use of evaluative assertion analysis for the study of decision makers.[6] The failure to differentiate might be an indicator that the Kissinger coders failed to code Kissinger's statements in the same way that Holsti coded those of Dulles, and thus that the method lacks reliability and replicability.[7] Assuming adequate and competent training of coders, a failure to differentiate would not mean a failure of reliability, but could indicate that the methodology cannot provide access to the perceptions of decision makers. The methodology would be therefore, not telling us what we think it is telling us, and would lack validity.

It is apparent from Table 6 that Dulles's general evaluation of the Soviet Union is far more negative than Kissinger's.[8] The mean of the six-month aggregation scores for Dulles is –2.83, with no single score more positive than –2.33, and with six of the periods more negative than –2.90. With –3.00 the most negative score possible, Dulles's overall evaluation of the Soviet Union was clearly and consistently "bad." Kissinger's general evaluation is very different: Its mean score for ten half-year periods from 1972 to 1976 is –0.068, which is essentially a neutral score, being so close to 0.00. For four of these periods, Kissinger's general evaluation is positive, while the negative evaluations are never worse than –0.863. Compare this to Dulles's two periods in which the evaluation is actually –3.00 and the magnitude of difference is very clear. A t-test of Kissinger's mean general evaluation and Dulles's mean general evaluation confirms the differences in the two men's evaluations of the Soviet Union.[9]

If the dual subject evaluations are included in Kissinger's score, the general evaluation is even more positive. The mean for Kissinger's DS general evaluation is +0.294, still hovering about the neutral point, but slightly positive. Again, a difference of means test shows the differences between Kissinger and Dulles to be statistically significant.[10]

Hypothesis 1 may also be discussed in terms of the hostility dimension. We would expect that Kissinger saw the Soviet Union as less hostile than Dulles did, and the results bear out this expectation. Again, all of Dulles's six-month scores are negative, and have a mean hostility score of –1.71. On the other hand, Kissinger's eleven periods produce seven positive (or "friendly") scores and an overall mean of –0.057. This may also be interpreted as a neutral overall perception of Soviet hostility. The DS hostility score is again slightly more positive, at +0.44. Both of Kissinger's scores are significantly different from Dulles's on a difference of means test.[11] Finally, aggregation of Kissinger's hostility assertions over the entire period yields a hostility score of –0.56 (with DS hostility being –0.06)—once more, approximately the same scores as for the six-month aggregations. In sum, Hypothesis 1 is confirmed: Kissinger's images of the Soviet Union, as operationalized by his general evaluation and hostility assertions, are more positive than the images held by Dulles.

This comparison is clearly useful in matching Kissinger's opera-

Table 6.   General evaluation and hostility scores for Dulles and Kissinger on the Soviet Union, in six-month aggregations

		Score	
Secretary	Aggregation	General Evaluation	Hostility
Dulles	Jan.-June 1953	−2.81	−2.01
	July-Dec. 1953	−2.92	−1.82
	Jan.-June 1954	−2.69	−2.45
	July-Dec. 1954	−3.00	−1.85
	Jan.-June 1955	−2.83	−0.74
	July-Dec. 1955	−2.33	−0.96
	Jan.-June 1956	−2.91	−1.05
	July-Dec. 1956	−3.00	−1.72
	Jan.-June 1957	−2.79	−1.71
	July-Dec. 1957	−2.93	−2.09
	Jan.-June 1958	−2.86	−2.03
	July 1958-Feb. 1959	−2.90	−2.10
	Mean:	−2.83	−1.71
		$N = 12$	$N = 12$
Kissinger	Jan.-June 1971	—[a]	—
	July-Dec. 1971	—	+0.833
	Jan.-June 1972	+0.069	−0.455
	July-Dec. 1972	+1.000	+0.158
	Jan. June 1973	+0.875	+1.343
	July-Dec. 1973	−0.787	+0.250
	Jan.-June 1974	+0.333	+0.136
	July-Dec. 1974	−0.145	+0.069
	Jan.-June 1975	−0.143	+0.242
	July-Dec. 1975	−0.347	−0.834
	Jan.-June 1976	−0.863	−1.386
	July-Dec. 1976	−0.667	−0.982
	Mean:	−0.068	−0.057
		$N = 10$	$N = 11$

[a] Dashes indicate periods which had *no* public statements containing evaluations.

tional code and evaluative behavior to Dulles's. But, is Dulles too extreme a case for comparison (i.e., most similar vs. most different designs for comparison)? In another study, Kissinger and Dulles were contrasted to John F. Kennedy.[12] Kennedy's operational code indicated an individual who was flexible because he was still learning, who was not inclined to dogma, and who saw the Soviet Union as dangerous but *educable*. Kissinger's images of the Soviet Union were also more positive than Kennedy's (and more open). Kennedy fell almost exactly between Dulles and Kissinger, in a historical continuum from the 1950s to the 1970s. The conclusions of the Dulles-Kennedy-Kissinger study reinforce the view that the operational-code and evaluative assertion analyses are complementary, and reinforce the view of the general validity of both approaches.

Because Kissinger has a mix of positive and negative views of the Soviet Union that is missing in Dulles (or Kennedy), we can see patterns in Kissinger's images. Kissinger's images are best in the 1972-73 period, at the height of post-summit détente. Note also the worsening of both his general evaluation and his hostility images in the 1975-76 period (see Figure 3). This drop-off is attributed to Soviet behavior in Angola. (Further discussion of this negative trend in Kissinger's evaluations of the Soviet Union is presented in the next two chapters.)

CLOSED AND OPEN IMAGES OF THE SOVIET UNION

A major aim of Holsti's study of Dulles was to investigate how "open" or "closed" Dulles's images of the Soviet Union were. Holsti notes that a belief system, with its component images, is not static, but dynamic, constantly interacting with new information being provided by the environment. How this information influences the decision maker depends upon the degree to which the belief system is open or closed. Holsti quotes Rokeach:

> At the closed extreme, it is new information that must be tampered with—by narrowing it out, altering it, or constraining it within isolated bounds. In this way the belief-disbelief system is left intact. At the open extreme, it is the other way around: New information is assimilated *as is* . . . thereby producing "genuine" changes in the whole belief-disbelief system.[13]

On the basis of the material in Part I, especially the operational-code analyses, we may hypothesize that Kissinger differs from Dulles in regard to the openness of his images of the Soviet Union. Although the categories or boxes that Kissinger created to think about, understand, and explain the phenomena of international relaxations were unchanging, the nations, leaders, and policies that were put into those boxes *could* change; the Soviet Union (and China) were moved from one category to another after time and new information indicated that a change was the best way to reflect "reality." Thus, we posit *Hypothesis 2:* Kissinger will exhibit a more open and flexible image of the Soviet Union than did Dulles, in that changes in the general evaluation of the Soviet Union will be related to changes in Kissinger's perceptions of the Soviet Union on the other three scales.

In the study of Dulles, Holsti first demonstrated that there *was* a relationship between Dulles's perception of Soviet hostility and his perceptions of Soviet success and Soviet capabilities (see the top of Table 7). Using Spearman rank-order correlations, Holsti discovered a negative relationship between hostility and success and hostility and capabilities: as Dulles perceived the Soviet Union to be more successful, or perceived it to be stronger, he also perceived it to be more hostile. As Soviet policy "failed" (e.g., in the 1955-56 period), or Soviet power waned, he perceived the Soviet Union to be less hostile. Soviet decision makers were seen to be more friendly because of failure and weakness.[14]

Dulles's exaggeration of a natural tendency to see an opponent as less hostile or threatening when the opponent is weak or a failure is reflected in the Kissinger data. Using Spearman correlations, and presenting both DS and non-DS variables, we find that eight of the twelve correlations are negative. However, none of the correlations is statistically significant (the largest, $r = -.31$, being between hostility and capabilities). Kissinger, then, displays a similar tendency, but in a very diluted form.

Two additional analyses may be noted. While Holsti did not do so, it seemed appropriate to use Pearson product-moment correlations in addition to the rank-order correlations. While some relationships change slightly, the results presented at the bottom of Table 7 do not alter the substantive interpretations. Again, eight of twelve correlations are negative (and on the average, slightly larger), and none is statistically significant. The other additional analysis examined whether the aggregation of data into the arbitrary time periods distorts the results. The Pearson analyses were also performed using the *document* as the unit of analysis. For each document, the hostility, general evaluation, success, and capability scores were calculated. Then, using all the documents, the various correlations were calculated, running hostility against success, hostility against capabilities, etc., within each document. The four correlations are consistent with the results presented in Table 7.:

> hostility and success, $r = -.14$
> hostility and capabilities, $r = -.04$
> DS hostility and DS success, [15] $r = .29$
> DS hostility and DS capabilities, $r = .03$

Table 7. Correlations between perceptions of hostility and perceptions of capabilities and success: Dulles's and Kissinger's images of the Soviet Union

Correlations for:	Aggregation		
	3-month	6-month	12-month
Dulles—Spearman Correlations			
Hostility and Success	−.58[a]	−.71[a]	−.94[a]
Hostility and Capabilities	−.55[a]	−.76[a]	−.94[a]
Kissinger—Spearman Correlations			
Hostility and Success	.04	−.27	−.09
Hostility and Capabilities	−.23	−.04	−.31
DS Hostility and DS Success	.12	.01	.26
DS Hostility and DS Capabilities	−.01	−.20	−.26
Kissinger—Pearson Correlations			
Hostility and Success	−.24	.09	−.20
Hostility and Capabilities	−.22	−.15	−.19
DS Hostility and DS Success	.05	.08	.51
DS Hostility and DS Capabilities	−.01	−.20	−.30

[a]Significant at .01 level.

In sum, then, the Kissinger data only hint at the strong negative relationship that the Dulles data produce between hostility and the two continua of success and capabilities.

Of course, Kissinger considered the Soviet Union a legitimate state, with legitimate security interests. Kissinger also recognized that, as a superpower, the Soviet Union could be expected to act like one (Kissinger's ability to empathize and identify with an opponent are important factors here). Unless Soviet behavior became revolutionary, challenging the elements in Kissinger's belief system that were associated with his concept of legitimacy, Soviet success or Soviet strength would not necessarily affect Kissinger's evaluations of Soviet hostility. To do so would entail a "zero-sum" mentality, which, as we have already noted, was not consistent with Kissinger's operational code.

So far, the analysis does not demonstrate a closed image on the part of Dulles. The results are simply consistent with other analyses of Dulles, including the operational-code analysis, which demonstrate his cynical views of non-hostile Soviet behavior (i.e., that it results from failure and/or weakness). Continuing the analysis, Holsti shows that, while hostility co-varies with success and capabilities, there are *no* such rela-

Table 8.   General evaluation and hostility correlations: Dulles and Kissinger view the Soviet Union

Correlations for:	Aggregation		
	3-month	6-month	12-month
Dulles—Spearman Correlations			
General Evaluation and Hostility	−.10	−.03	−.10
Kissinger—Spearman Correlations			
General Evaluation and Hostility	.32[a]	.49[a]	.37
DS General Evaluation and DS Hostility	.42[b]	.63[b]	.37
Kissinger—Pearson Correlations			
General Evaluation and Hostility	.30[a]	.65[b]	.78[b]
DS General Evaluation and DS Hostility	.47[b]	.75[b]	.67[b]

[a] Significant at .10 level.
[b] Significant at .05 level.

tionships with general evaluation. That is, no matter how his perception of Soviet hostility changes, there is no change in Dulles's good-bad evaluation of the Soviet Union. This is clearly seen in the top section of Table 8. Holsti discusses this finding:

> This lack of any significant relationship between hostility and general evaluation is not unexpected, for it is completely consistent with the factors already considered, particularly Dulles' tendency to impute relatively good Soviet behavior to necessity rather than any real desire to end the Cold War. So long as good behavior is attributed to necessity, there is no need to attribute it to virtue.[16]

The picture of Dulles's perceptions of the Soviet Union is completed by Figure 2, which reproduces Holsti's graph of the four evaluative scales.[17] The major feature of this figure is the very negative general evaluation line, and its failure to co-vary in any way with the other evaluations.

The comparison of the Dulles data with Kissinger's general evaluation of the Soviet Union and Soviet hostility is striking. The twelve correlations in Table 8 (six Spearman, six Pearson; DS data, and non-DS data) all are positive, and ten are statistically significant. These data indicate the existence of an open image of the Soviet Union—with Kissinger's evaluation varying positively with his perceptions of Soviet hos-

Figure 2. Dulles's perceptions of the Soviet Union

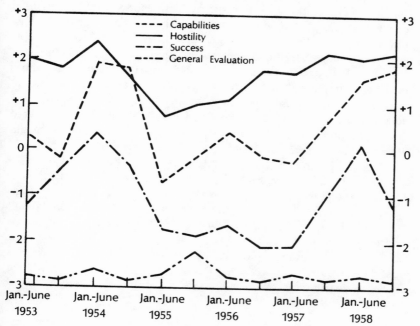

tility. Thus, Kissinger's evaluations of the Soviet Union seem to be behavior dependent, and not based on preconceived notions of implacable evil or an inexorable master plan. Kissinger's good-bad general evaluation varies with his hostility evaluation: perceptions of Soviet "goodness" are associated with Soviet "friendliness," Soviet "badness" is positively associated with Soviet "hostility." As would be expected, this relationship is generally stronger with the dual subject data set.

Finally, the general evaluation-hostility relationship can also be tested by Pearson correlations, using the document as the unit of analysis. The results are entirely consistent with the results above: the general evaluation-hostility correlation is .31; the DS general evaluation-DS Hostility correlation is .43 (both significant at the .01 level). The overall relationship among the four evaluation scales for Kissinger is presented in Figure 3, which presents a much more complex graph than that created by Dulles's evaluative assertions. No scale is consistently negative, as in Dulles's general evaluation. There are many more peaks and valleys along all four scales, with the general evaluation scale approximately straddling the neutral line around 0.00.

Kissinger once characterized Dulles's image of the Soviet Union as an "inherent bad faith of the Communists" model.[18] Dulles's closed image of the Soviet Union is consistent with this characterization. Kissinger's belief system, based upon a very different set of core concepts —revolutionary vs. legitimate states—produces a very different image of the Soviet Union, once it has been decided which of these labels applies to it. The simple notion that Kissinger could re-evaluate nations and leaders in terms of these concepts, especially whether their behavior was consistent with a stable international order, and that he never considered any condition immutable, is a strong indicator that Kissinger's images would be more open and flexible than those of Dulles.

Dulles's inherent bad faith model was mainly built upon three dichotomies he saw in the Soviet Union.[19] Dulles contrasted the "good" Russian people with the "bad" Soviet leaders; the "good" Russian national interest with "bad" international Communism; and the "good" Russian state with the "bad" Soviet Communist Party. As a way of verifying these interpretations, Holsti analyzed the *specific* terms or labels that Dulles used to refer to the Soviet Union in hostile and friendly contexts, and he discovered a pattern in Dulles's use of labels.[20] The following distribution occurs in Dulles's use of the terms 'Soviet,' 'communist,' and 'Russian':

	Hostile Context	*Friendly Context*
Soviet	59.1%	82.9%
Communist	37.3	0.0
Russian	3.6	17.1

The interesting finding is that the term 'Communist' appears in over a third of the hostile references, but is never used in a friendly context. On the other hand, references to 'Russian' are almost five times as likely to appear in a friendly context as in a hostile one. This distribution indeed confirms, at least in part, the dichotomies that Holsti claimed Dulles saw. Would such specific use of terms be expected of Kissinger? For Kissinger's terminology to be consistent with the analyses of him that we have made so far, we would expect that since he has a more open and flexible image of the Soviet Union, Kissinger would not exhibit systematic patterns in the terms used to characterize the Soviet Union.[21]

In the initial run-through of the Kissinger documents, this hypothesis was checked. First, it was found that Kissinger employed a far more varied set of terms than Dulles did, including consistent use of terms

Figure 3. Kissinger's perceptions of the Soviet Union

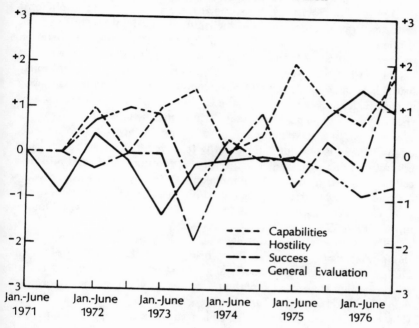

other than Soviet, Communist, and Russian. He used terms like 'power,' 'great power,' and 'superpower,' especially in the DS assertions. He also personalized a large number of references, using "Party Secretary Brezhnev," "Brezhnev," and the names of other officials, such as Gromyko, or "Moscow" or "the Kremlin." All of these terms, including Soviet, Communist, and Russian, were completely intermixed in the various documents—no pattern emerged in their use.[22] As expected, Kissinger did not systematically apply different labels to the Soviet Union to indicate his likes and dislikes.

CONCLUSION

The differences between Kissinger and Dulles that were suggested by Kissinger's operational-code analysis, as well as his psychological and intellectual background, were supported by the simple analyses described in this chapter. The two men show basic differences in their image of the Soviet Union, and these differences make Kissinger's evaluations stand out more clearly. Kissinger's more positive images (compared also with those of JFK) match the movement from cold war to détente in U.S.–Soviet relations. Since these men operated in different historical eras, another aspect of their differences should be touched on. While each man made his personal contribution to the relations between the superpowers, each had to conduct diplomacy within the context of his day. It has been suggested that Dulles might have had to use fairly brutal language simply to make Stalin and his immediate successors pay attention. Kissinger, who from the beginning was much more used to speaking in the accepted diplomatic tradition, during an era of growing cooperation, may have needed only to express "concern" over an issue, or to change his position only slightly, to have an effect on Soviet leaders.[23] In addition, Kissinger had been able to establish cordial informal relationships with Soviet decision makers, so that when it was necessary for him to display irritation or anger, his message came through much more clearly (e.g., see references to his working relationship with Dobrynin in *White House Years*).

This chapter also presents a portion of Kissinger's descriptive material for America's primary rival in world politics. The comparisons with Dulles and the descriptive material give us further confidence in evaluative assertion analysis as a methodology for providing access to foreign-policy decision makers. Finally, the behavior of the Soviet Union, Kissinger's images of the Soviet Union, and his concept of détente interact in a complex fashion. A complete understanding of this interaction requires an additional set of comparisons—the comparisons of Kissinger's images of the Soviet Union with his images of another major contemporary international actor, the People's Republic of China.

7

Perceptions of the
Soviet Union and China

For both Dulles and Kissinger, as American foreign-policy decision makers, the Soviet Union was the primary object and main focus of United States foreign policy. To Dulles, the Soviet Union was the center of a monolithic force called international Communism. To Kissinger, American-Soviet relations were the core of any stable international order. Of all the international actors, it was the Soviet Union that had to be enmeshed within a web of interdependence with the West, so that it too would have a stake in the existing international order. It is not surprising, then, that the Nixon(Ford)–Kissinger era has been characterized as an era in which the Soviet Union was the centerpiece of American policy in international affairs.[1] It has also been argued that the Nixon-Kissinger concern with balance and order in U.S.–Soviet relations led to a policy that slighted America's allies.[2] Stanley Hoffmann has similarly argued that American mistakes in the India-Pakistan war of 1971, in Angola, and in the conflict between Greece and Turkey over Cyprus were in part due to Kissinger's "exaggerated stress on the connection between the local situation and the great powers context."[3] George Ball, a vocal critic of the Nixon-Kissinger foreign policy, said of the manipulation of states in the U.S.–Soviet struggle: "The concept underlying such a strategy was Ptolemaic, pre-Copernican; it perceived the United States as the center of the cosmos with other nations in orbit around it."[4]

If, indeed, the Soviet Union was the central feature of U.S. policy, and the other elements of that policy were all related to and revolved around U.S.–Soviet relations, what would be the place or role of the People's Republic of China? If American relations with nations other than the Soviet Union were based on America's Soviet policy, then America's policy toward China would in some way be related to U.S.–

Soviet relations. Therefore, we might expect Kissinger's images of the Soviet Union and China to be related in some manner. That is, we might expect Kissinger's Soviet and Chinese hostility and general evaluation perceptions to co-vary across time. The way that they might co-vary will depend very much on the manner in which Kissinger perceived China. China, too, was a legitimate international actor in Kissinger's belief system. The question, though, is whether China was seen as an enemy or simply as an aspiring great power competitor. Was it seen as a potential ally, or as a state that could be used in the manipulation of U.S.–Soviet relationships?

On a number of occasions, when questioned on this topic, Kissinger had explicitly asserted that it was not American policy to play the Soviet Union off against China, that the proper policy toward the two Communist powers should be one of "meticulous honesty with both of them so that neither believes that we are trying to use one against the other."[5] This thought, from a 1974 interview, is echoed in 1976: "The worst mistake we could possibly make is to give the Chinese the impression that we are using them for our purposes,"[6] and in 1978: "They [China] are not going to be anybody's card. . . . I do not think we can specifically 'play the Chinese card' to suit our purposes."[7] In discussing "triangular diplomacy" in his memoirs, Kissinger stresses that it did not mean a "crude attempt to play off the Chinese against the Soviet Union."[8]

If this truly was Kissinger's position, then Kissinger's public evaluative assertions of each nation would probably not be related, and each would be kept separated within the panoply of American foreign policy. However, it is known that in the classic politics of the triad (discussed in chapter 7), A seeks to play B against C, while B and C each play A against the other similarly. The politics of the triad argue that Kissinger's images of the Soviet Union and China *should* be related to each other.

IMAGES OF THE SOVIET UNION AND CHINA: BASIC DATA AND COMPARISONS

The first basic comparison between the Soviet Union and China is presented in chapter 5, where it is demonstrated that the Soviet Union was by far the more central attitude object for Kissinger, in terms of the frequency with which he referred to it. Analyses of the frequency with which the Soviet Union or China appeared in the documents and of the total number of assertions devoted to each demonstrated the greater salience of the Soviet Union. Thus, one assumption made in this chapter, that the Soviet Union is the central focus of U.S. policy, is partially confirmed in the context of relative Sino-Soviet saliency.

Chapter 5 also shows that the Soviet Union was referred to more frequently than China, regardless of the category of evaluative assertion, and regardless of the DS or non-DS distinction. This greater saliency also holds across time. More assertions are made about the Soviet Union for each year from 1972 through 1976, with an even greater disparity shown in the DS data.[9] At the level of six-month aggregations, the same holds for nine of the ten half-yearly periods with the non-DS data, and for all ten periods uisng the DS data. As the main focus of U.S. concern, the Soviet Union is consistently the more salient object in Kissinger's public statements.

However, studies of saliency and government information-processing capabilities suggest that there might be some inverse relationship between the saliency of the Soviet Union and China. If information or attention capabilities are limited, then as a government (or individual) pays more attention to one nation, it will pay less attention to others. This proposition may be investigated on the individual level, to see whether it is true for Kissinger's perceptions of the Communist powers. If it were true, one would expect a negative correlation between the number of assertions about each country across time. However, this *does not* happen. Using three-month aggregations from 1972 to 1976 ($N=20$), correlations of .32 and .23 are obtained for non-DS and DS data, respectively. Note that both correlations are positive (but neither is statistically significant). We may conclude that, while the Soviet Union is the more salient object, increased references to it do not decrease the number of references to China.

How does the salience of the Soviet Union affect Kissinger's perception of the Soviet Union in relation to China? As the primary object of U.S. foreign policy and its primary opponent, how is the Soviet Union perceived? *Hypothesis 3* proposes that the Soviet Union will be perceived as stronger and more successful than China (these attributes being part of the basis for Soviet salience). *Hypothesis 4* proposes that because the Soviet Union may be stronger and more successful, it is indeed perceived as a greater threat, and thus the Soviet Union will be perceived as acting in a more hostile manner, and be given a more negative general evaluation than China. Before the comparisons called for by these hypotheses are investigated, the basic data for the three-month, six-month, and yearly aggregations are presented in Tables 9 and 10. The comparisons discussed below, and the analyses of Figures 4 and 5, are based on the data in these tables.[10]

For the comparisons of the average scores for the three-month aggregations shown in Table 9, it should be kept in mind that looking at the 1972-76 period as a whole masks some important trends for both

Table 9.   Perceptions of the Soviet Union (USSR) and China (PRC)—
three-month aggregations

Aggregation	Capabilities		Gen. Evaluation		Hostility		Success	
	USSR	PRC	USSR	PRC	USSR	PRC	USSR	PRC
1971								
Jan-March	—	—	—	—	—	—	—	—
Apr-June	—	—	—	—	—	—	—	—
July-Sept	—	—	—	—	—	—	—	—
Oct-Dec	—	-1.333	—	-0.083	+0.833	+0.875	—	—
1972								
Jan-March	—	—	-1.333	-0.167	+2.000	+0.143	—	—
Apr-June	+0.996	—	+0.130	—	-0.375	+1.000	-0.308	—
July-Sept	—	—	+1.000	—	+1.576	—	—	—
Oct-Dec	—	—	—	—	—	—	—	—
1973								
Jan-March	+1.000	-1.000	0.000	+0.389	+1.667	+1.000	—	—
Apr-June	—	+1.750	—	+1.194	+0.750	—	—	—
July-Sept	+1.514	-0.667	-1.515	+0.833	+0.917	+1.000	—	—
Oct-Dec	+1.042	0.000	-0.214	-0.500	+0.199	+1.500	-1.889	—
1974								
Jan-March	+0.667	-2.000	+0.189	—	+0.441	+2.000	—	—
Apr-June	+0.056	-2.000	+0.727	-2.000	-0.100	+1.430	-0.143	—
July-Sept	+0.342	—	-0.173	+1.000	-0.756	+0.510	+1.250	+1.000
Oct-Dec	+0.485	+2.500	-0.111	+1.500	+0.564	+1.613	0.000	+1.000
1975								
Jan-March	+1.487	+3.000	+1.556	—	+0.312	+1.250	-2.000	—
Apr-June	+2.576	+2.125	-0.426	+0.241	+0.194	+1.077	-0.400	0.000
July-Sept	+0.538	+3.000	0.000	-0.750	-0.364	+2.500	-0.381	—
Oct-Dec	+1.264	+0.333	-0.758	+2.089	-1.081	+2.060	+1.500	+3.000
1976								
Jan-March	+0.882	+1.037	-0.750	+1.538	-1.413	+1.813	-0.233	—
Apr-June	+0.140	-1.222	-1.044	+0.667	-1.255	+1.080	-0.322	+2.000
July-Sept	+2.100	+2.000	-1.800	+1.867	-1.085	+1.521	—	—
Oct-Dec	+0.750	+2.000	-0.100	+2.472	-0.874	+1.667	+2.000	+2.000

countries. Of these trends, which are graphed in Figures 4 and 5, the most striking is the worsening image of the Soviet Union in 1975-76, and the concurrent improvement of China's image (on all four scales). Historically, during these two years Kissinger grew increasingly angry with the Soviets over the Cuban/Soviet intervention in Angola. Kissinger's view of détente, and its relationship to his concept of order and stability, was rudely challenged by the Soviet Union: "The principal element in the deterioration of relations with the Soviet Union is Soviet actions in

Table 10. Perceptions of the Soviet Union (USSR) and China (PRC)—
half-year and yearly aggregations

Aggregation	Capabilities		Gen. Evaluation		Hostility		Success	
	USSR	PRC	USSR	PRC	USSR	PRC	USSR	PRC
1972	+0.996	—	+0.107	−0.167	+0.448	+0.250	−0.308	—
Jan-June	+0.996	—	+0.069	−0.167	+0.448	+0.250	−0.308	—
July-Dec	—	—	+1.000	—	+0.158	—	—	—
1973	+1.350	−0.667	−0.384	+0.071	+0.510	+1.105	−1.889	—
Jan-June	+1.000	−1.000	+0.875	+0.389	+1.343	+0.983	—	—
July-Dec	+1.396	−0.400	−0.787	−0.166	+0.250	+1.385	−1.889	—
1974	+0.302	−0.500	+0.080	+0.667	+0.106	+1.323	+0.500	+1.000
Jan-June	+0.200	−2.000	+0.333	−2.000	+0.136	+1.485	−0.143	—
July-Dec	+0.393	+2.500	−0.145	+1.429	+0.069	+1.167	+0.909	+1.000
1975	+1.363	+2.020	−0.252	+0.883	−0.303	+1.667	−0.039	+1.800
Jan-June	+1.986	+2.200	−0.143	+0.241	+0.242	+1.118	−0.667	0.000
July-Dec	+1.095	+1.700	−0.347	+1.491	−0.834	+2.101	+0.303	+3.000
1976	+0.727	+1.203	−0.809	+1.851	−1.336	+1.620	−0.238	+2.000
Jan-June	+0.675	+0.470	−0.863	+1.375	−1.386	+1.636	−0.265	+2.000
July-Dec	+1.714	+2.000	−0.667	+2.197	+1.982	+1.605	+2.000	+2.000

Angola. We pointed out at the time, and we repeat, that we consider those actions irresponsible, inconsistent with the principles that govern the conduct between our nations."[11] The Soviets were, in Africa, "for the first time, massively introducing military equipment and starting a cycle of upheavals similar to the impact of their first introduction of military equipment into the Middle East."[12] World order and world stability required that the U.S. and the Soviet Union avoid conflict. Africa had, tacitly, been set off-limits for superpower intervention—at least in Kissinger's concept of détente. The Soviets, in 1975-76, were crossing those limits.

The trends displayed in the figures, and Kissinger's disapproval of Soviet behavior, seem to be the key to Kissinger's perceptions of Soviet hostility as set out in Hypothesis 4. The relationship between Kissinger's evaluation of Soviet hostility and his evaluation of Soviet capabilities, success, and general evaluation was events-dependent, as discussed in the last chapter. Here, Hypothesis 3 is used to set up the comparison between perceptions of Soviet and Chinese hostility—proposing that perceptions of greater Soviet capability and success would lead to perceptions of greater hostility. However, it appears that the arguments set out in chapter 6, not Hypothesis 3, are the more convincing, as Hypothesis 3 cannot be confirmed when tested with data based on the three-month

Figure 4. Trends in general evaluation scores for the Soviet Union and China

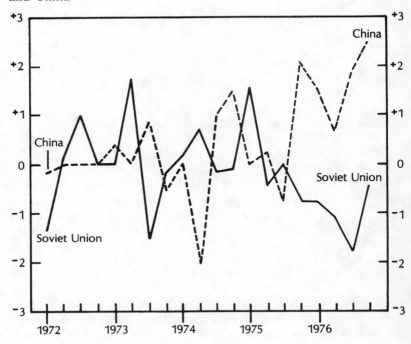

aggregation of assertions. The mean score for Soviet capability is +0.99, while the average score for Chinese capability is +0.52. Although the Soviet score is higher, as hypothesized, the difference is not statistically significant (see Table 11). Even with the DS data, the relationship does not change.[13]

Within the data sets, there is a particularly interesting trend for China. From 1971 through the middle of 1974, Kissinger either makes no references to Chinese capabilities, or else the statements produce negative scores. However, for the nine three-month periods from the end of 1974 through 1976, in part the period of growing displeasure with the Soviet Union, only one score is negative. This trend, which would affect the overall comparison, is events-dependent, as noted above.

In terms of Hypothesis 3, a revealing comparison is made by looking only at the twenty-one documents (across the entire time period) in which Kissinger makes reference to both Soviet and Chinese capabilities. In these documents, the average score for Soviet capabilities is +1.59,

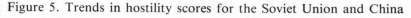

Figure 5. Trends in hostility scores for the Soviet Union and China

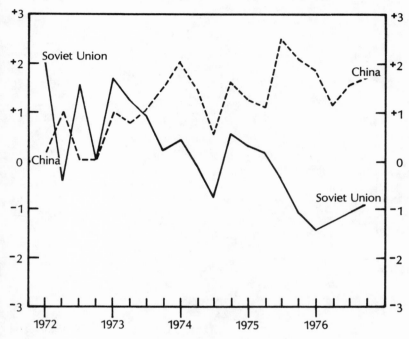

while for the Chinese it is a mere +0.01. The evidence, then, is mixed. While the difference of means is not statistically different, the Soviet Union is perceived as stronger, with the higher Chinese scores occurring during the period of Kissinger's growing unease over Soviet activities. When references to capabilities occur in the same document, Soviet capabilities are seen as much greater. There are, then, indications that Kissinger's public statements reflected an image of a stronger Soviet Union.

For success, the evidence is similarly unclear. On the basis of fewer assertions concerned with success, and fewer three-month periods that had any success assertions, China is perceived as far more successful. The Soviet mean is −0.77, compared to a mean of +1.50 for China (significantly different). *All* the references to Chinese success start in late 1974 and go through 1975-76. While there is some basis for saying that the Soviet Union is perceived as stronger, there is none to indicate that it was perceived as being more successful.

Three separate lines of argument support Hypothesis 4. Soviet be-

Table 11.   Soviet-Chinese comparisons, based on averages of three-month aggregation scores

Perception	Soviet Union	China
A. Capabilities	N^a = 16 $\overline{X}$ = +0.99 SD = .6705	N = 15 $\overline{X}$ = +0.52 SD = 1.763
	t = .8125 df^b = 18.26–18 sig^c = not significant	
B. General Evaluation	N = 19 $\overline{X}$ = −0.15 SD = .930	N = 14 $\overline{X}$ = +0.61 SD = 1.188
	t = 1.913 df = 20.93–21 sig = .05	
C. Hostility	N = 20 $\overline{X}$ = +0.13 SD = 1.002	N = 18 $\overline{X}$ = +1.33 SD = .564
	t = 4.4798 df = 31.84–32 sig = .0005	
D. Success	N = 12 $\overline{X}$ = −0.077 SD = 1.127	N = 6 $\overline{X}$ = +1.5 SD = .957
	t = 2.886 df = 13.33–13 sig = .01	

[a]N indicates the number of 3-month periods during which assertions were made about the country in question in the category in question.

[b]df = degrees of freedom, calculated by the formula:

$$df = \frac{[S_1^2/(N_1 - 1) + S_2^2/(N_2 - 1)]^2}{[S_1^2/(N_1 - 1)]^2 \, 1/(N_1 + 1) + [S_2^2/(N_2 - 1)]^2 \, 1/(N_2 + 1)}$$

See Hubert M. Blalock, *Social Statistics* New York: McGraw-Hill, 1980), 175–76.

[c]One-tailed.

havior in Africa clearly seems to have affected Kissinger's views of the Soviet Union and China. Second, there is evidence that the Soviet Union is perceived to be the stronger nation on the capabilities dimension. The more salient Soviet Union, the only other superpower and the only other nation capable of globally challenging the United States, generates a somewhat greater set of capability perceptions. In terms of the balance of power, which is central to Kissinger's belief system (i.e., in terms of the ability of an actor to upset international stability), Hypothesis 4 is most plausible. Indeed, this hypothesis may be proposed from a very different, third perspective—Kissinger's personal style and intellectual disposition. As a high-ranking State Department colleague noted, although Kissinger saw the Soviets as America's major antagonist and competitor, Kissinger viewed the Chinese from a more positive *personal* angle, judging them far more congenial and impressive.

State Department officials who were with Kissinger in China contrasted his attitude toward the two Communist powers.[14] The U.S.–Soviet relationship was characterized as an adversary relationship, which required a broader range of "tough" behavior. When the Soviets aroused Kissinger's hostility, through a variety of actions perceived as antithetical to a peaceful world order, it was said that Kissinger became blunt and "brutal" in his dealings with them. (Hostile actions included the Soviet submarine base in Cuba and the Soviet role in the 1970 clash between Syria and Jordan, in the Middle East negotiations in general, in which the Soviets were sometimes perceived as engaged in "sabotage," and of course, in Angola.) On the other hand, it was observed that Kissinger was rarely taken to the point where he had to be brutal or harsh with the Chinese. It was said that Kissinger was elated by his early contacts with the Chinese, in terms of their style and mode of thought. He found the Chinese to be utterly pragmatic, non-ideological in their discussions, and masters of "realpolitik," ready to conspire with him. As we have seen from the operational-code analysis, this style was indeed far more complementary to Kissinger's own. The Soviet style of diplomacy was characterized as "picky"—a constant quibbling over each and every point, major and minor, in the hope of obtaining some advantage or locating some loophole. The Chinese, it was claimed, did not negotiate in this manner. Instead, they preferred to speak in global, strategic, and long-range terms, which Kissinger appreciated and valued. Kissinger, it was said, found the Chinese to be cosmopolitan, intellectual, and haughty—all qualities to his liking. While Chou En-Lai epitomized this style (being a true statesman whom Kissinger admired), many others, such as Deng Xiaobing, also fit this description.[15] In general, Kissinger

found the Chinese intellectual and bargaining styles more congenial
This factor may also be included in the rationale for a hypothesis propos
ing more positive images of China along the hostility and general evalu
ation dimensions.

The difference of means tests reported in Table 11 support Hypothe
sis 4. Kissinger's general evaluation of the Chinese is statistically signifi
cantly more positive than that of the Soviet Union. Table 9 shows that
starting in mid-1974, only one of the three-month periods produces a
negative general evaluation score for China. This relationship hold:
regardless of the level of analysis used or the data set employed.[16]

If the twenty-one documents in which Kissinger refers to both the
Soviet Union and China in terms of general evaluation are investigated
the Chinese again came out on top: Soviet mean$=-0.70$; Chinese mean
$=+0.23$ (significant at the .05 level). In addition, because of the impor
tance of the hostility and general evaluation dimensions, evaluative asser
tion scores were calculated for the whole period. *All* the general
evaluation assertions about the Soviet Union and China were taken to
generate *one score*[17] for the entire time period:

Soviet general evaluation -0.24
Chinese general evaluation $+1.05$
Soviet DS general evaluation $+0.06$
Chinese DS general evaluation $+1.25$

This level of analysis produces the greatest difference in general evalu
ation scores. It seems clear that, on a good-bad continuum, Kissinge
saw China much more positively. The Soviet Union, at best, achieves a
neutral evaluation. The Chinese, however, are clearly in the range of
positive, or good, evaluations. This portion of Hypothesis 4 may be
considered to be confirmed

The same relationships emerge when the Soviet Union and China are
compared on the hostility dimension. From Table 9 it can be seen that
on a friendship-hostility scale, every three-month score for China i:
positive. Kissinger perceived China as friendly across the entire time
period. This positive image, like the other scales, improved during 1975
76. The average for Chinese hostility during the 1975-76 period was
$+1.62$, while the average Chinese hostility for the earlier 1972-74 period
was $+1.09$. From Table 11 it is apparent that Kissinger's assertions on
the hostility dimension are much more positive for China than for the
Soviet Union, with the Chinese average of three-month scores $+1.33$ and
the Soviet mean $+0.13$ (statistically significant at the .0005 level). This
relationship also holds for the DS data,[18] and the other levels of analysis
Using the sixty-eight documents that contained hostility references to

both nations, China averaged +1.16, against a Soviet average of −0.15 (significant at the .0001 level). Finally there are the evaluation scores based upon all the hostility assertions for the entire time period:

Soviet hostility   −0.56
Chinese hostility   +1.35
Soviet DS hostility   −0.59
Chinese DS hostility   +1.48

On the hostility dimension, the Soviet Union does not reach even a neutral image, but is within the low hostile range. The Chinese, however, are seen as friendly, well over the +1.00 mark. On the basis of the above analysis, Hypothesis 4 may be considered fully supported. Kissinger indeed held more positive general evaluation and hostility images for the Chinese than he did for the Soviet Union.

DYNAMICS OF THE SOVIET AND CHINESE IMAGES

At this point the analysis returns specifically to questions of "triangular relations" (to use Kissinger's phraseology), or the triad. As noted earlier, the general expectation in a triadic situation is that A will attempt to play B against C. In the specific context of the present chapter, the question is whether the United States was playing a triadic game with the Russians and the Chinese. This question may be approached only indirectly, by asking: Were Kissinger's evaluative assertions about the Soviet Union and China patterned in such a way as to indicate favor toward one Communist power when disfavor was being indicated about the other?

Three possibilities (within a linear frame of reference) exist. There could be no relationship between Kissinger's perceptions of the Soviet Union and China. This would be in agreement with Kissinger's explicit declarations that U.S. policy was not concerned with playing the Soviet Union and China against each other, and it would be an indicator that, even if the Soviet Union were the most important object of American foreign policy, other important objects were not related to Soviet-American policy. The second possibility is that Kissinger's perceptions of the Soviet Union and China are positively related. This would mean that positive evaluations of one were accompanied by positive evaluations of the other, and the converse—that negative evaluations of one were matched by negative evaluations of the other. This relationship could support the "Soviet Union-as-central" argument, but it would mean that Kissinger perceived the situation as dyadic, not triadic. A dyadic view, by lumping perceptions of (and perhaps behavior toward) the Soviet Union and China together, would seem to indicate a monolithic world

Table 12.   Correlations between perceptions of the Soviet Union and China

	Correlation					
	3-month		6-month		12-month	
Perceptions	Spearman	Pearson	Spearman	Pearson	Spearman	Pearso
Soviet general evaluation with Chinese general evaluation	$-.51^a$	$-.46^a$	$-.45^b$	$-.47^b$	$-.71^b$	$-.77$
Soviet hostility with Chinese hostility	$-.39^a$	$-.41^b$	$-.46^b$	$-.37^c$	$-.77^a$	$-.69$

[a] Significant at .05 level.
[b] Significant at .10 level.
[c] NS.

Communism image.[19] On the basis of the analysis in Part I, it is very unlikely that Kissinger would demonstrate a dyadic set of images. Therefore, the third possibility is the one formalized as *Hypothesis 5:* Kissinger's evaluative assertions about the Soviet Union and China, on the general evaluation and hostility scales, will be negatively associated. That is, as Kissinger's images of one Communist state become more negative, those of the other become more positive. As images of one become more positive, those of the other become more negative.

This hypothesis is based on several factors, including traditional triadic behavior, the centrality of the Soviet Union in U.S. foreign relations, and the lack of a monolithic Communism image in Kissinger's belief system. It also challenges Kissinger's explicit statements about not playing the Soviets and Chinese against each other. Finally, the study of Kissinger's personality and interpersonal style indicate that, in his private interactions, Kissinger would have been very likely to say very negative things about the Chinese when with the Russians, and negative things about the Russians when with the Chinese. Some of this private style may become apparent in the public statements also.[20]

Returning to Figures 4 and 5, Hypothesis 5 can be investigated using the two graphs, especially Figure 4, which indicate that as one nation's score rises, the other's drops. This pattern leads to large absolute gaps between Chinese and Soviet scores, starting in the October– December 1975 period for general evaluation, and the July–September 1975 period for hostility. The trend is confirmed by the correlations in Table 12. For general evaluation, all six correlations (for three-, six-, and twelve-month aggregations, both Spearman and Pearson correlations) are negative and significant. For hostility, all six correlations are again negative, with al

Figure 6. Trends in Kissinger's perceptions of China, 1971-1976

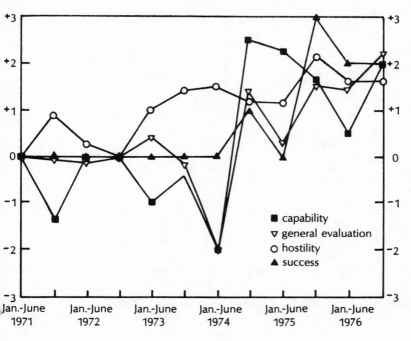

but one statistically significant. The hypothesis that Kissinger's perceptions of the Soviet Union and China are negatively associated is clearly
confirmed. Figures 4 and 5 show that, occasionally, as perceptions of the
Soviet Union become more positive, those of China become more negative, but the dominant relationship displayed is that negative perceptions
of the Soviet Union are associated with positive perceptions of China.

It is evident that Kissinger's perceptions of the two Communist
powers are related, and that the basic strategy of the triad is indicated.
There is, however, further evidence that buttresses these conclusions and
also makes a stronger case for the assertion that the Soviet Union is
perceived as the most central and most dangerous opponent, around
which other policy revolves. The evidence begins with an analysis of
Kissinger's perceptions of China on all four scales and of how these
scales relate to each other. The analysis is presented graphically in Figure
6 (which is analogous to Figure 3 for the Soviet Union). First, obviously
Kissinger's general evaluation is again an open image, varying markedly
across time, as do all the other scales. A test for openness employed in
chapter 6 was the relationship between general evaluation and hostility.

Table 13. Perceptions of China: General evaluations and hostility correlations

	Correlation					
	3-month		6-month		12-month	
Perceptions	Spearman	Pearson	Spearman	Pearson	Spearman	Pearson
General evaluation and hostility	.25	.28[a]	.36	.46[a]	.81[b]	.94[b]
General evaluation and DS hostility	.52[b]	.45[b]	.69[b]	.73[b]	.78[b]	.60

[a] Significant at .10 level.
[b] Significant at least at .05 level.

For the Soviet Union, general evaluation and hostility were positively related, and this relationship holds also for Kissinger's perceptions of China. Of the twelve correlations presented in Table 13, all are positive, and nine are significant. Again, the good-bad image of China is open, rising and falling in association with perceptions of Chinese hostility.

Recall also from the previous chapter that Kissinger's perceptions of Soviet hostility were *negatively* related to Soviet strength and success, although with far smaller magnitude than the relation exhibited by Dulles's perceptions. That is, Kissinger's perceptions of increased Soviet capabilities and Soviet success were associated with perceptions of greater hostility, and perceptions of decreased success or strength were accompanied by a rise of perceptions of friendship. In the case of China, on the other hand, these perceptions are *positively* related! As Table 14 shows, Kissinger's general evaluation of China and his perceptions of Chinese hostility are positively, strongly, and significantly related to his perceptions of Chinese capabilities and Chinese success.[21]

Thus, when the Chinese are perceived as more successful and more capable, Kissinger's general evaluation improves, and his perceptions of Chinese friendliness increase. This is *not* the manner in which one would view an enemy or opponent, unless one wanted to treat (and/or actually treated) that opponent in such a way as to play it against a third nation. Alternatively, China may not even have been seen as an opponent, as it is possible to argue from the data in Table 11 and the discussion of Hypothesis 4. Indeed, it is possible to argue that China is an informal "coalition partner" of the United States. This view is developed in the next chapter, in the discussion of the triadic relationships among the United States, the Soviet Union, and China.

Table 14.   Perceptions of China: Correlations of general evaluation and hostility with capabilities and success

Perceptions	Correlation					
	3-month		6-month		12-month	
	Spearman	Pearson	Spearman	Pearson	Spearman	Pearson
General evaluation and capabilities	.32[a]	.38[b]	.74[b]	.77[b]	.60	.69[a]
General evaluation and success	.62[b]	.62[b]	.82[b]	.76[b]	.94[b]	.94[b]
Hostility and capabilities	.33[a]	.30[a]	.28	.26	.66[a]	.58
Hostility and success	.33[a]	.32[a]	.76[b]	.70[b]	.88[a]	.84[b]

[a] Significant at .10 level.
[b] Significant at least at .05 level.

SUMMARY: PLAYING OFF TWO COMMUNIST POWERS

To review briefly the several separate pieces of evidence and to see how they fit together, first recall that, for the Soviet Union, there are negative associations between success and strength when they are related to general evaluation and hostility. In addition, Soviet general evaluation and hostility are positively associated. That is, as the main opponent, the Soviet Union is preferred to be less successful and less strong, and when it is perceived to be acting in a hostile manner, it is then given a more negative general evaluation. Second, the Soviet Union and China are negatively related on both general evaluation and hostility. That is, as the Soviets are seen as more "bad," the Chinese are perceived as being less "bad." As the Soviets are seen as being more hostile, the Chinese are seen as being less hostile. In addition, looking at several averages and overall scores, China is the attitude object receiving the more favorable general evaluation and hostility evaluation. Third, for China, in striking contrast to the Soviet Union, there is a positive relationship between strength and general evaluation and hostility. There is also a positive relationship between Chinese success and China's general evaluation and hostility. As noted, this means that China is more favorably evaluated and is seen as more friendly as its strength and success increase.

The overall conclusion is that, while Soviet strength and success are unfavorably perceived, Chinese strength and success are positively perceived. This occurs at the same time that the Soviet Union and China have a negative relationship for general evaluation and hostility—unfavorable evaluations of the Soviet Union are associated with favorable evaluations of China. Furthermore, China is the preferred attitude object in terms of hostility and general evaluation. Adding in the evidence concerning Soviet saliency (the simple frequency measures), the picture strongly indicates that the Soviet Union is perceived much more as an enemy. *The Soviet Union is perceived as the main opponent, and the increase in the success or strength of a third power is seen as a good thing to offset Soviet strength and influence.*

Therefore, two things are clear. First, for Kissinger, the Soviet Union is the central object of U.S. policy and is certainly more salient than China. Second, in his public statements about the Soviet Union and China Kissinger *is* setting one against the other. These results could have been expected from the biographical and operational-code analyses, and indeed those analyses informed the development of the working hypotheses employed in this chapter. Therefore, we have systematic empirical evidence of Kissinger's images of the Soviet Union and China, evidence that supports earlier impressions.

8

The Superpower Triad:
Perceptions and Behavior

An important issue in the application and utility of psychological or cognitive approaches in the study of foreign policy is the relationship between psychological factors and behavior. Chapters 2 and 3 set out the elements of Kissinger's belief system and some of the psychological/psychoanalytic influences on that belief system. Chapter 3 also presents evidence to indicate that Kissinger's belief system was directly related to Kissinger's behavior when he assumed a foreign-policy decision-making role—allowing him to act out the role of the statesman.

The last two chapters have also shown that Kissinger's belief system, as delineated by the operational-code analysis, was related to his subsequent "attributional behavior," that is, his evaluations of the Soviet Union and China. Employing important belief system concepts, such as legitimate vs. revolutionary states and the concept of behavior that would threaten the stability of a legitimate world order, we have also taken an initial look at how attributional behavior (i.e., images and perceptions) changed across time and how the images of the Soviet Union and China related to one another.

A final relationship between psychological (and individual) factors and behavior is investigated in the present chapter. Here, Kissinger's images of the Soviet Union and China are compared to actual foreign-policy output in the world arena.[1] The ultimate step in linking psychology/beliefs and behavior is the investigation of the relationships between Kissinger's images and the foreign-policy behavior of the U.S., the Soviet Union, and China. This investigation turns to the triangular, or triadic, nature of these relationships, as discovered in the last chapter.

ELABORATION OF THE TRIAD

Theodore Caplow defines the triad as "a social system containing three related members in a persistent situation. . . . The members of a triad need not be single persons. They may be three collectivities each acting as a unit."[2] Caplow further indicates that the triad, in addition to being one of the most familiar social contexts, is also the building block of all social organization. The most basic and important properties of the triad are:

> Every triad contains three relationships: AB, BC and AC. The triad is the only social group that has an equal number of members and relationships. . . . The most significant property of the triad is its tendency to divide into a coalition of two members against the third. The appearance of particular coalitions can be predicted with considerable accuracy if the relative power base of the three members be known.[3]

In addition, Caplow points out a variety of "catalytic effects," which occur when the presence of a third party affects a previously dyadic relationship. As has been noted, the central international relationship during the Kissinger era was the dyad of the United States and the Soviet Union, but Kissinger perceived China as an additional player, indeed as a catalyst:

> The simpler catalytic effects follow sociological principles that we first discover for ourselves in nursery school—the presence of an antagonist increases one's affection for a friend and the presence of a friend increases one's hostility toward a common antagonist.[4]

David Wilkinson notes that a third party becomes a relevant force by altering the payoff matrix of outcomes, or by changing the number of choices available to the members of the original dyad.[5] Each of these possibilities is applicable to great-power interaction. Although during his tenure as a major foreign-policy decision maker Kissinger explicitly denied that the United States took advantage of China as a catalyst, this was not his pre-1968 position. As early as 1959, and in *The Necessity for Choice,* Kissinger speculated that the rivalry between the two Communist powers could be manipulated by the United States to American advantage.[6]

Caplow outlines eight types of triads, based on the distribution of power among the units:

Type 1: $A = B = C$
Type 2: $A > B$; $B = C$; $A < (B + C)$
Type 3: $A < B$; $B = C$
Type 4: $A > (B + C)$; $B = C$
Type 5: $A > B > C$; $A < (B + C)$
Type 6: $A > B > C$; $A > (B + C)$
Type 7: $A > B > C$; $A = (B + C)$
Type 8: $A = (B + C)$; $B = C$

On this basis, he attempts to predict the coalitions most likely to form. The two triads most relevant to the U.S.-Soviet-Chinese situation are Caplow's Types 3 and 5. In Type 5, in terms of the present analysis, A could be used to represent the U.S., B to represent the Soviet Union, and C to represent China. In the Type 3 triad, A would represent China, and the U.S. and the Soviet Union are B and C. The difference between Type 5 and Type 3 is in the estimation of the comparative power of the United States and the Soviet Union.

In terms of the behavioral consequences of coalition formation, it seems to make little difference whether the United States is more powerful than the Soviet Union or actual parity exists. For Type 5, it is predicted that A (the U.S.) would join either B or C, while C (China) would join either A or B. B (the Soviet Union) would seem to have little incentive to join A, but a strong incentive to join C. The expected coalitions are thus AC (U.S.-China) or BC (Soviet Union-China). For a Type 3 coalition, China (A) could improve its position by joining either B or C, each of whom should welcome the addition of A. Because neither B nor C could improve its position through a coalition, the expected coalitions are AB (China-U.S.) or AC (China-Soviet Union). For both types of triad, then, the expected coalitions are similar. Wilkinson cites game-theory experiments whose results indicate that for Type 5, BC coalitions (Soviet Union-China) are most likely, with AC (U.S.-China) next most likely. For Type 3, the experiments show that indeed AB and AC, coalitions (China-U.S. and China-Soviet Union) occur more often than BC.[7]

The triad analyses provide another perspective from which to derive expectations of how Kissinger's perceptions are related to U.S., Soviet, and Chinese behavior. One thing is clear from the triadic coalition analyses—simply on the basis of the distribution of power (and ignoring other possible factors), there are no incentives for the U.S.-Soviet Union coalition. Thus, regardless of the coalition type, or the coalition that forms, the U.S. and the Soviet Union will most likely be opponents. This reinforces the Soviet Union-as-central-opponent thesis.

ELABORATION OF EVENTS DATA: COPDAB

One of the issues that surfaced in Part I concerned the relevance of a psychological approach to the study of foreign policy. In part, criticism of psychological approaches is directed at the assumption that perceptions of decision makers are related to the behavior of nations. As noted, a variety of arguments may be brought forward to challenge this assumption—the lack of effect or control on the part of any single individual, the influence of an extensive process of bureaucratic politics, the attribution of either too much or too little rationality to decision makers, the discounting of group decision making (outside of the bureaucratic politics framework) and processes such as "group-think," or the importance of actions, not words, as the important indicators to be studied.

In order to conduct at least partial tests of the relationship between perceptions and behavior in general, and between Kissinger's perceptions of the Soviet Union and China with U.S.-Soviet-Chinese behavior in particular, a data set recording international events was required. With this data set, a chronology of events (and characteristics of those events, such as frequency, or levels of conflict and cooperation) can be mapped over Kissinger's images in order to determine the extent that they co-vary. After a survey of a number of data sets, the Conflict and Peace Data Bank (COPDAB), developed at the University of North Carolina under the direction of Edward E. Azar, was selected for use.[8]

The COPDAB data set has several characteristics that recommend it for use in this study. The most important is the organization of the data into *directed dyads*. That is, each event is coded in terms of one nation (or actor) directing its activities toward another. With these data not only is it possible to investigate all three of the pairs derived from the triad, but also each pair can be broken into its two directed dyads: U.S. actions toward the Soviet Union and Soviet actions toward the U.S., U.S. actions toward China and Chinese actions toward the U.S., and Soviet actions toward China and Chinese actions toward the Soviet Union.[9]

Second, each event is scaled along the Azar-Sloan scale for internation events. This is a 15-point scale, where a value of 1 is given to the most cooperative event between two nations, and a point value of 15 is given to the most conflictive event (see Table 15). The scale permits the events data to be operationalized in several ways for use in the present study. The first event variable to be used is the average Azar-Sloan score of all events from one nation to another (e.g., U.S. to Soviet Union) during some specified period of time. For example, a mean score of 10.8 for U.S. actions toward China for a three-month period would mean that, in aggregate, U.S. behavior ran toward the conflictual, being almost three points above the neutral 8 point on the Azar-Sloan scale.

Table 15. Azar-Sloan scale of inter-nation events and weighted values

Weighted Value	Point Value	Event(s)
102	15	Nation A initiates or engages in very hostile war actions against Nation B and occupies territory of the latter + causes many deaths and dislocations + captures enemy soldiers.
65	14	Nation A engages in limited hostile acts against Nation B; bombards military units or hits territory of B; minor costs to B.
50	13	Nation A engages in subversion against Nation B; they engage in small clashes (air or border) and police acts, skirmishes or blockades.
44	12	Nation A breaks up diplomatic relations with B; A incites riots or rebellion in B (either through aid to rebels or radio war); terrorists or demonstrators in A bomb B's property, nationalize B's companies.
29	11	Nation A increases its military capabilities and politico-economic resources to counter Nation B's actions or the latter's contemplated actions; A places sanctions on B or hinders B's movement in waterways or on land and attempts to cause economic problems for B.
16	10	Nation A engages in verbal threats, warnings, demands and accusations against B; verbal, hostile behavior (to imply major dissatisfaction with B).
6	09	Nation A expresses mild disaffection toward B's policies, objectives, goals, behavior with A's government objection to these protestations; A's communique or note dissatisfied with B's policies in third party.
1[a]	08	Nations A and B demonstrate indifference to each other's policies, moves, actions or make no comment-type statement toward one another (an act among sub-groups not aimed at government); non-governmental visitors.
6	07	Nations A and B communicate, meet or propose talks regarding problems of mutual interest; A's officials visit B; there are public supports in A toward B (with officials or A favoring such support); issue joint communiques; appoint ambassador (routine).
10	06	Nation A supports B's policies, recognizes B's regime, etc., or solicits support of B against a third party.
14	05	Nation A establishes friendship, cultural, or similar limited agreements with B; start of diplomatic relations; head of state of A visits or meets B; A thanks B for aid.
27	04	Nation A extends economic aid to B; draws up economic pacts; gives assistance and famine relief; industrial and economic assistance to B.
31	03	Nation A extends military aid to B; military technical assistance to strengthen B; gives B facilities and special privileges.
47	02	Nations A and B establish international or dyadic alliance; economic market; joint military command and maneuvers.
92	01	Nations A and B unite voluntarily into one nation-state.

[a] Neutral point

COPDAB also enables the simple *frequency* of conflictual and cooperative events to be summed for any specific period of time. The absolute numbers of conflictual and cooperative events between one nation and another are the second and third event variables used. The last event variable is constructed from the frequency of conflictual, cooperative, and neutral events. This is the Policy Style (PS) index, as developed by Theodore Rubin.[10] As Rubin notes, the concept of relations between nations must emphasize quality as well as sheer magnitude of interaction. Quality implies "the mix of positive (friendly), negative (unfriendly) and neutral actions of a pair toward one another."[11]

Instead of being a complete analysis of all of Kissinger's statements with international events, the analysis covers a sample period of three years taken from the middle of his tenure as a top-level foreign-policy decision maker (from 1972 to 1974). The sample is sufficient to test the hypotheses dealing with the various triadic relationships.[12]

PERCEPTIONS AND BEHAVIOR: ALTERNATIVE EXPECTATIONS

In what ways are Kissinger's perceptions related to subsequent American foreign-policy behavior? In what ways do Soviet and Chinese behavior affect subsequent perceptions of those countries by Henry Kissinger? Earlier, content analysis was discussed as a methodology that could facilitate comparisons. Content analysis, as Holsti notes, may also be used to analyze a text "in order to make inferences about the causes or antecedents of the message."[13] In the present chapter, much of the analysis is concerned with Kissinger's textual assertions within the context of Soviet and/or Chinese behavior as antecedents.

A number of possible relationships between behavior and perceptions have been proposed, either explicitly or implicitly, in the above discussions. The simplest position is that there is no relationship between perceptions and events. This hypothesis will be employed as a null hypothesis (a fallback position) if none of the other possibilities is confirmed.[14] The second, most straightforward possiblity eschews the more complex triadic relationships and assumes that there are merely two dyadic relationships. Here, the U.S. and Kissinger, despite the comparisons drawn between the Soviet Union and China in the previous chapter, see and treat each major Communist power as an opponent in world politics. There is no interaction among U.S.-Soviet-Chinese behavior, so that we posit expectations for each opponent separately. *Hypothesis 6* reflects this position, stating that, as Kissinger's perceptions of the Soviet

Union become more positive, subsequent U.S. behavior toward the Soviet Union will also become more positive. As Kissinger's perceptions of the Soviet Union become more negative, subsequent U.S. behavior toward the Soviet Union will also become more negative. The same two assertions are posited for China.

A second set of relationships may also be drawn from the dyadic view of perceptions and behavior. This view of behavior between nations may be termed a "mutuality of reactions." This mutuality is operationalized by *Hypothesis 7:* The more negative the behavior directed *toward* the U.S. by the Soviet Union, the more negative will be Kissinger's subsequent perceptions of the Soviet Union. The more positive the behavior directed toward the U.S. by the Soviet Union, the more positive will be Kissinger's subsequent perceptions of the Soviet Union. These same assertions are also posited for China. Hypothesis 7 proposes a like response between Soviet (or Chinese) behavior and Kissinger's public assertions—hostility to match hostility, friendliness to match friendliness, etc.,[15] and the relations based on mutual reactions are similar for the Soviet Union and China.

Triadic relationships are somewhat more complex. Instead of simple U.S.-Soviet and U.S.-Chinese relationships, a classic "power politics" triad is substituted, in which each member plays the other two against each other as expediency dictates—there are no preferences for one nation or the other on any systematic basis. One version of this view is described by Robert Osgood:

> The U.S.-Soviet *modus vivendi* is to be achieved within a more complex balance of power and influence in which People's Republic of China will play a key role. The tactical elaboration of this tripolar relationship constitutes the major innovation of the Nixon Strategy. The administration sees Soviet fear of China's political rivalry and ideological heresy, and China's fear of Soviet military confrontation in the north and encirclement in the south, moving the Soviet Union toward a genuine détente with the United States and its European allies, while bringing China into the international diplomatic arena as a counterpoise to Soviet ambitions. The resulting moderation of Soviet behavior, it is hoped, will be matched by the normalization of China's foreign relations, as both states realize their great stake in the new pattern of international politics. Moreover, Sino-Soviet antipathy, if it can be kept within peaceful bounds, is expected not only to constrain both countries but also to give them an incentive to improve relations with the United States.[16]

Accordingly, *Hypothesis 8* proposes that the more negative Soviet behavior toward the United States becomes, the more positive are Kissinger's subsequent perceptions of China. The more positive Soviet behavior is toward the United States, the more negative are Kissinger's subsequent perceptions of China. The same two relationships are also proposed for Chinese behavior toward the United States, and Kissinger's subsequent perceptions of the Soviet Union. Hypothesis 8 sets out relationships, then, whereby the good behavior of one Communist power leads to negative perceptions of the other, and hostile behavior of one leads to positive perceptions of the other. Again, there is no favoritism; Kissinger's reactions are assumed to reinforce or to alter the behavior of one attitude object by appropriate public statements about the other.

The next step is to posit a set of relationships between Kissinger's perceptions of one Communist power and subsequent U.S. behavior toward the other one. *Hypothesis 9* proposes that positive perceptions of the Soviet Union will be followed by negative U.S. behavior toward China. Similarly, Kissinger's negative perceptions of the Soviet Union will be related to subsequent positive behavior toward China by the U.S. Once again, the same propositions are also asserted, but reversed, for China.

Finally, there is the possibility of a triadic situation with one relationship biased toward cooperation (or more positive perceptions and behavior) and one relationship biased toward opposition or enmity. For example, Caplow's Type 3 and Type 5 triadic power structures suggest that a United States-China coalition would be more likely than a U.S.-Soviet combination. A bias toward a U.S.-China relationship is also clearly the conclusion reached in chapter 6, based upon Kissinger's comparative images of the Soviet Union and China. In addition, there is what Kissinger came to call a "dual policy" in America's relations with the Soviet Union, as discussed in chapter 3. While Kissinger most clearly articulated this policy during 1975 and 1976, after Angola, it has been part of his conception of U.S.-Soviet relations from the start of his decision-making tenure. (This dual policy included firm U.S. response to Soviet provocation, but also a willingness to cooperate.)

The expectation, from the "bias" perspective, then, would be more positive U.S. behavior toward China, displayed in a more systematic or consistent manner, and systematically linked to Kissinger's perceptions. The specific relationships to be expected are set out in Hypotheses 10 and 11. *Hypothesis 10,* investigating one of the sets of possible interrelationships derived from the above discussion, proposes that Chinese behavior will be responded to by positive perceptions from Kissinger. That is, the more positive Chinese behavior is toward the U.S., the more positive subsequent perceptions of China will be. However, negative Chinese behavior toward the United States will *not* be systematically responded to with negative perceptions. Here perceptions will either continue to be positive, or else no pattern will emerge. Negative Soviet behavior, on the other hand, will be responded to with negative perceptions, as the dual policy suggests. Positive Soviet behavior will not be rewarded by positive assertions in Kissinger's public statements about the Soviet Union.

Hypothesis 11 proposes that negative Soviet behavior toward the United States will be related to more positive subsequent perceptions of China. Positive Soviet behavior will either produce no pattern in Kissinger's perceptions of China, or produce still more positive perceptions. Continuing the "biased" triad concept, positive Chinese behavior toward the U.S. will be followed by negative assertions about the Soviet Union (as an encouragement or reward). Negative Chinese behavior will produce no pattern, or possibly even more negative assertions about the Soviet Union. The relationships set out in Hypotheses 10 and 11 are different in that they propose selective responses by Kissinger to Soviet and Chinese behavior. In general, only negative Soviet behavior will produce systematic reactions in Kissinger's assertions; on the other hand, only positive Chinese behavior will be followed by patterns in Kissinger's evaluative assertions. As an overall summary, the various relationships proposed by Hypotheses 6 through 11 are diagrammed in Figure 7.

PERCEPTIONS AND BEHAVIOR: ANALYSES

Each data analysis of Hypotheses 6 to 11 is presented twice—lagged and with no lag. The lagged analysis was set up to tap explicitly the "perception-to-action" and the "action-to-perception" relationships. When the data are aggregated for two-month periods, the lag is two months. For such analysis, $N = 17$. However, it could be argued that the lagged analysis might be misleading. A two-month lag might be too much time in the study of perceptions; the actual lag might be only a matter of one or several days. Accordingly, the analyses were also performed with no lag ($N = 18$).[17]

A second issue is specifically directed toward interpreting the tables to follow. Along with the foreign-policy behavior variables in each table there will appear a (+) or (−). These signs indicate the direction of the correlation *expected,* given the hypothesis under investigation and the form of the foreign-policy behavior variable. Table 16 briefly recapitu-

Figure 7.
Hypotheses of
expected relation-
ships between
perceptions and
behavior

KEY

X ——→ Y: behavior directed from nation X toward nation Y

(+) = positive behavior

(−) = negative behavior

K ---→ Y: evaluations by Kissinger of nation Y (perceptions of nation Y)

(+) = positive evaluations/perceptions

(−) = negative evaluations/perceptions

Example:

X ——→ Y: X directs positive behavior toward Y

K ---→ Y: Kissinger has negative evaluations of Y
(−)

Hypothesis	IF	THEN
6	K ---→ USSR (+)	US ——→ USSR (+)
	K ---→ USSR (−)	US ——→ USSR (−)
	K ---→ PRC (+)	US ——→ PRC (+)
	K ---→ PRC (−)	US ——→ PRC (−)
7	USSR ——→ US (−)	K ---→ USSR (−)
	USSR ——→ US (+)	K ---→ USSR (+)
	PRC ——→ US (−)	K ---→ PRC (−)
	PRC ——→ US (+)	K ---→ PRC (+)
8	USSR ——→ US (−)	K ---→ PRC (+)
	USSR ——→ US (+)	K ---→ PRC (−)
	PRC ——→ US (−)	K ---→ USSR (+)
	PRC ——→ US (+)	K ---→ USSR (−)
9	K ---→ USSR (+)	US ——→ PRC (−)
	K ---→ USSR (−)	US ——→ PRC (+)
	K ---→ PRC (+)	US ——→ USSR (−)
	K ---→ PRC (−)	US ——→ USSR (+)
10	PRC ——→ US (+)	K ---→ PRC (+)
	PRC ——→ US (−)	K ---→ PRC (+) or no pattern
	USSR ——→ US (−)	K ---→ USSR (−)
	USSR ——→ US (+)	K ---→ USSR (−) or no pattern
11	USSR ——→ US (−)	K ---→ PRC (+)
	USSR ——→ US (+)	K ---→ PRC (+) or no pattern
	PRC ——→ US (−)	K ---→ USSR (−)
	PRC ——→ US (+)	K ---→ USSR (−) or no pattern

Table 16.   Events-data variables

---

1. Azar-Sloan Scale of Inter-Nation Events (A-SINE): Each event is scaled from 1 to 15. The event scores over a two-month period are averaged. The *lower* the score, the more cooperative the behavior. The *higher* the score, the more conflictual the behavior.

2. CONFLICT: The absolute number of conflictual events directed from one nation to another (abbreviated as No. CON).

3. COOPERATION: The absolute number of cooperative events directed from one nation to another (abbreviated as No. COOP).

4. Policy Style: Policy Style (PS) index, which ranges from +1.00 to −1.00. The higher a positive value, the more cooperative the behavior directed toward another nation; the higher a minus score, the more hostile or conflictual the behavior directed toward another nation.

Application: Notation for events directed
from the United States

Toward China	Toward the Soviet Union
US to PRC/A-SINE	US to USSR/A-SINE
US to PRC/No. CON	US to USSR/No. CON
US to PRC/No. COOP	US to USSR/No. COOP
US to PRC/PS	US to USSR/PS

---

lates the foreign-policy behavior variables involved in the following analyses.

With these preliminary instructions, Hypothesis 6 may now be investigated. As is shown in Figure 7, Hypothesis 6 posits an investigation of the relationship between Kissinger's perceptions of each Communist power and the subsequent American foreign-policy behavior toward that nation. Hypothesis 6 is based upon two separate dyadic relationships, and the assumption that the quality of U.S. foreign-policy behavior followed the quality of Kissinger's perceptions. Neither the data for the Soviet Union nor the Chinese data provides strong evidence to support Hypothesis 6. Out of thirty-two possible correlations for the Soviet Union (Table 17), only four are statistically significant, and in the predicted direction. The other six significant correlations are in the "wrong" direction. All the correctly predicted significant correlations occur with the hostility variables. The hypothesis fares as badly with the Chinese analysis (Table 18): only three correlations are statistically significant. Interestingly, all three are in the predicted direction and involved the general evaluation variables.

Clearly, the relationship between perceptions and behavior is *not* the

Table 17.   Correlations: Kissinger's perceptions of the Soviet Union and subsequent U.S. behavior toward the Soviet Union

	Event-data Variable (U.S. to U.S.S.R.)							
	A-SINE (−)		No. CON (−)		No. COOP (+)		PS (+)	
Perception	Lagged	No Lag	Lagged	No Lag	Lagged	No Lag	Lagged	No Lag
Hostility	.38	−.42[b]	.76[a]	−.07	.57[a]	.09	−.24	.40[b]
General evaluation	−.09	.44[a]	−.09	−.22	−.08	−.36	−.02	−.66[a]
DS hostility	.05	.02	.63[a]	−.04	.64[a]	−.08	.00	−.05
DS general evaluation	−.19	.56[a]	−.12	−.13	−.05	−.35	.04	−.68[a]

[a] Significant at .05 level.
[b] Significant at .10 level.

straightforward, dyadic one proposed by Hypothesis 6, which posits that behavior reflects previous perceptions. However, even the sparse results presented in Tables 17 and 18 indicate differences in the perception of the treatment of the two Communist powers. The hostility dimension appears to be more central in relations with the Soviet Union (as the more powerful and primary opponent), while general evaluation seems of more importance in regard to China.

Another set of dyadic relationships is proposed by Hypothesis 7. These "mutuality" relationships anticipate that Soviet or Chinese behavior toward the United States will be followed by matching assertions from Kissinger—negative behavior will generate negative perceptions, and positive behavior will generate positive perceptions. In other words, Hypothesis 7 proposes that Kissinger's images respond to Soviet or Chinese behavior, as is strongly suggested in the operational-code analysis. Hypothesis 7 is treated in Tables 19 and 20.

Again the results are mixed, but do not as a whole support the hypothesis. First, it is obvious from Table 19 that Hypothesis 7 does not hold for China (and thus the hypothesis must be rejected), since no relationships of any magnitude emerge from the analysis. (In some regards the results for China are much more consistent with later hypotheses—Kissinger's perceptions do not seem to change as a result of Chinese foreign-policy actions toward the United States.) We know that Kissinger's evaluations of China are generally good, but the variation that exists in those perceptions cannot be explained by the variation in Chinese behavior toward the U.S. The U.S. does not appear to be in a simple mutual reaction relationship with China. (This is developed at greater length in the discussion of Hypotheses 10 and 11 below.)

If Kissinger's images do not systematically vary with Chinese behav-

Table 18.   Correlations: Kissinger's perceptions of China and
subsequent U.S. behavior toward China

| | Event-data Variable (U.S. to China) | | | | | | | |
| | A-SINE (−) | | No. CON (−) | | No. COOP (+) | | PS (+) | |
Perception	Lagged	No Lag	Lagged	No Lag	Lagged	No Lag	Lagged	No Lag
Hostility	−.05	−.18	.07	−.02	−.27	.13	−.28	−.03
General evaluation	.20	.08	−.23	−.18	.16	−.13	.63[a]	.12
DS hostility	−.04	−.27	−.06	−.19	.19	.08	−.08	.15
DS general evaluation	.16	−.04	−.29	−.24	.52[a]	−.13	.58[a]	.21

[a] Significant at .05 level.

ior (disconfirming Hypothesis 7), what happens to our earlier assertion
of the openness of Kissinger's images, which have been characterized as
events-dependent? Table 20 shows that they *are* events-dependent with
the behavior of the Soviet Union, for which the correlations are much
higher than for China. Fourteen of the sixteen lagged correlations are in
the predicted direction, and four of them are statistically significant. All
of the six significant correlations in the table are in predicted direction. The USSR to US/A-SINE variable, measuring the level of conflict
in the Soviet Union's behavior toward the U.S., produces all four of the
correctly predicted correlations (negative correlations) when Soviet behavior is lagged before Kissinger's assertions. Three of the correlations
are significant; therefore, as Soviet behavior became more conflictual,
Kissinger perceived greater Soviet hostility and evaluated the Soviet
Union in a more unfavorable manner. Although this relationship is not
enough to support Hypothesis 7, the mutuality of reaction effect is much
more pronounced for the Soviet Union than for China, and is clearly
indicative of an open, events-dependent set of images. However, Hypothesis 7 and the model of U.S.-Soviet-Chinese relations that it represents
do not adequately describe the patterns of events and perceptions that
exist.

Hypothesis 8 was derived from a power politics explanation of perceptions and behavior, assuming no preference in triadic relations. It
proposes that there is an inverse relationship between one nation's behavior and Kissinger's subsequent perceptions of the other: negative Soviet
behavior would be followed by positive perceptions of China, and positive Soviet behavior would be followed by negative perceptions of China.
The same holds for Chinese behavior and perceptions of the Soviet
Union.

Again, the results cannot be considered to confirm the hypothesis.

136   Content-Analytic Study

Table 19. Correlations: Chinese behavior toward the United States and subsequent evaluative assertions by Kissinger

| Event-data Variable | Perception | | | |
	Hostility	General Evaluation	DS Hostility	DS General Evaluation
PRC to US/A-SINE (−)				
Lagged	.17	−.04	.23	.10
No Lag	−.24	−.03	−.04	.10
PRC to US/No. CON (−)				
Lagged	.06	−.25	.04	−.21
No Lag	−.09	.19	−.02	.20
PRC to US/No. COOP (+)				
Lagged	.03	−.14	−.10	−.18
No Lag	.01	−.04	.00	−.05
PRC to US/PS (+)				
Lagged	.07	−.22	−.08	−.26
No Lag	.25	−.11	−.02	−.26

(see Tables 21 and 22). For the Soviet Union and China combined, there are a total of fourteen statistically significant correlations—but ten are in the wrong direction! This means that more cooperative behavior by one is matched by more favorable or positive perceptions of the other. All six of the "wrong" correlations that occur with Soviet behavior appear in the lagged analysis. Thus, Soviet behavior toward the United States is *followed* by similar assertions by Kissinger about China. These results, coming mostly through the general evaluation variables, do not fit the reasoning behind Hypothesis 8 (but again more closely match the expectations of Hypothesis 11).

Hypothesis 9 was developed as a follow-on set of relationships to those proposed in Hypothesis 8. It continues the notion of inverse behavior toward and perceptions of the two Communist powers—playing each against the other. This hypothesis (like Hypothesis 6) is involved with perceptions preceding behavior. The expectations are that perceptions of one opponent will be followed by the reverse type of behavior by the United States toward the other; that is, favorable perceptions by Kissinger of China would be followed by negative American actions toward the Soviet Union. For Hypothesis 9, as for the others, no clear patterns of significant association emerge (see Tables 23 and 24). Only fifteen correlations are statistically significant for the two nations combined, and of these statistically significant relationships, eleven are not in the

Table 20. Correlations: Soviet behavior toward the United States and subsequent evaluative assertions by Kissinger

| | Perception | | | |
Event-data Variable	Hostility	General Evaluation	DS Hostility	DS General Evaluation
USSR to US/A-SINE (−)				
Lagged	−.06	−.43[a]	−.55[b]	−.52[b]
No Lag	.08	−.31	.11	.05
USSR to US/No. CON (−)				
Lagged	.01	−.32	−.26	−.45[a]
No Lag	.02	−.42[a]	−.09	−.21
USSR to US/No. COOP (+)				
Lagged	.37	.09	.33	−.12
No Lag	.13	−.03	−.03	−.10
USSR to US/PS (+)				
Lagged	.06	.34	.35	.39[a]
No Lag	.03	.09	−.07	−.21

[a] Significant at .10 level.
[b] Significant at .05 level.

Table 21. Correlations: Soviet behavior toward the United States and Kissinger's subsequent evaluative assertions about China

| | Perception of China | | | |
Soviet Event-data Variable	Hostility	General Evaluation	DS Hostility	DS General Evaluation
USSR to US/A-SINE (+)				
Lagged	−.02	−.47[a]	−.17	−.55[a]
No Lag	−.16	.09	.31	.46[a]
USSR to US/No. CON (+)				
Lagged	.08	−.49[a]	−.05	−.50[a]
No Lag	.03	.24	.23	.36
USSR to US/No. COOP (−)				
Lagged	.38	−.18	.19	−.22
No Lag	.08	−.04	−.05	−.13
USSR to US/PS (−)				
Lagged	.11	.39[b]	.14	.44[b]
No Lag	.01	−.23	−.40[b]	−.55[a]

[a] Significant at .05 level.
[b] Significant at .10 level.

predicted direction. The fairly clear *verbal* "playing off" of the two Communist powers that was identified earlier does not similarly emerge when foreign-policy events are added to the analysis. Therefore, none of the straightforward perception-behavior relationships that have been proposed has been confirmed.

Aspects of the hypotheses that have already been investigated are combined in Hypotheses 10 and 11. Both hypotheses are concerned with Kissinger's differential responses to Soviet and Chinese behavior. Hypothesis 10 proposes a bias in favor of Chinese behavior: that is, positive Chinese behavior would evoke positive reactions from Kissinger, but positive Soviet behavior would not, and on the other hand, negative Soviet behavior would evoke negative reactions from Kissinger, but negative Chinese behavior would not. An added dimension of the analyses of Hypotheses 10 and 11 is the comparison of Kissinger's evaluative assertions about the Soviet Union with his assertions about China. Whereas the other hypotheses depended on the existence of a certain relationship for both Communist powers, the analyses here may also draw on the *relative* strength of the relationships that occur for each one.

In order to evaluate Hypothesis 10, we return to Tables 19 and 20. As we know, few systematic significant relationships are found in the tables. However, by comparing the Soviet Union and China, some support for Hypothesis 10 may be found. The USSR to US/No.CON variable in Table 20 indicates that Soviet conflictual behavior indeed evokes negative evaluative assertions from Kissinger. Six of the eight correlations are in the predicted direction, two are significant, and in aggregate, the correlations are much larger and more consistently in the predicted direction than those from Table 19 for PRC to US/No.CON. There appears to be no substantial evidence from Table 19 that Chinese conflictual behavior is followed by unfavorable evaluative assertions from Kissinger.

The second section of Hypothesis 10 is also supported by evidence in Tables 19 and 20. The number and strength of the correctly predicted correlations for USSR to US/A-SINE and USSR to US/PS provide this evidence. The correlations produced by PRC to US/A-SINE and PRC to US/PS are much weaker and have more incorrectly predicted directions. The parts of Hypothesis 10 that deal with favorable or positive behavior toward the United States cannot be confirmed. Neither country reveals a pattern for the No.COOP variable. Therefore, Kissinger responds to hostile Soviet behavior in a more "mutual reaction" manner than he uses for hostile Chinese behavior, and, as predicted, there is no pattern of response to hostile or negative Chinese behavior toward the

Table 22. Correlations: Chinese behavior toward the United States and Kissinger's subsequent evaluative assertions about the Soviet Union

Chinese Event-data Variable	Perception of Soviet Union			
	Hostility	General Evaluation	DS Hostility	DS General Evaluation
PRC to US/A-SINE (+)				
Lagged	.07	.02	.02	.02
No Lag	−.03	−.63[a]	.04	−.40[b]
PRC to US/No. CON (+)				
Lagged	.02	−.35	−.22	−.41[b]
No Lag	−.02	−.33	−.09	−.26
PRC to US/No. COOP (−)				
Lagged	.16	−.08	.23	−.21
No Lag	.54[a]	−.34	.24	−.48[a]
PRC to US/PS (−)				
Lagged	.09	.20	.20	.12
No Lag	.36	−.09	.03	−.37

[a] Significant at .05 level.
[b] Significant at .10 level.

U.S. Furthermore, there is no indication that Kissinger responded systematically to cooperative or positive acts toward the United States.

This suggestion of differential perceptions and behavior is continued in Hypothesis 11. Here, negative behavior by the Soviet Union is posited to lead to more positive perceptions of China, while negative Chinese behavior is expected to produce either no pattern or even more unfavorable perceptions of the Soviets. Indeed, in Table 22 it is the case that for correlations of the PRC to US/No.CON variable with perceptions of the Soviet Union, seven of eight correlations are negative, with one being statistically significant. On the whole, these results indicate that Kissinger's response to increased Chinese conflictual acts was a more unfavorable image of the Soviet Union (especially as compared to the results produced by USSR to US/No.CON in Table 21). The remaining results are very mixed.

Hypothesis 11 also proposes that cooperative behavior directed at the United States by China would be followed by unfavorable perceptions of the Soviet Union, but the evidence in Table 22, for PRC to US/No.COOP is mixed and cannot be used to support the hypothesis. It was also proposed that positive Soviet behavior would be followed by no pattern or even more favorable evaluative assertions of China. Cer-

Table 23.   Correlations: Kissinger's perceptions of the Soviet Union and subsequent U.S. behavior toward China

Perceptions of the Soviet Union	Event-data Variable (U.S. to China)							
	A-SINE (+)		No. CON (+)		No. COOP (−)		PS (−)	
	Lagged	No Lag	Lagged	No Lag	Lagged	No Lag	Lagged	No Lag
Hostility	−.01	−.42[a]	.07	−.16	.04	.54[b]	.13	.21
General evaluation	.12	.05	.10	.32	−.13	−.14	.16	−.64[b]
DS hostility	.03	−.18	−.27	.36	.65[b]	.21	.50[b]	−.10
DS general evaluation	.13	.10	.03	.15	.20	−.29	.20	−.44[b]

[a] Significant at .10 level.
[b] Significant at .05 level.

tainly, more favorable perceptions of China do not appear; in fact, there is *no* pattern (Table 21, USSR to US/No.COOP). (Once more the relationship proposed by Hypothesis 8—that positive Soviet behavior would be followed by unfavorable evaluations of China—*does not hold.*)

While Hypothesis 11 did not involve consideration of how Kissinger's perceptions were followed by U.S. foreign-policy behavior, several of the results presented in Tables 23 and 24 support the rationale behind this consideration. Although we have established few substantial linkages between Soviet behavior and subsequent Kissinger perceptions, some tentative inferences about U.S. behavior subsequent to those perceptions may be drawn. Hypothesis 11 suggested that positive Soviet behavior might be followed by favorable perceptions of China. This relationship was not confirmed. However, from Table 23 it can be seen that more favorable perceptions of the Soviet Union could have led to more cooperative behavior toward China, since the US to PRC/No.-COOP variable produces two strong and significant positive correlations with perceptions of Soviet hostility.[18] Some additional evidence is simply that there are no patterns between perceptions of the Soviet Union and conflictual action directed toward China (US to PRC/No.CON). Hypothesis 11 similarly notes that negative Soviet behavior toward the United States *will not* be associated with increased unfavorable perceptions of China.

Table 24 gives evidence to support the perceptions-to-behavior version of Hypothesis 11, which suggests that friendly and cooperative Chinese behavior would be followed by unfavorable perceptions of the Soviet Union. In Table 24, more friendly perceptions of China are followed by more conflictual acts toward the Soviets (US to USSR/No.-

Table 24. Correlations: Kissinger's perceptions of China and subsequent U.S. behavior toward the Soviet Union

| | Event-data Variable (U.S. to U.S.S.R.) | | | | | | | |
| | A-SINE (+) | | No. CON (+) | | No. COOP (−) | | PS (−) | |
Perceptions of China	Lagged	No Lag	Lagged	No Lag	Lagged	No Lag	Lagged	No Lag
Hostility	.24	−.43[a]	.52[b]	−.01	.37	.18	−.22	.33
General evaluation	−.68[b]	.09	.15	.21	.39[a]	.18	.78[b]	−.16
DS hostility	.07	−.22	.46[b]	−.02	.40[a]	.07	−.05	.21
DS general evaluation	−.51[b]	.26	.13	.17	.34	.07	.61[b]	−.24

[a] Significant at .10 level.
[b] Significant at .05 level.

CON). Another proposed relationship in Hypothesis 11—that negative Chinese behavior would lead to no patterns or even more unfavorable perceptions of the USSR—also finds some support in Table 24. The "reversed" correlations that occur with US to USSR/A-SINE and US to USSR/PS indicate the unfavorable perceptions of China are associated with unfavorable behavior toward the Soviet Union. Thus, the anomalies in Tables 23 and 24 in terms of Hypothesis 9 can be explained by the "biased" triadic relationships embodied in Hypothesis 11. When hypothesis 11 attempts to identify a relationship between external events directed toward the United States and Kissinger's images of external objects, it is not confirmed. However, when the existence of those images is assumed—as is done in Tables 23 and 24, which begin with perceptions—then the basic relationships proposed by Hypothesis 11 *are* supported.

On the whole, simple dyadic "mutual reaction" relationships do not emerge as a distinct pattern, either with Kissinger's perceptions preceding U.S. behavior or with Soviet/Chinese behavior preceding Kissinger's perceptions. Simple playing-off behavior, discovered in the previous chapter in relation to perceptions only, does not occur when behavior is introduced as an additional factor. However, weak evidence points to a Chinese bias, as set out in Hypotheses 10 and 11: only certain types of behavior and/or perceptions are responded to, others are ignored.

CONCLUSION

Several substantive and methodological conclusions are possible at this point. As a partial answer to questions regarding the influence of the individual in foreign policy, it is apparent that Kissinger's images are *not* congruent with American foreign-policy behavior. Although Kissinger was the dominant foreign-policy decision maker during the period under investigation, his words—and the evaluative assertions that they contained—did not simply and directly reflect American behavior toward the Soviet Union and China. Although the two are related in many ways, perceptions and behavior have complicated, often indirect, relationships that are obviously affected by a number of other variables. Perceptions alone cannot be used to predict American foreign-policy behavior. Behavior directed toward the United States cannot alone be used to predict Kissinger's evaluations of a particular foreign-policy attituded object. (This latter point is clear from analyses presented in chapter 6, where it was asserted that Soviet behavior in Africa was a major factor in Kissinger's perceptions during the 1975-76 period.[19]) What can be said is that there are few direct, uncomplicated relationships between dyadic behavior and dyadic perceptions.

It is also worthwhile to repeat that a number of simple perception-behavior relationships were rejected. Various threads of support for Hypotheses 10 and 11 were uncovered, particularly for Hypothesis 11. Recall also that these hypotheses reflect expectations that are based in part on the "perceptions-only" analysis presented in chapter 6. In sum, chapter 6 and the present one permit us to describe both Kissinger's perceptions and American behavior as supporting a set of relationships in which the United States is biased toward China within a U.S.-Soviet Union-China triad. The "rewards" or "punishments" or positive/cooperative or negative/conflictual American words/actions were not distributed equally between the two Communist powers. The centrality of the Soviet Union as America's principal opponent is reflected in the more positive and rewarding behavior directed at China.

Although Kissinger denied using a Chinese "card," his evaluations clearly show that he played the Soviet Union and China against each other. This chapter also indicates that Kissinger and the United States followed the politics of the triad. Kissinger summarizes these tendencies in *White House Years:*

> Triangular diplomacy, to be effective, must rely on the natural incentives and propensities of the players. It must avoid the *impression* [emphasis added] that one is "using" either of the contenders against the other. . . . The hostility between China and the Soviet Union served our purposes best if we maintained closer relations with each side than they did with each other.[20]

The Context of
Perceptions and Behavior

Clearly, both events and perceptions are the results of a complex of factors affecting foreign policy. This complex is, in effect, the context of a foreign-policy document and reflects factors both internal to the decision-making process and external to the nation-state. This chapter examines aspects of this context. First, especially given the weak direct linkages between perceptions and behavior noted in chapter 8, it might be useful to investigate the proposed U.S.–Soviet Union–China relationships by skipping the perceptual stage. In this chapter some rudimentary analyses are performed using *only* the foreign-policy events data. These analyses permit a more complete appreciation of the roles and interrelationships of perceptions and words in the area of international affairs. Second, although chapter 8 more than others has looked at the dynamics of changing relationships over time, two important changes, noted earlier but not yet systematically investigated, are changes in the international environment and changes in Kissinger's governmental role. The former are relevant in the external (or international) foreign-policy context; the latter are relevant in the internal (domestic) foreign-policy context.

EVENTS DATA ANALYSIS

Hypothesis 7 sets out a series of dyadic relationships, which are termed "mutual reaction." While this term did not describe American relationships with either the Soviet Union or China in the context of Kissinger's reactions, as given in his public statements, to behavior directed at the U.S., the hypothesis can be tested using only the foreign-policy *behavior* variables. Table 25, part A, builds upon the evidence of mutuality that did emerge earlier with regard to Soviet conflictual behavior and firmly supports the hypothesis. The clearest demonstration of U.S.–Soviet mutuality is seen on the diagonal of Table 25. All four correlations are positive and are over .35, and three are statistically significant. Particularly impressive are the relationships between the two No.CON variables ($r=.77$), and the two No.COOP variables ($r=.78$). Within two-month periods, the two superpowers match each other in terms of both conflictual and cooperative acts toward each other as measured by two summary variables (a mean and a ratio) and two variables based on absolute numbers of events.[1]

Another point of interest appears in part A of Table 25. The correlations of US to USSR/No.COOP with USSR to US/No.CON and of US to USSR/No.CON with USSR to US/No.COOP are both strongly positive. The mutuality hypothesis would predict these correlations to be negative. However, a number of foreign-policy analyses have suggested that nations that interact frequently, especially major powers, will have high levels of conflict and cooperation.[2] These research findings are supported by the positive correlations between numbers of conflictual and cooperative acts. They simply mean that the United States and the Soviet Union were in a period of high mutual interaction, as would be expected from the saliency of the Soviet Union in U.S. foreign policy.

Examining part B of Table 25 for a "mutual reaction" pattern with China provides a very different result. There is none of the mutual hostility that is found in the U.S.–Soviet relationship. The outstanding relationship in the U.S.–China analysis is that between the two No.COOP variables ($r=.93$). Clearly, there is a mutual cooperation relationship between the United States and China. On the basis of this correlation, the US to PRC/No.COOP with PRC to US/PS relationship can be seen as supporting evidence, as can the US to PRC/A-SINE with PRC to US/A-SINE relationship. The one seeming anomaly is the strong postive relationship between US to PRC/PS and PRC to US/A-SINE. This means either that cooperative U.S. behavior is responded to by hostile Chinese behavior, or that conflictive Chinese behavior still elicits cooperative U.S. behavior. This set of possibilities is problematic in terms of Hypothesis 7, but not in terms of Hypothesis 11. The latter proposes that the United States, desiring to maintain a U.S.–China "coalition," would ignore hostile Chinese behavior and respond cooperatively regardless of the Chinese foreign-policy stimuli. Thus, we have cooperative mutuality, and indications of systematic cooperative American behavior. This policy would seem to be natural for an era of emerging normalcy; an American desire to open up and normalize relations, and to maintain a Sino-American front against the Soviet Union. This pattern also indicates the possibility that in U.S. foreign policy, "words are

Table 25.   Events only: Correlations for U.S.–Soviet and U.S.–Chinese events-data variables[a]

A. U.S.–Soviet Union Correlations

U.S. Events-data Variable	Soviet Events-data Variable			
	USSR to US/ A-SINE	USSR to US/ No. CON	USSR to US/ No. COOP	USSR to US/ PS
US to USSR/A-SINE	.39[b] (+)	.16 (+)	−.27 (−)	−.40[b] (−)
US to USSR/No. CON	.30 (+)	.77[c] (+)	.57[c] (−)	−.18 (−)
US to USSR/No. COOP	.12 (−)	.76[c] (−)	.78[c] (+)	−.05 (+)
US to USSR/PS	−.21 (−)	.01 (−)	.23 (+)	.36 (+)

B. U.S.–China Correlations

U.S. Events-data Variable	Chinese Events-data Variable			
	PRC to US/ A-SINE	PRC to US/ No. CON	PRC to US/ No. COOP	PRC to US/ PS
US to PRC/A-SINE	.38[b] (+)	.28 (+)	.19 (−)	.00 (−)
US to PRC/No. CON	−.15 (+)	−.16 (+)	.01 (−)	.16 (−)
US to PRC/No. COOP	.06 (−)	.08 (−)	.93[c] (+)	.64[c] (+)
US to PRC/PS	.64[c] (−)	.16 (−)	.30 (+)	.04 (+)

[a] No lag. (+) and (−) indicate expected direction for "mutual reaction" hypothesis.
[b] Significant at .10 level.
[c] Significant at .05 level.

cheap." As shown in Tables 19 and 20, some (albeit small) negative correlations occur that indicate that uncooperative Chinese behavior could bring forth unfavorable evaluations in Kissinger's public statements. However, in United States foreign-policy behavior, even this minimal negative reaction to Chinese behavior seems to disappear. While the Chinese were chided in unfavorable public references, American actions maintained a cooperative and friendly pattern.

In the triadic analyses, the power politics rationale underlies Hypotheses 8 and 9. This rationale is based upon a set of triadic relations with no systematic biases or preferences. At this stage in the analyses, it should be expected that this assumption is unsupported. Indeed, just as the unbiased triad was not supported by the earlier analysis including perceptions, it cannot be supported using only events data (see Table 26). In Table 26, only three of sixteen correlations fit expectations; all four of the significant correlations are in the wrong direction. Again, the wrong correlations fit much more closely the relationships set out in Hypothesis 11, in which differential treatment is proposed.

Finally, the last relationship is the biased triad proposed by Hypoth-

Table 26.   Correlations between U.S. behavior toward the Soviet Union and behavior toward China[a]

U.S.–Soviet Events-data Variable	U.S.–China Events-data Variable			
	US to PRC/ A-SINE	US to PRC/ No. CON	US to PRC/ No. COOP	US to PRC/ PS
US to USSR/A-SINE	.14 (−)	.17 (−)	−.39[b] (+)	−.40[b] (+)
US to USSR/No. CON	.21 (−)	.01 (−)	.12 (+)	.16 (+)
US to USSR/No. COOP	.24 (+)	−.07 (+)	.39[b] (−)	.36 (−)
US to USSR/PS	−.20 (+)	−.34 (+)	.29 (−)	.48[c] (−)

[a] (+) and (−) indicate expected direction of the correlation if the U.S. actually was "playing off" the Soviet Union and China.
[b] Significant at .10 level.
[c] Significant at .05 level.

eses 10 and 11. In testing the other hypotheses, both here and in the previous chapter, the data indicate support for Hypothesis 11 while disconfirming the other propositions. Also, in the previous chapter some evidence was found to indicate (with no lag) that Soviet actions toward the United States affected Kissinger's perceptions of China. Do the basic relationships proposed by Hypothesis 11 hold for the analysis of events only? The top two rows of Table 27, part A, give results that conform to the expectations of Hypothesis 11—especially the correlations with US to PRC/No.CON. As the Soviet Union directs conflictual behavior at the U.S., the U.S. directs less conflictual behavior at China. In the third row, there is evidence to support another part of Hypothesis 11: that, as the Soviets direct positive behavior at the U.S., the U.S. will behave toward China with no systematic pattern, or will direct positive behavior at China. The correlation between the two No. COOP variables supports this interpretation. As developed in the previous chapter, the United States punished the Soviet Union for hostile or uncooperative behavior, but it would not reward the Soviets for cooperative behavior. Just as Kissinger's dual policy stressed firm response to Soviet provocation or adventurism, the other side of the policy was to engage the Soviet Union within the existing international system—involving the U.S.S.R. in economic and political webs of interdependence. Thus, it was hoped that the Soviets would develop a set of self-imposed constraints based on the costs of conflict within an interdependent system. Neither of the paths in the dual policy called for American applause when the Soviets simply acted as any legitimate state would be expected to act. The

Table 27.   Events only: Correlations between Soviet/Chinese behavior toward the U.S. and U.S. behavior toward the other Communist power

A. Soviet behavior toward U.S.

Soviet–U.S. Events-data Variable	U.S.–China Events-data Variable			
	US to PRC/ A-SINE	US to PRC/ No. CON	US to PRC/ No. COOP	US to PRC/ PS
USSR to US/A-SINE	−.26 (−)	−.41[a] (−)	−.08 (+)	.18 (+)
USSR to US/No. CON	.00 (−)	−.38[a] (−)	.10 (+)	.36 (+)
USSR to US/No. COOP	.17	−.07	.62[b]	.31
USSR to US/PS	.23	.33	.16	−.12

B. Chinese behavior toward U.S.

China–U.S. Events-data Variable	U.S.–Soviet Events-data Variable			
	US to USSR/ A-SINE	US to USSR/ No. CON	US to USSR/ No. COOP	US to USSR/ PS
PRC to US/A-SINE	−.21 (−)	.28	.34	.37 (−)
PRC to US/No. CON	.26 (+)	.82[b] (+)	.77[b] (−)	−.03
PRC to US/No. COOP	−.35	.18	.42[a] (−)	.31
PRC to US/PS	−.44[b] (−)	−.16	.05	.26 (−)

Note: (+) and (−) indicate expected direction of correlation if Hypothesis 11 is correct.
[a] Significant at .10 level.
[b] Significant at .05 level.

furthest Kissinger would go was a form of Charles Osgood's GRIT strategy (Graduated and Reciprocated Initiatives in Tension-reduction), set out in three principles of U.S. policy toward the Soviet Union—the principle of concreteness, the principle of restraint, and the principle of linkage.[3]

China is more difficult to analyze (Table 27, part B). Patterns in the direction predicted by Hypothesis 11 are indicated, but no overall confirmatory pattern is discernible. Of the four significant correlations for it in Table 27, two are in the predicted direction. Given the strength of the "wrong" US to USSR/No.COOP correlations, one possible explanation is that major powers interact frequently and have high levels of cooperative and conflictual behavior.

CHANGING THE FOREIGN-POLICY ENVIRONMENT

Cold War and Détente. In the comparison of Kissinger's images of the Soviet Union to those of John Foster Dulles, attention was drawn to the different foreign-policy environments of their respective tenures. In simple terms, a period of cold war was contrasted to a period of détente. This contrast was merely asserted, with the understanding that something had indeed occurred to change Soviet-American relations. A general relaxation of tensions and improvement of relations were used to help explain and test (in terms of face validity) the differences between Kissinger's and Dulles's images. On the other hand, the normalization of relations in détente could be seen as a factor that complicated the analysis of perceptions and behavior. One would expect the analysis to be much more direct and clearer during periods of high mutual tension and hostility.

As an important factor in the external foreign-policy environment, is a period of détente truly different from other periods of Soviet-American relations? Two brief analyses demonstrate that real distinctions can be made. The first analysis is a content analysis, based on words. The second analysis is based on a broader sweep of COPDAB data. The content analysis, by Kjell Goldmann, was performed on governmental statements in a study to measure fluctuations in international tension: "We regard tension as essentially synonymous with mutual threat perceptions . . . tension exists between two actors, or coalitions of actors to the extent that they expect conflict behavior to occur between themselves."[4] This definition of tension usefully operationalizes the basic understanding of what both cold war and détente mean. Tension, as measured by Goldman, fluctuates between +1.00 and −1.00, with +1.00 being the most friendly or least tense situation, and −1.00 indicating the highest level of tension. Figure 8 presents the "amount of tension" that occurred among the United States, the Soviet Union, and China in three specific time periods.

As Figure 8 shows, there was indeed substantial change in tension among the triad members across time. For the United States–Soviet Union dyad in particular, the mutual −0.9 scores of the "early" cold war period were moderated during the "late" cold war (to −0.7 and −0.3), and finally become positive in the 1972-75 period of détente (+0.3 for the U.S.–Soviet Union, and +0.6 for the Soviet Union–U.S.). It is interesting (especially with regard to Hypothesis 11) that Sino-American tensions did not change much during the cold war years, but, in the period of détente, the U.S.–China score became strongly positive (+0.7). In the same period, however, the China–U.S. tension score remains at −1.0 (hostile). This is a useful confirmation of the proposed American bias toward China. Goldmann's analysis confirms the U.S. shift to positive reactions to China, regardless of Chinese words directed at the United States. Finally, Goldmann's analysis outlines the decline in Sino

Figure 8. Cold war and détente: Goldmann's
analysis of tension fluctuations

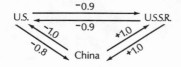

Early Cold War System: 1950-54

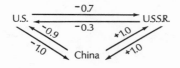

Late Cold War System: 1955-61

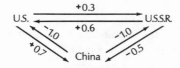

Current System: 1972-75

Soviet relations—moving from +1.0 mutual scores in the early periods
to –1.0 China–Soviet Union and –0.5 Soviet Union–China scores in the
1972–75 period.[5]

The improvement of U.S.–Soviet relations can be described through
the analysis of events as well as of words. Using COPDAB data, summary measures can be derived to describe specific time periods. Table 28
displays American behavior toward the Soviet Union and China, with
the data broken down by administrations, and comparing the Nixon
years (1969–73) to the preceding twenty years. The foreign-policy behavior variables here include the *average* number of conflictual and cooperative events (Avg. No.CON and Avg.No.COOP) for the years indicated.
In addition, a simplified version of the Policy Style index is used, which
is a ratio of conflictual to cooperative events: Avg.No.CON/Avg.No.-
COOP. The higher the ratio, the more conflictual is the relationship; the
lower the ratio, the more cooperative the relationship.

Part A of Table 28 chronicles a steadily improving overall set of

Table 28.   U.S. behavior toward the Soviet Union and China, 1948-1973

A. Behavior toward the Soviet Union

Behavior Variable	Truman 1948-52	Eisenhower 1953-60	Kennedy 1961-63	Johnson 1964-68	Cumulative 1948-68	Nixon 1969-73
			Time Period			
Avg. No. CON	77.0	59.12	59.0	29.8	56.4	35.0
Avg. No. COOP	12.0	38.25	52.66	35.6	32.9	68.2
$\dfrac{\text{Avg. No. CON}}{\text{Avg. No. COOP}}$	6.4	1.54	1.12	0.83	1.71	0.51

B. Behavior toward China

Behavior Variable	Truman 1949-52	Eisenhower 1953-60	Kennedy 1961-63	Johnson 1964-68	Cumulative 1949-68	Nixon 1969-73
			Time Period			
Avg. No. CON	18.0	18.0	18.0	20.8	18.7	7.6
Avg. No. COOP	1.5	7.5	4.3	9.8	6.4	28.2
$\dfrac{\text{Avg. No. CON}}{\text{Avg. No. COOP}}$	12.0	2.4	4.2	2.1	2.92	0.26

relations between the United States and the Soviet Union. The ratio of conflictual to cooperative acts directed by the U.S. toward the Soviet Union declines in each successive period, reaching 0.51 in the Nixon years, 1969–73.[6] For the Nixon period, this ratio means that almost twice as many cooperative acts were directed toward the Soviet Union as conflictual ones. The average number of cooperative acts under Nixon is substantially greater than in any other administration. The contrast of the Nixon years with the Truman years is striking: the former average less than half as many conflictual acts and almost six times as many cooperative acts. Thus the Truman ratio is the highest, at 6.4, and Nixon's is the lowest. The ratio for the Eisenhower years is the second highest, at 1.54, and although it is a definite improvement on the Truman period, this period, in which Dulles operated, was unmistakably a time of greater conflict and lesser cooperation than the period in which Kissinger practiced diplomacy.

A similar distinction can be made for American behavior toward China (Table 28, part B). The differences between the Nixon administration and the other administrations are even greater when China is the foreign-policy object. If détente means the reduction of tension and hostility, with the growth of cooperation and general normalization of

Table 29.   Soviet and Chinese behavior toward the U.S., 1948-1973

A. Soviet Behavior toward the U.S.

Behavior Variable	Truman 1948-52	Eisenhower 1953-60	Kennedy 1961-63	Johnson 1964-68	Cumulative 1948-68	Nixon 1969-73
			Time Period			
Avg. No. CON	88.2	68.4	86.7	70.8	76.3	45.2
Avg. No. COOP	14.4	58.6	67.3	37.6	44.3	68.2
Avg. No. CON / Avg. No. COOP	6.13	1.17	1.29	1.88	1.72	0.66

B. Chinese Behavior toward the U.S.

Behavior Variable	Truman 1949-52	Eisenhower 1953-60	Kennedy 1961-63	Johnson 1964-68	Cumulative 1949-68	Nixon 1969-73
			Time Period			
Avg. No. CON	15.3	24.3	20.7	202.0	66.4	118.2
Avg. No. COOP	1.0	10.4	2.0	6.6	6.3	19.0
Avg. No. CON / Avg. No. COOP	15.3	2.34	10.4	30.6	10.53	6.22

relations, then as measured both by words and by deeds, the period of détente that Kissinger was creating as well as operating in was clearly different from the cold war in the quality of its international interactions.

This conclusion is supported by the data presented in Table 29. Soviet behavior toward the U.S. (part A) is most cooperative during the Nixon years. The frequency of conflictual events is lowest during 1969–73, the only period in which the Soviet Union directed more cooperative behavior than conflictual behavior toward the United States. Again, the Nixon years have the lowest ratio, 0.66, while the highest ratio, 6.13, belongs to the era of Stalin and the early cold war. The Chinese patterns are more difficult to discern. Chinese behavior toward the United States is "better" if one compares the ratio during the Nixon years, 6.22, to the 15.3 of the Truman period, and the full 1948–68 ratio of 10.53. However, the frequency of interaction with the United States is very low, especially during the 1949–52 period. Also, excluding the Johnson years, China had the highest number of conflictual events with the U.S. under Nixon. However, since this time also saw the largest number of cooperative events, the overall ratio is better than all except that for the Eisenhower years. Again, while U.S.–Soviet behavior appears to fit a pattern of mutuality, the Sino-American pattern is more complicated. American actions toward China became more cooperative, while Chinese behavior fluctuated. Note that this pattern also supports Hypothesis 11: Favorable American behavior is continued, regardless of the Chinese response. Still, the cooperative American behavior of the Nixon years elicits the greatest frequency of cooperative Chinese behavior.

The basic point that emerges from the behavioral analyses, as well as from Goldmann's content analysis, is the improved climate in international affairs. This is especially true for Soviet-American relations. Verbally and behaviorally, the international climate is more positive during the period of détente than during the coldest of the cold war years under Truman or Eisenhower. These comparisons outline the overall external environment within which the present study must be placed, and which affected both events and perceptions.

Role Factors. In the general analysis of foreign policy or the comparative study of foreign policy, the issue of the "relative potency" of various factors or influences on foreign policy has been raised. One feature of the *internal* context of foreign policy is the influence of role on the policy-making process, but the literature contains few studies that specifically investigate this feature. Henry Kissinger underwent what might be considered a major role change when he was sworn in as secretary of state on September 22, 1973. While it is important to remember that he retained his position as assistant for National Security affairs, one should not, *a priori,* discount the effect of this additional, prestigious role.[7] Furthermore, there are the "bureaucratic politics" arguments that Kissinger now was responsible for a completely new organization, an organization whose interests were now supposed to be his interests, and for which he was supposed to care.[8]

There are various ways to investigate whether there were significant changes or differences in Kissinger's perceptions of the Soviet Union and China after he became secretary of state. The results of two fairly simple approaches are displayed in Table 30. Part A contrasts (but does not test) the differences in the total evaluative assertion scores that can be calculated for all assertions Kissinger made before and after he became secretary of state. The evaluations of the Soviet Union are more negative in the latter period, while the evaluations of China are more positive. However, if we compare means, based on the average evaluation scores from *each document* during the two periods (part B), only two of the eight differences are statistically significant. Only perceptions of Soviet hostility (and DS hostility) are significantly different.

A more complex but appropriate technique is the use of regression

Table 30.   Effect of role change on perceptions

A. Single evaluative assertion scores

Perception	Before becoming secretary of state	After becoming secretary of state
Soviet Union		
General Evaluation	−0.16	−0.26
DS General Evaluation	+0.30	−0.01
Hostility	+0.81	−0.67
DS Hostility	+1.16	−0.26
China		
General Evaluation	+0.24	+1.18
DS General Evaluation	+0.58	+1.38
Hostility	+0.90	+1.45
DS Hostility	+1.24	+1.69

B. Difference of means test, by document

Perception	Pre-secretary	Post-secretary	t	DF	Significance[a]
Soviet Union					
General Evaluation	+0.50	−0.01	1.13	15.8	.27
DS General Evaluation	+0.82	+0.25	1.30	19.8	.21
Hostility	+1.19	−0.39	5.07	25.3	.00*
DS Hostility	+1.48	−0.03	5.90	32.4	.00*
China					
General Evaluation	+0.35	+1.13	1.12	42.0	.27
DS General Evaluation	+0.52	+1.22	1.37	14.3	.19
Hostility	+0.91	+1.33	1.19	25.4	.24
DS Hostility	+1.23	+1.53	.96	21.7	.35

[a] An asterisk indicates significance at the .01 level.

for an interrupted time-series analysis. Briefly, this involves two sets of regressions: one that includes the period up to the "intervention" (here the change of role) and a second regression that covers the entire time under analysis. The independent variable is the date or time period (using the two-month aggregations). The dependent variable is the evaluation score of the category under consideration. From the two regressions one can then calculate Chow's F,[9] which tests whether any of the parameters in the model changed from the point of intervention. If the Chow's F is significant, one can reject the null hypothesis ("no difference"), and one can conclude that there has been a difference since the intervention. The results of this analysis are presented in Table 31. The data used were the thirty-six two-month aggregation periods of Kissinger's assertions. There are sixteen observation periods before the intervention, and twenty

Table 31.   Time-series analysis of effect of role change

Perception	Chow's F (DF = 20,15)	Significance[a]
Soviet Union		
General Evaluation	3.90	.05
DS General Evaluation	1.81	None
Hostility	1.18	None
DS Hostility	2.49	.05*
China		
General Evaluation	47.38	.05
DS General Evaluation	2.24	None
Hostility	1.27	None
DS Hostility	0.96	None

[a] An asterisk means that the Durbin-Watson statistic indicates autocorrelation.

afterwards (the first secretary of state period is September–October 1973). Only three of the eight variables have significant Chow F statistics. For the general evaluation of both the Soviet Union and China, the intervention seems to make a difference.[10] The other tests indicate no effect of the change in role.

Before these results are interpreted, a second internal factor that may be of import by itself, as well as for the secretary of state analyses, should be considered. This second major change in the internal environment was the resignation of President Richard Nixon and the succession of Gerald Ford. This also may be seen as an informal change in Kissinger's role. The relationship between Kissinger and Nixon was noted earlier. It is not possible to state unreservedly that Nixon was the "senior partner" in the Nixon-Kissinger foreign-policy team, but the evidence at hand points to this conclusion. Although Kissinger has consistently maintained that the president should always be recognized as bearing the ultimate responsibility in foreign affairs,[11] it may be proposed that under Ford, Kissinger became the senior partner in foreign-policy matters. This would constitute an informal, but important, role change.

Even within the context of presidential succession, then, one could hypothesize a major change in Kissinger's role. The breakpoint at the change in president should then be studied in the same way as Kissinger's change to secretary of state. Accordingly, Table 32 presents data on Kissinger's perceptions during the Nixon and Ford administrations. The simple comparisons show much the same pattern as before. In part A it can be seen that perceptions of the Soviet Union become more unfavorable, while those of China become more positive. The differences are perhaps even more pronounced than those found with the secretary of state breakpoint. In part B, the two presidential periods are more distinct than the periods before and after Kissinger became secretary of state. Seven of eight comparisons of means are statistically different. Therefore, the difference produced by the change in presidents is of greater consequence than the differences produced by Kissinger's becoming secretary of state. However, the time-series analyses shown in part C give the same results as before. A significant change is found for general evaluation, for both the Soviet Union and China. None of the other variables shows parameter changes at the intervention point.

Depending heavily on the time-series analyses, the overall conclusion seems to be that neither of the role changes, as such, made much difference to Kissinger's perceptions of the two Communist powers. *Although the two intervention points occurred ten months apart, the time-series analyses are similar.* Yet, the other comparisons do show some differences. For both the secretary of state and presidential breakpoints, the *later* periods show more negative perceptions of the Soviet Union and more positive perceptions of China. This tendency is even more marked in the presidential analysis, where the intervention point is ten months later. This seems to indicate that *some* change indeed took place. However, the time-series analyses indicate that *neither* of the role changes is the important factor. The increasing strength of the differences of means tests at the presidential breakpoint also indicate that the change, whatever it was, took place after August 1974, when Nixon left and Ford took office. The evidence that emerges is that Angola, marking the beginning of Soviet/Cuban intervention in Africa, is the situation that led to the strongly negative view of the Soviet Union that Kissinger began to express in 1975. Given the indefiniteness of when, where, and how the Soviet/Cuban activity began, time-series analysis of this change is not undertaken. Note, however, that these results confirm the conclusions drawn in chapter 6.

Although the general conclusion is that the apparent role changes experienced by Kissinger had no effect on his images of the Soviet Union and China, one could argue that Kissinger had been secretary of state in all but name, and that the events of September 1973 merely formalized the situation rather than altering it. Similarly, it can be argued that Kissinger's basic powers and tasks did not change at all with presidents —he continued doing what he had been doing in the Middle East and elsewhere.

Table 32. Kissinger's perceptions under Nixon and Ford

A. Single evaluative assertion scores

Perception	Nixon Presidency	Ford Presidency
Soviet Union		
General Evaluation	+0.07	−0.45
DS General Evaluation	+0.45	−0.26
Hostility	+0.35	−0.87
DS Hostility	+0.75	−0.45
China		
General Evaluation	−0.12	+1.38
DS General Evaluation	+0.21	+1.54
Hostility	+0.98	+1.55
DS Hostility	+1.18	+1.82

B. Difference of means tests, by document

Perception	Nixon Period	Ford Period	t	DF	Significance
Soviet Union					
General Evaluation	+0.72	−0.26	2.71	59.1	.01
DS General Evaluation	+0.90	+0.02	2.59	87.1	.01
Hostility	+0.53	−0.48	4.27	90.9	.00
DS Hostility	+0.95	−0.19	5.58	127.8	.00
China					
General Evaluation	+0.34	+1.29	−1.74	23.4	.09
DS General Evaluation	+0.45	+1.36	−1.79	24.1	.09
Hostility	+0.97	+1.39	−1.29	55.3	.20
DS Hostility	+1.13	+1.64	−1.92	52.3	.06

C. Time-series analysis

Perception	Chow's F ($DF = 15, 20$)	Significance[a]
Soviet Union		
General Evaluation	3.63	.05
DS General Evaluation	1.94	None
Hostility	1.02	None
DS Hostility	0.95	None*
China		
General Evaluation	3.54	.05
DS General Evaluation	1.37	None
Hostility	1.49	None
DS Hostility	1.05	None

[a] An asterisk means that the Durbin-Watson statistic indicates autocorrelation.

A more "theoretical" answer is that Kissinger's images changed only when *events* led him to reconsider, reclassify, and recategorize nations and their leaders within the framework of his belief system. The role changes described here did not require Kissinger to change his image of the Soviet Union, while Angola was a severe challenge to his image of the Soviet role in an ordered structure based on détente. One tentative but certainly not conclusive finding of the work here is that idiosyncratic variables are more influential than role for a high-level decision maker, especially one who is faced with general information overload, complex situations, and unanticipated events, but who has a well-developed and firmly held belief system.

10

A World Perceived:
Conclusions

As a study of Kissinger the *individual* decision maker, this text provides various forms of access to Kissinger—biographical, psychobiographical, operational-code, and evaluative assertion analyses—and permits the comparison and partial validation of the methodologies used to provide that access. This study of Kissinger is meant to illuminate individual/psychological factors in the foreign-policy process, and in American foreign policy from 1969 to 1976, focusing particularly on the U.S.–Soviet Union–China triad. Part I describes Henry Kissinger the individual, and looks at the connections between personality, beliefs, and decision-making behavior. In Part II, substantive foreign-policy tasks are oriented around a set of comparisons that examine decision makers (Dulles and Kissinger), images of opponents (Soviet Union and China), and finally, influences on foreign policy behavior.

The psychohistorical analysis of Kissinger's personality provides several important patterns for understanding the intellectual concepts that Kissinger developed as an academic, and which, through "projective biography," he used to guide his own behavior as a policymaker. Therefore, the psychohistorical analysis informed the operational-code analysis of Kissinger's belief system. The concern with order and stability, the need to avoid chaos, and the need to set limits on the aspirations of states and leaders were captured in various concepts central to Kissinger's belief system. While the limits were best if they were self-imposed by the opponent, they would also be imposed from the outside if necessary. Therefore, the use of negotiations and force in tandem also derived from Kissinger's concept of limits. Thus, many of the positions and actions taken by Kissinger the policymaker are accounted for by the belief system and psychohistorical analyses. (Other elements of Kissinger's style predict his distrust of bureaucracy and his subsequent use of back channels, bureaucratic end-runs, and White House control of the foreign-policy structure. His policy positions on Eurocommunism, China, and situations like Angola derived from Kissinger's positions on order, limits, and legitimacy rather than on Communism per se.) Détente is the clearest example of a policy that is predictable from psychohistorical and operational-code analyses.

Looking at détente as a central Soviet-American foreign policy issue, we have outlined its psychobiographical origins and intellectual roots in Kissinger's belief system and its compatibility with Kissinger's character and style. We have outlined the mixed cooperative and coercive elements of détente and how they derived from Kissinger's concept of limits. In détente, the limits on Soviet behavior were to be either self-imposed through positive incentives or imposed by the United States by threatened costs. This understanding of détente highlights the Kennanesque character of Kissinger's policy and the possibility that détente has been as misunderstood as Kennan's original conception of containment. We noted that détente was attacked from both the right and the left: from the right because it called for cooperative actions with the Soviet Union, from the left because it called for coercive actions toward the Soviet Union. Kissinger's views of how the Soviet Union should be treated, with cooperation and positive incentives as well as threatened costs, need to be evaluated and considered in future policy toward the Soviet Union, as an alternative to the inchoate policy of the Carter administration and the cold-war revival of the Reagan administration.

The discussion of détente, of the centrality of the Soviet Union in U.S. policy, and of the use of China as an informal coalition partner in a biased triad all show how the Nixon-Kissinger period differed from both the preceding cold war years and the Carter period that followed. It is now clear that détente was not just an historical era that "happened," but was closely linked to Kissinger's beliefs about how the world should be organized to obtain a stable structure of peace and avoid chaos.

Kissinger's belief system could also be systematically linked to his attributional behavior; his belief system could be used to generate hypotheses and explanations of his evaluations of the Soviet Union and China. Ultimately, however, Kissinger's perceptions of the Soviet Union and China were only indirectly related to American foreign-policy behavior as measured by the COPDAB data set. Kissinger's images (or attributions) were highlighted by comparisons with those of John Foster Dulles, whose operational code differed drastically from Kissinger's. Even without recourse to comparisons with Dulles, it was apparent that the Soviet Union was Kissinger's central attitude object in his foreign-policy calculations. Kissinger's images of the Soviet Union and China were clearly open. Evaluations of the Soviet Union averaged out to be neutral, but varied from highly positive to highly negative, and were events-dependent across time. Evaluations of China were much more positive, and indeed, the evaluations indicated that China *was not perceived as an enemy.*

Comparative analysis of Kissinger's Soviet and Chinese images revealed that Kissinger perceived the Soviet Union as stronger (but *not* more successful) than China. The Soviet Union was also perceived as more hostile than China, and was evaluated more negatively on the general evaluation dimension. An investigation of the interrelationships between Kissinger's images of the two Communist powers indicated that perceptions of the Soviet Union and China were negatively correlated with one another. The negative relationships displayed on the hostility and general evaluation dimensions supported the hypothesis that Kissinger, in his rhetoric, was indeed playing one against the other, as predicted by the politics of the triad. Despite explicit statements to the contrary, Kissinger was using his public rhetoric about the Soviet Union and China to influence the Soviets.

Although the relationship between perceptions and a state's foreign-policy behavior is not clear and direct, but highly complex, evidence emerges from our analyses that indicates the existence of an informal U.S.–China "coalition," as predicted by Theodore Caplow's analysis of triads. In this case, Kissinger and the United States were biased positively toward China and negatively against the Soviet Union—even in the era of Soviet-American détente. While U.S. behavior toward the Soviet Union was more cooperative in the Nixon period than in earlier periods, and Kissinger pursued a web of interdependence with the Soviet Union, a dual policy of the use of negotiation as well as force was also pursued against the United States' single most powerful opponent and the greatest possible threat to world order. To use the Chinese in this triadic situation was one of those opportunities that Kissinger the academic called upon the good statesman not to lose. Kissinger the policy-maker, as indicated in the perceptual data, the events data, and his memoirs, clearly did not miss this opportunity.

This analysis differs from other analyses of Kissinger's policies and their success. George Liska, for example, has argued that Kissinger wasted the chance to pursue a "Bismarckian" policy (a flexible system of checks and balances to forestall the rise of a challenging power), but instead followed a "Metternichean" policy of preserving the status quo.[1]

In so doing, Liska argues, Kissinger missed exploiting the potential of China. The analyses presented here indicate otherwise. Kissinger followed what Liska terms a "Bismarckian" policy, and its flexibility allowed Kissinger to use inter-nation balances to create order and to deter de-stabilizing "revolutionary" moves by major adversaries. Similarly, the present analysis also differs from William Pfaff's liberal critique of Kissinger, which states that Kissinger sought "preponderance" rather than "balance."[2]

Another purpose of this study was to investigate the relative effect of idiosyncratic factors, especially as contrasted to role factors, on foreign policy. Given the nonroutine or crisis situations the foreign-policy decision maker must handle,[3] the cognitively complex situations of foreign policy in general, the relative freedom of high-level foreign-policy decision makers, and the characterization of Kissinger as a "Machiavellian" personality that thrives on "free-agent" activities, we expected that idiosyncratic factors would be more potent than role factors in his case. The overall conclusion from this study of Kissinger is that individual or idiosyncratic factors appear to have had much more effect than role did. Analyses of Kissinger's formal change of role to secretary of state, and the change of presidents, support this conclusion. As a high-level decision maker with a clearly defined and strongly held belief system and a powerful personality and personal style, and with the great leeway given him by the two presidents under whom he served, Kissinger felt role constraints were of much less import than personal factors. Yet, as the analysis of events data shows, translating images into foreign-policy behavior (or having foreign-policy behavior faithfully reflect those images) is not a direct and straightforward process. Much of this complexity must be related to the existence of bureaucratic politics and the effect of role *at other levels* of the governmental apparatus; especially the level concerned with the implementation of policy.

Although focusing on Henry Kissinger, the present study also adds to a more general understanding of foreign-policy processes and American foreign-policy during the Nixon/Ford years. In noting that individual factors were more important than role factors, we have highlighted the ability of individuals, such as Kissinger, to overcome, to some extent, governmental or bureaucratic constraints. This is closely related to the basic assumptions and processes of Graham Allison's Model III, "Governmental Politics."[4] Model III is based on the interaction of individuals. Influence, activity, and the outcome of their interaction are based upon the individual characteristics of the participants, such as personality, experience, and relationships with other actors. Kissinger's relationship with Nixon, his ability to go beyond the role of National Security adviser, his use of empathy and identification, and his past experiences (even negative ones) were all part of his success in governmental politics and his central place in the foreign-policy process.

Appendix:
The Use of Content Analysis

The use of content analysis raises questions concerning its applicability as a research methodology. The general issue of *validity* is addressed in Part II, as Kissinger's assertions about the Soviet Union and China are analyzed in various ways, including comparisons to international events, to the images held by John Foster Dulles, and to Kissinger's own operational code. Kissinger's images are also investigated over time. All of these analyses help to indicate whether the methodology has been able to measure the phenomena it was supposed to measure.

A second major issue is *reliability,* particularly in a methodology that requires judgments at each of several steps in a coding process. The following section reports on the inter-coder reliability achieved in the Kissinger content analysis. Related issues specifically relevant to content analysis of the public statements of a political figure are the variation in these public statements in different contexts, and the possibility of multiple authorship or ghost writing of documents. Another problem is that the decision maker may not say what he "really means" in his public statements. These issues may be studied by evaluation of patterns of public statements of different types or for different audiences.

Although evaluation of a variety of documents and different audiences ensures that across a long period of time a broad pattern will emerge, it is very useful to examine whether different types of documents reflect different messages. This examination may reveal to what extent one should depend upon the overall results and/or the results of the analysis of specific types of documents. For matters of substantive interpretation it is also useful to see to what degree messages were altered to fit the specific audience. Ole Holsti notes that studies have demonstrated that "John Foster Dulles effectively identified the distinguishing characteristics of his audience and directed his political appeals to those attributes."[1] Here, the general question of audience is separated into two analyses. The first analysis investigates the patterns of evaluations produced by different types of documents in three categories: prepared statements, extemporaneous statements, and Congressional testimony. The second analysis is concerned with audience in terms of Kissinger's location at the time a statement was made: in the United States, outside the United States (all areas except the Soviet Union and China), in the Soviet Union, and in China.

RELIABILITY

In his doctoral dissertation, Holsti notes that evaluative assertion analysis may be an unusually quick content analysis technique and one with a high degree of reliability.[2] In the study of John Foster Dulles, reliability was demonstrated by a high degree of replicability when the same coder returned to documents that had been coded previously. This general observation is supported by the coding experiences encountered in the Kissinger study—individual coders demonstrated high intra-coder reliability.

One major difference between the Kissinger and Dulles studies is the use of multiple coders in the Kissinger analyses. More than six weeks of coder training on many sample documents preceded the coding actually reported in the study. Daily meetings to identify and correct problem areas culminated in a test coding of six documents.[3] The results of this test coding are reported below. Spot checks of randomly selected documents were made during the entire document-coding process to ensure continued inter-coder reliability.

In an evaluative assertion analysis several different aspects of coding require reliability checks.[4] For this study, as noted, the coders were searching for *evaluative* assertions about the Soviet Union and China in Kissinger's public statements. The first aspect that needs to be checked, therefore, is inter-coder agreement in identifying and locating the same assertions from the documents. Issues that arose in identifying assertions concerned clear understanding of terms like "opponents," "adversaries," or even "Communists" from antecedent sentences. References to single individuals (such as Brezhnev or Mao) were used or discarded in terms of antecedent text (as well as those statements that merely said "they," "those," "its," etc.).

Osgood et al. provide a percentage of agreement index to describe agreement in isolating the same assertions:

$$\frac{2\ (AO_{1,2})}{AO_1 + AO_2}$$

Here, "AO_1 is the total number of AO's isolated by Coder 1 . . . , AO_2 is the total number of AO's isolated by Coder 2, and $AO_{1,2}$ is the total number of AO's isolated by both."[5] For the three coders involved in the Kissinger coding, the percentage of agreement between coders A and B was 0.79, for B and C it was 0.73, and for A and C, 0.82. This averages out to an agreement level of 0.78.

A second issue, more specific to this study, is agreement on the categorization of the assertions into the four dimensions or scales of evaluation that had been employed by Holsti, and which were selected for use in the Kissinger study also. As noted in chapter 4, rules for placing statements in these four categories were derived by personal communication with Holsti and from his writings on the Dulles study. In the sample documents, the three Kissinger coders were in complete rank agreement. Each coder placed the largest number of assertions in the hostility category; the next largest number went into success; general evaluation was third; and capabilities was last. What is especially convincing about the perfect agreement obtained on the test documents is the fact that these rankings were not the same as those obtained for all documents, for both the Soviet Union and China. For the total study, the most assertions fell into the hostility category, followed by capabilities, general evaluation, and, finally, success. Thus the coders were sensitive to, and agreed on, the specific content of the test documents and did not simply chance upon or reflect a general trend in the documents as a whole.

Finally, evaluative assertion analysis depends upon the direction (indicating associative or disassociative; positive or negative), and the value (+3.00 to −3.00) of the verb connectors (c) and evaluators (cm or AO_2; here as used previously, AO_2 indicates a second attitude object). As noted, the evaluative assertion score in any one category would be calculated from the total number of assertions, and the total sum would be calculated from the total sum of the multiplications (c X cm of AO_2). This score also depends upon the aggregation of assertions—either from a single document, over some subperiod of time, or from the entire period under study.

For Osgood et al., the common meaning evaluators (cm) are adjectives or nouns "about whose meaning or significance all users of the English language must agree if they are able to communicate with one another."[6] However, there is a problem here, which is particularly accentuated by the AO_2's (second attitude objects), concerning the agreement among "all users."[7] The coders had to be particularly sensitive to words specific to Kissinger, e.g., "legitimate," "revolutionary," etc., and to his judgments concerning specific countries or individuals that might be AO_2's. Therefore, all coders read extensively in the biographical and analytic material reviewed in Part I. There were also regular sessions in which coding problems were raised, discussed, and agreed upon. These were most often concerned with the values for AO_2's.

For all the assertions identified across all these documents, a single evaluative assertion score was calculated. The scores were satisfactorily close for all three coders: –0.18, –0.38, and –0.54. All were negative and only slightly below zero. Looking at all the DS and non-DS categories, but without DS success (for which there were no assertions in these documents), there are seven categories of assertions. Following Osgood et al., we can calculate correlations between each pair of coders for each category, for a total of twenty-one correlations (seven categories and three coder pairs). Fifteen of these correlations were over $r = .75$, and thirteen exceeded $r = .85$. Coders A and C, for example, averaged a correlation agreement of $r = .91$. Spot checks of all these reliability tests made during the document-coding period were consistently higher, if only marginally so in some cases. The test-document reliability measures were discussed at length, since they provided the basis for the decision to commence the full coding process.

AUDIENCE: TYPE OF DOCUMENT

As is shown in Table A.1, eight categories of documents were developed after a review of all the public statements of Kissinger that had been located. In Table A.1, the overall evaluation score for all the evaluative assertions located in each type of document is provided, but, as noted earlier, these scores cannot be compared statistically. Therefore, the eight categories were collapsed into three, and a mean of scores *by document* was calculated (see Table A.2). This creates a sample large enough to allow statistical comparison of means. And, inasmuch as the present analysis is based upon document type, use of the mean scores calculated from document scores is appropriate. Speeches, toasts, arrival/departure remarks, and articles/letters were combined into prepared statements. News conferences, question-and-answer sessions after speeches, and interviews combined to make up extemporaneous statements. The third category is Congressional testimony.

In Table A.1, only one major type of document stands out as consistently high or low—toasts. For both the Soviet Union and China, toasts

Table A.1. Evaluative assertions by document type

				Assertion				
Document Type	Cap	DS Cap	Gen Eval	DS Gen Eval	Host	DS Host	Success	DS Success
A. Soviet Union								
Speeches	+.475	+.557	−.817	−.288	−.829	−.133	−.403	+.056
	(197)	(211)	(40)	(52)	(246)	(366)	(38)	(48)
Toasts	−3.00	+2.43	+2.33	+2.30	+1.54	+1.66	0	0
	(3)	(7)	(3)	(10)	(11)	(60)	(0)	(0)
Arrival/departure	+2.50	+2.83	0	+3.00	+1.389	+1.456	0	0
remarks	(2)	(6)	(0)	(1)	(12)	(19)	(0)	(0)
Articles/letters	0	0	0	0	−1.762	−1.762	0	0
	(0)	(0)	(0)	(0)	(7)	(7)	(0)	(0)
News Con-ferences	+.910	+1.056	+.228	+.474	−.134	+.378	+.481	+.333
	(122)	(161)	(63)	(102)	(453)	(722)	(18)	(30)
Q & A sessions	+1.526	+1.600	0.0	+.455	−1.310	−1.111	−.810	−.810
	(57)	(60)	(8)	(11)	(102)	(111)	(7)	(7)
Interviews	+1.344	+1.267	−.461	−.371	−.030	−.239	−1.292	−1.294
	(31)	(40)	(39)	(44)	(124)	(162)	(16)	(17)
Congressional	+.738	+.889	−.315	−.315	−.928	−.511	+.208	+.201
testimony	(181)	(196)	(91)	(91)	(433)	(579)	(56)	(58)
B. China								
Speeches	+2.762	+2.762	+.154	+.815	+1.813	+1.654	+2.00	+2.00
	(14)	(14)	(13)	(27)	(57)	(127)	(1)	(1)
Toasts	0	+1.00	+2.667	+2.378	+2.540	+2.273	+3.00	+3.00
	(0)	(1)	(9)	(15)	(21)	(33)	(3)	(3)
Arrival/departure	0	0	+3.00	+3.00	+2.00	+2.00	0	0
remarks	(0)	(0)	(1)	(1)	(1)	(1)	(0)	(0)
Articles/letters	0	0	0	0	0	0	0	0
News Con-ferences	+.424	+.424	+1.047	+1.182	+.096	+1.592	+2.00	+2.00
	(11)	(11)	(43)	(53)	(124)	(236)	(1)	(1)
Q & A sessions	+.167	+.167	+1.800	+1.879	+1.783	+1.634	0	0
	(8)	(8)	(5)	(11)	(20)	(31)	(0)	(0)
Interviews	+.615	+.615	+.869	+1.075	+1.505	+1.508	+1.00	+1.00
	(13)	(13)	(28)	(31)	(68)	(80)	(1)	(1)
Congressional	−.625	−.625	+.400	+4.00	+2.90	+.689	+.333	+.333
testimony	(8)	(8)	(5)	(5)	(31)	(44)	(3)	(3)

Note: Numbers in parentheses are total numbers of assertions (N). Cap = capability; Gen Eval = general evaluation; Host = hostility.

Table A.2. Difference of means tests: Comparisons among prepared, extemporaneous, and Congressional hearings documents

Comparison	Variable[a]	Mean	t	DF	Significance
A. USSR					
Prepared vs.	Cap	1.492/1.064	1.25	56.26	.218
Extemporaneous	DS Cap	1.745/1.349	1.37	76.89	.176
	Eval	.007/.037	−.06	23.17	.953
	DS Eval	.712/.174	1.25	47.90	.216
	Host	−.179/.093	−.31	92.15	.755
	DS Host	.339/.130	−.83	108.81	.410
	Success	−1.104/−.555	−.67	11.53	.518
	DS Success	−.043/−.344	.37	11.21	.718
Prepared vs.	Cap	1.492/.811	1.74	42.41	.090[b]
Hearings	DS Cap	1.747/.874	2.40	41.33	.021[c]
	Eval	.007/.223	−.55	23.49	.728
	DS Eval	.712/.223	.89	24.07	.382
	Host	−.179/−.944	2.07	76	.042[c]
	DS Host	.340/−.388	2.00	87	.048[c]
	Success	−1.104/.379	−1.69	12.42	.116
	DS Success	−.043/.397	−.49	13.58	.631
Extemporaneous	Cap	1.064/.811	.71	41.84	.482
vs. Hearings	DS Cap	1.349/.874	1.40	36.33	.170
	Eval	.037/.223	−.40	15.31	.698
	DS Eval	.174/.223	−.10	14.93	.918
	Host	.093/−.944	2.61	14.1	.010[c]
	DS Host	.130/−.388	1.91	44.04	.063[b]
	Success	−.555/.379	−1.33	21.32	.197
	DS Success	−.344/.397	−1.13	18.90	.271
B. China					
Prepared vs.	Cap	2.788/−.490	5.14	23.92	.000[c]
Extemporaneous	DS Cap	2.639/−.490	4.93	24.67	.000[c]
	Eval	1.633/.777	1.37	19.35	.186
	DS Eval	1.316/1.041	.52	26.70	.610
	Host	1.986/1.105	2.76	74	.007[c]
	DS Host	1.971/1.423	2.25	89	.027[c]
	Success	2.500/1.500	1.41	2.00	.293
	DS Success	2.500/1.500	1.41	2.00	.293
Prepared vs.	Cap	2.788/−.792	3.90	4.48	.017[c]
Hearings	DS Cap	2.639/−.792	3.75	4.45	.020[c]
	Eval	1.633/.750	1.07	7.79	.316
	DS Eval	1.316/.750	.73	6.41	.491
	Host	1.989/−.076	4.61	31	.000[c]
	DS Host	1.971/.468	3.89	37	.000[c]
	Success	2.500/.333	1.66	2.60	.195
	DS Success	2.500/.333	1.66	2.60	.195

Table A.2. Continued

Comparison	Variable[a]	Mean	t	DF	Significance
B. China (continued)					
Extemporaneous	Cap	−.490/−.792	.31	5.43	.767
vs. Hearings	DS Cap	−.490/−.792	.31	5.43	.767
	Eval	.777/.750	.04	4.73	.971
	DS Eval	1.041/.750	.42	4.44	.697
	Host	1.105/−.076	1.99	8.99	.078[b]
	DS Host	1.423/.468	1.72	10.53	.113
	Success	1.500/.333	.90	2.60	.436
	DS Success	1.500/.333	.90	2.60	.436

Note: Mean scores for each category of documents calculated from document scores.
[a] Cap = capability; Eval = general evaluation; Host = hostility.
[b] Significant at .10 level.
[c] Significant at .05 level.

were very positive, more so for the Soviet Union. Congressional testimony stands out as a consistently more negative set of evaluations. Simply in terms of numbers of assertions, news conferences and speeches are the largest, followed by Congressional testimony and interviews. Therefore, in the three combined categories, the averages will be based upon similar numbers of assertions.

Table A.2 presents the difference of means tests between pairs of combined document types. Interestingly, differences appear only for capability and hostility assertions. For the Soviet Union, there is no difference between Kissinger's evaluations in prepared as compared to extemporaneous statements. (As noted in chapter 4, Kissinger had an active hand in the preparation of speeches.) That is, there is no discernible difference between the images projected in previously prepared statements and extemporaneous comments made in a variety of circumstances. Kissinger's consistency of thought and the influence of a clearly articulated belief system are supported. For China, his prepared statements give evaluations that are of a stronger and more friendly China than is given in extemporaneous statements. This finding fits partially with the analysis in chapter 8 of a bias toward China that apparently is somewhat more calculated and comes through more strongly in prepared statements.

For both the Soviet Union and China, the eleven significant differences between Congressional testimony (hearings) and other types of document indicate more negative evaluations before Congress. This trend is consistent across all Congressional comparisons. (Holsti found

Table A.3.   Comparison of assertions by location (type of audience)

Location Comparison	Variable[a]	Mean	t	DF	Significance
A. Soviet Union—comparison of means (whole period by *document*)					
In U.S. vs.	Cap	1.113/1.242	−.29	18.68	.776
outside U.S.	DS Cap	1.267/1.661	−1.07	28.48	.295
	Eval	−.199/.167	−.58	8.79	.578
	DS Eval	−.047/.758	−1.56	22.79	.132
	Host	−.370/−.243	−.48	183	.634
	DS Host	−.033/.166	−.80	202	.424
	Success	−.544/−.880	.17	6.12	.869
	DS Success	−.312/−.475	.17	6.12	.869
In U.S. vs.	Cap	1.113/.933	.31	4.72	.771
in U.S.S.R.	DS Cap	1.267/1.722	−.99	11.25	.344
	Eval	−.199/1.792	−3.28	72	.002[b]
	DS Eval	−.047/1.763	−3.69	84	.000[b]
	Host	−.370/1.839	−5.24	9.31	.001[b]
	DS Host	−.033/1.732	−4.66	165	.000[b]
	Success	−.544/2.667	−6.92	3.66	.002[b]
	DS Success	−.312/2.778	−8.34	13.17	.000[b]
In U.S. vs.	Cap	1.113/0	6.74	81.00	.000
in China	DS Cap	1.267/3.000	−11.55	91.00	.000
	Eval	−.199/1.000	−5.76	65.00	.000
	DS Eval	−.047/−.167	.10	1.07	.936
	Host	−.370/1.250	−2.14	1.05	.279
	DS Host	−.033/.033	−.05	2.03	.964
	Success	−.544/0	−1.68	31.00	.102
	DS Success	−.312/0	−1.05	37.00	.300
Outside U.S. vs.	Cap	1.242/.933	.44	8.84	.669
in U.S.S.R.	DS Cap	1.661/1.722	−.11	19.81	.913
	Eval	.167/1.792	−2.53	14.00	.024[b]
	DS Eval	.758/1.763	−1.78	29.00	.086[c]
	Host	−.243/1.839	−4.12	18.08	.001[b]
	DS Host	.166/1.732	−3.04	63.00	.003[b]
	Success	−.880/2.667	−2.86	3.42	.064[c]
	DS Success	−.475/2.778	−3.49	5.57	.013[b]
Outside U.S. vs.	Cap	1.242/0	2.98	14.00	.010
in China	DS Cap	1.661/3.000	−3.98	20.00	.001
	Eval	.167/1.000	−1.39	7.00	.206
	DS Eval	.758/−.167	.74	1.35	.596
	Host	−.243/1.250	−1.85	1.35	.316
	DS Host	.166/.033	.10	2.17	.929
	Success	−.880/0	−.74	3.00	.514
	DS Success	−.475/0	−.53	5.00	.622

Table A.3.   Continued

Location Comparison[d]	Variable[a]	Mean	t	DF	Significance
In U.S.S.R. vs. in China	Cap	.933/0	1.66	4.00	.172
	DS Cap	1.722/3.000	−2.94	9.00	.017[b]
	Eval	1.792/1.000	3.37	7.00	.012[b]
	DS Eval	1.763/−.167	1.62	1.09	.352
	Host	1.839/1.250	.69	1.65	.561
	DS Host	1.732/.033	2.59	15.0	.021[c]
	Success	2.667/0	8.00	1.00	.079[b]
	DS Success	2.778/0	12.50	2.00	.006[b]

B. China—comparison of means (whole period by *document*)

Location Comparison[d]	Variable[a]	Mean	t	DF	Significance
In U.S. vs. outside U.S.	Cap	.514/2.089	−2.35	6.71	.051[b]
	DS Cap	.514/2.089	−2.35	6.71	.051[b]
	Eval	.602/1.714	−1.72	10.11	.116
	DS Eval	.750/1.778	−1.89	14.49	.079[b]
	Host	1.182/1.167	.03	12.69	.977
	DS Host	1.400/1.717	−1.05	22.97	.307
	Success	1.000/0	1.58	5.00	.175
	DS Success	1.000/0	1.58	5.00	.175
In U.S. vs. in China	Cap	.514/0	1.12	26.00	.272
	DS Cap	.514/1.000	−1.06	26.00	.300
	Eval	.602/2.285	−3.81	17.54	.001[b]
	DS Eval	.750/2.223	−2.07	41.00	.045[b]
	Host	1.182/2.083	−2.27	9.33	.049[b]
	DS Host	1.400/1.959	−1.14	84	.256
	Success	1.000/3.000	−3.16	5	.025[b]
	DS Success	1.000/3.000	−3.16	5	.025[b]
Outside U.S. vs. in China	Cap	2.089/0	4.29	2.00	.050[b]
	DS Cap	2.089/1.000	2.23	2.00	1.55
	Eval	1.714/2.285	−.89	9.16	.399
	DS Eval	1.778/2.223	−.82	12.18	.426
	Host	1.167/2.083	−1.50	15.91	.153
	DS Host	1.717/1.959	−.72	19.50	.480
	Success	0/3.000	0	0	.500
	DS Success	0/3.000	0	0	.500

[a] Abbreviations as in Table A.2.
[b] Significant at .10 level.
[c] Significant at .05 level.
[d] Three comparisons, in U.S. vs. in U.S.S.R., in U.S.S.R. vs. in China, and outside U.S. vs. in U.S.S.R., were not possible because no assertions about China were made in the Soviet Union.

that Dulles's evaluations were more hostile before the American public than before Congress.[8] The results in Table A.2 indicate that this was not the case for Kissinger.) To some extent, Kissinger found it useful to make more negative comments about the two Communist powers before the Congress. It was noted earlier that in *A World Restored,* Kissinger discusses the need for statesmen to educate the people and governments they lead in order to help them understand the statesman's "vision."[9] This education is necessary to achieve a domestic consensus on the statesman's foreign policy and to legitimize the consensus within the government. Kissinger's central criticism of Castlereagh was that he failed to create this consensus, by being too far ahead of his domestic support. Kissinger's desire to educate is evident in the many long, lecturelike explanations found in his press conferences and speeches (e.g., on the nature of détente). That he toned down his references to Russia and China before Congress was perhaps a result of his desire to legitimize his policies by not being too far ahead of the American lawmakers, that is, by not being too far beyond their experiences and understanding.

Nevertheless, the overall impression is of remarkable consistency across document types, as compared in Table A.2. No differences are found for general evaluation or success assertions. For the Soviet Union, only six of twenty-four comparisons are significantly different. Besides the apparent playing down of Soviet and Chinese strength before Congress (or, rather, stressing their capabilities elsewhere), there are few differences. In general, this finding increases our confidence in the use of content analysis for the study of a foreign-policy decision maker.

AUDIENCE: KISSINGER'S LOCATION WHEN STATEMENTS WERE MADE

Again, the comparisons made here are between mean evaluation scores, using the document as the unit of analysis. For the four locations—in the U.S., outside the U.S. (excluding Russia and China), in the Soviet Union, and in China—there are six possible comparisons. The six comparisons for the evaluations of the Soviet Union are presented in Table A.3, part A.

Although trends occur (e.g., all the assertion categories except Soviet success are evaluated more positively in U.S. than outside U.S.), only two comparisons show significant differences. These two are: In U.S. vs. in U.S.S.R. and Outside U.S. vs. in U.S.S.R. With the exception of capabilities, all the differences of means are significant. As would be expected, the means produced by evaluations made in the Soviet Union are more positive than the others. Kissinger evaluated the Soviet Union more favorably in his public statements while he was there.[10] Thus, although Kissinger does not "reward" the Soviet Union in general (see chapter 7) he does speak favorably of it when visiting that country, giving an immediate "reward" for Soviet hospitality and willingness to negotiate.

Because Kissinger made no assertions about China while in the U.S.S.R. part B of Table A.3 contains only three comparisons. The pattern of speaking more favorably about a country while in that country is not as strong for China as for the In U.S.S.R. assertions about the Soviet Union. The most distinct result is the more positive nature of the In China assertions as compared to the In U.S. assertions. There is also an interesting but less prominent trend for Kissinger to evaluate China more positively outside the U.S. than in U.S.

Therefore, there is a difference in Kissinger's evaluations when they are compared on the basis of location. Apparently he preferred to speak well of his hosts, whether in the Soviet Union or China. When comparing the evaluations made in U.S. to those made in the Soviet Union or in China, it should be kept in mind that toasts in general were more positive (and many of them would have been made at formal occasions during visits to China or the Soviet Union), and that Congressional testimony in general was more negative (and, naturally, occurred in the United States). These comparisons reinforce some of the conclusions from earlier chapters. They also reveal some of the differences and consequences of comparing different types of documents. In conjunction with the discussion of reliability, they provide confidence in the use of content analysis as a methodology for this study. These are issues that are raised in various critiques of the methodology, and they require attention and analysis.

Notes

CHAPTER 1

1. Henry Kissinger, "The Meaning of History: Reflections on Spengler, Toynbee and Kant (BA thesis, Harvard University, 1951), 127.

2. Stephen Walker describes how an individual's belief system may be a function of personality antecedents and motives (such as the need for power, affiliation, or achievement) that form during the individual's socialization and cognitive development in childhood. See Stephen G. Walker, "The Motivational Foundations of Political Belief Systems: A Re-Analysis of the Operational Code Construct." Paper presented at the annual meeting of the Amercian Political Science Association, Washington, D.C., 1980.

3. Stephen G. Walker, "Cognitive Maps and International Realities: Henry A. Kissinger's Operational Code" (Paper presented at the annual meeting of the American Political Science Association, San Francisco, 1975), 1-2.

4. Albert Eldridge, "The Crisis of Authority: The President, Kissinger and Congress (1969-1974)" (Paper presented at the annual meeting of the International Studies Association, Toronto, 1976), 31.

5. Henry Brandon, *The Retreat of American Power* (Garden City: Doubleday, 1973), 23.

6. Eldridge, "The Crisis of Authority," 20.

7. To date, two volumes of Kissinger's memoirs have been published: *White House Years* (1979) and *Years of Upheaval* (1982), both by Little, Brown of Boston. A third volume is forthcoming. Most of the relevant examples and anecdotes regarding Kissinger's views of the Soviet Union and China appear in *White House Years,* with additional supporting examples to be found in *Years of Upheaval.*

8. Graham T. Allison, *The Essence of Decision* (Boston: Little, Brown, 1971). See Chapter 5, "Model III: Governmental Politics."

9. *White House Years,* 805.

10. Two exceptions are Walker and Eldridge, previously cited. See also: Eldridge, "Pondering Intangibles: A Value Analysis of Henry Kissinger." Paper presented at the symposium, "The Theory and Practice of Henry Kissinger's Statesmanship," College Park, Maryland, 1975; and Walker, "The Interface Between Beliefs and Behavior: Henry Kissinger's Operational Code and the Vietnam War," *Journal of Conflict Resolution* 21 (1977): 129-68.

11. An initial overview indicates that Kissinger, as a single individual, could, and did, have an impact on the creation of American foreign policy. Bruce Mazlish, in *Kissinger, The European Mind in American Policy* (New York: Basic Books, 1976), quotes Abba

Eban's observation that Kissinger's "personal role refutes the view that history is the product of impersonal forces and objective conditions in which the personal factor doesn't matter." (p. 4)

12. Holsti's research on Dulles was used as a model for the present study for several reasons. First, Holsti studied the role of perception in relation to inter-nation conflict. Second, his work was useful in illuminating a vital figure in a particular era of world politics. Finally, Holsti's study has been the most well-known and widely cited study on the influence of idiosyncratic factors in foreign policy. For example, Pat McGowan has cited the study of the individual as one of the "neglected problems" in the comparative study of foreign policy (see "The Future of Comparative Studies: An Evangelical Plea," in James N. Rosenau, ed., *In Search of Global Patterns* [New York: Free Press, 1976], 229). The present study of Kissinger was designed to address this neglected problem and to add to the relatively small body of literature concerning the empirical analysis of the individual-/idiosyncratic factor in foreign policy.

13. See Kenneth Boulding, "Future Directions in Conflict and Peace Studies," *Journal of Conflict Resolution,* 22 (1978):348.

14. James N. Rosenau, "Pre-Theories and Theories of Foreign Policy." In R. Barry Farrell, ed., *Approaches to Comparative and International Politics* (Evanston, Ill.: Northwestern University Press, 1966), 27-92.

15. There are, however, two articles directed specifically toward the role–idiosyncratic question: James N. Rosenau, "Private Preferences and Political Responsibilities: The Relative Potency of Individual and Role Variables in the Behavior of U.S. Senators" (in J. David Singer, ed., *Quantitative International Politics* [New York: Free Press, 1968], 17-50), and Glenn H. Stassen, "Individual Preference Versus Role-Constraint in Policy Making: Senatorial Response to Secretaries Acheson and Dulles" (*World Politics,* 25 (1972):96-119). In later works, Rosenau combined both idiosyncratic and role influences into an "individual" factor, reflecting the close relationship of the two.

16. McGowan, "The Future of Comparative Studies," 228.

17. Robert Axelrod has listed a number of factors affecting individual cognitive processes that require further study. These include: Project 2, The Effects of Role; Project 4, The Effects of Issue Domain; and Project 6, The Effects of Audience ("Projects," in Axelrod, ed., *The Structure of Decision* [Princeton, N.J.: Princeton University Press, 1976], 266-287). All of these factors are investigated in this book. For a discussion of content analysis as a research tool that is specifically related to this topic, see Harvey Starr, "The Operational Code and Other Forms of Content Analysis: Analyses of Henry Kissinger." Paper presented at the annual meeting of the International Society of Political Psychology, Boston, 1980.

18. Ole R. Holsti has observed that, "A possibly useful development would be to combine the theoretical and substantive richness of the operational code with some other forms of content analysis." (See Holsti, "Foreign Policy Decision Makers Viewed Psychologically: 'Cognitive Process' Approaches" [Duke University, 1975, Mimeographed] 36.) This is precisely the method of the present study, which uses both less formal (e.g., psychohistorical) and more formal (evaluative assertion analysis) variations of content analysis. See also Starr, "The Operational Code and Other Forms of Content Analysis."

19. See Allison, *Essence of Decision,* Ch. 1-4.

20. There is a long tradition of the study of cognitive factors related to decision making, and it is exemplified by Herbert Simon's *Administrative Behavior* (New York: Macmillan, 1947) and Richard Snyder, H.W. Bruck, and Burton Sapin's *Foreign Policy Decision Making* (New York: Free Press, 1962), which was originally published in 1954. In the last

few years, reviews and critiques have appeared that draw much of the earlier literature together and integrate it with the more recent work being done by political scientists, psychologists, and others. A short list of these reviews should begin with Ole R. Holsti's "Foreign Policy Decision Makers Viewed Psychologically," which appeared in a revised version in James N. Rosenau, ed., *In Search of Global Patterns,* as well as Holsti, "Foreign Policy Formation Viewed Cognitively" (in Axelrod, ed., *Structure of Decision*). The Axelrod book is recommended in its entirety for its introduction to different approaches to cognitive analysis, as is John Steinbruner's *The Cybernetic Theory of Decision* (Princeton, N.J.: Princeton University Press, 1974). Cognitive constraints on decision making are also reviewed in Ole Holsti and Alexander George's "The Effects of Stress on the Performance of Foreign Policy Makers" (in C.P. Cotter, ed., *Political Science Annual* [Indianapolis: Bobbs-Merrill, 1975]), Daniel Heradstveit and Ove Narvesen's "Psychological Constraints on Decision-making. A Discussion of Cognitive Approaches: Operational Code and Cognitive Maps" (*Cooperation and Conflict,* 13(1978):77-92), Michael Shapiro and G. Matthew Bonham's "Cognitive Processes and Foreign Policy Decision Making" (*International Studies Quarterly,* 17 (1973):147-74), and K. Brodin's "Belief Systems, Doctrines and Foreign Policy" (*Cooperation and Conflict,* (1972):97-112). Perhaps the best single application of cognitive constraints to the analysis of foreign-policy activity, containing an extensive bibliography of the psychological literature, is Robert Jervis's *Perception and Misperception in International Politics* (Princeton, N.J.: Princeton University Press, 1976). Two collections of materials germane to cognitive approaches and constraints are Margaret G. Hermann, ed., *A Psychological Examination of Political Leaders* (New York: Free Press, 1977), and Lawrence S. Falkowski, ed., *Psychological Models in International Politics* (Boulder, Col.: Westview, 1979).

21. Donald R. Kinder and Janet A. Weiss, "In Lieu of Rationality," *Journal of Conflict Resolution,* 22 (1978):707-78. This article is also useful as a review of major trends in the cognitive approach literature.

22. Rudolph Rummel, *Understanding Conflict and War.* Vol. 4, *War, Power, Peace* (Beverly Hills: Sage, 1979), 71-73.

23. Alexander George, "The Use of Information," Appendix D, Commission on the Organization of the Government for the Conduct of Foreign Policy, Vol. 2 (Washington, D.C.: U.S. Government Printing Office, 1975), 30-31.

24. Hermann, *Psychological Examination of Political Leaders,* 4-5.

25. Holsti, "Foreign Policy Decision Makers Viewed Psychologically," in *In Search of Global Patterns,* 131.

26. Based on Holsti, "Foreign Policy Makers Viewed Psychologically" (Duke University mimeo), 13-14. See also Fred Greenstein, "The Impact of Personality on Politics: An Attempt to Clear Away Underbrush," *American Political Science Review,* 61 (1967): 629-41.

27. Holsti, "Foreign Policy Makers Viewed Psychologically" (Duke University mimeo), 19, and Holsti and George, "The Effects of Stress," 275. How this intervening variable process might work is described by Jervis (*Perception and Misperception*): "We may be able to say, for example, that two kinds of situations, although not seeming alike to later scholars, will *appear* [emphasis added] similar to contemporary decision makers and will *be seen* [emphasis added] to call for similar responses." (p. 29)

28. See Harvey Starr, "Toward Minimizing Misperceptions," *Review of Politics,* 39 (1977):432, and Jervis, *Perception and Misperception,* 172.

29. See Holsti, "Foreign Policy Makers Viewed Psychologically" (Duke University mimeo), 5-12; Jervis, *Perception and Misperception* 3-10; or Brodin, "Belief Systems. . . ."

30. Jervis, *Perception and Misperception,* 3.
31. The following material is drawn from Harvey Starr, "The Kissinger Years: Studying Individuals and Foreign Policy," *International Studies Quarterly,* 24 (1980):465-96.
32. Stephen R. Graubard, *Kissinger, Portrait of a Mind* (New York: W.W. Norton, 1973), 11.
33. Stanley Hoffmann, *Primacy or World Order* (New York: McGraw-Hill, 1978), 41.
34. Graubard, *Kissinger,* 22, 27.
35. *White House Years,* 730-31. Jervis puts this view in context in *Perception and Misperception:* "If he is to decide intelligently how to act, a person must predict how others will behave. If he seeks to influence them, he needs to estimate how they will react to the alternative policies he can adopt. Even if his actions do not affect theirs, he needs to know how they will act in order to tailor his actions accordingly." (p. 32)
36. Mazlish, *Kissinger,* 197.
37. See Harvey Starr, " 'Opportunity' and 'Willingness' as Ordering Concepts in the Study of War," *International Interactions,* 4 (1978):363-87.

CHAPTER 2

1. Much of this introductory section is drawn from Harvey Starr, "The Kissinger Years: Studying Individuals and Foreign Policy," *International Studies Quarterly* 24(1980):470-72.
2. Ralph Blumenfeld, et al., *Henry Kissinger: The Private and Public Story* (New York, New American Library, 1974); Marvin Kalb and Bernard Kalb, *Kissinger* (New York: Dell, 1974); David Landau, *Kissinger: the Uses of Power* (New York: W. W. Norton, 1973).
3. John Stoessinger, *Henry Kissinger: The Anguish of Power* (New York: W. W. Norton, 1976).
4. See, for example, Edwin Weinstein et al., "Woodrow Wilson's Political Personality: A Reappraisal," *Political Science Quarterly* 93(1978):585-98, or Robert Tucker, "The Georges' Wilson Reexamined: An Essay on Psychobiography," *American Political Science Review* 71(1977):606-18, for a reappraisal of the Georges' work and commentary on the psychobiographical appraoch. For a rejoinder, see Alexander and Juliet George, "Dr. Weinstein's Interpretation of Woodrow Wilson: Some Preliminary Observations," *Psychohistory Review* 8(1979):71-72; Alexander and Juliet George, *Woodrow Wilson and Colonel House* (New York: Dover, 1964).
5. Mazlish states: "My approach throughout is interpretive. This fact must be underlined from the very beginning. By now there are a number of acceptable and sometimes fine studies and articles on Kissinger's thought, policies, or actual negotiations. Often weakened by an uncritical adulatory or condemnatory bias, such works are nonetheless fundamental in helping to establish some of the "facts" about Kissinger in his many guises. They rarely, however, center on Kissinger's personality in the sense I undertake here." (*Kissinger, The European Mind in American Policy* [New York: Basic Books, 1976], 8) Peter Dickson, in *Kissinger and the Meaning of History* (London: Cambridge University Press, 1978), also notes that: "Thus far, there have been five works in which a serious attempt has been made to understand and interpret [Kissinger's] personality. Yet the authors of these biographical studies seem to reveal more about themselves than Kissinger. No consensus concerning this controversial figure seems possible." (p. 17)
6. Dana Ward, "Kissinger: A Psychohistory," *History of Childhood Quarterly* 2 (1975):287.

7. In 1930, the Kissingers also took in a boarder, Jack Heiman, who moved to Fuerth from a small village in order to attend a Jewish school. He stayed for several years. Although he was three years older than Henry and four years older than Walter, Heiman appears to have been closer to the younger Kissinger.

8. Ralph Blumenfeld et al. (*Henry Kissinger* [New York: New American Library, 1974]) note: "As his father's shadow diminished, Henry slipped out from beneath it." (p. 42) Mazlish develops this theme at length.

9. Note that Kissinger never lost his accent, while Walter, only a year younger, speaks with no trace of one (see Mazlish, *Kissinger*, 40).

10. Blumenfeld et al., *Henry Kissinger*, 47.

11. See Mazlish, *Kissinger*, 47-54, for a discussion of Kraemer and his relationship with Kissinger.

12. Marvin and Bernard Kalb, *Kissinger* (New York: Dell, 1974), 52. The account does differ somewhat. In Blumenfeld et al., Kraemer is quoted as saying: "This young soldier reconstructed the city government in five, six days. There was nothing—no telephone, no food, nothing." (p. 64)

13. Richard Valeriani, *Travels with Henry* (New York: Houghton-Mifflin, 1979), 13. Valeriani, a network reporter, flew over half a million miles with the secretary of state.

14. Kalbs, *Kissinger*, 53.

15. See Kalbs, *Kissinger*, 54; Blumenfeld et al., *Henry Kissinger*, 79.

16. Interestingly, Walter Kissinger, who had risen to lieutenant, also chose to stay on in Korea an extra year after his discharge. He remained as a War Department foreign service officer (see Blumenfeld et al., *Henry Kissinger*, 78). Blumenfeld et al. quote an acquaintance of the brothers who noted that they did it, simply, for the money.

17. Kalbs, *Kissinger*, 54.

18. Dana Ward, "Kissinger: A Psychohistory," *History of Childhood Quarterly* 2(1975):311.

19. Biographers also like to point out that the class of '50 included James Schlesinger, who was to be a fellow cabinet member—and adversary—of Kissinger's in the Nixon and Ford administrations.

20. Friedrich's protégé, when Kissinger was in graduate school, was Zbigniew Brzezinski.

21. Blumenfeld et al., *Henry Kissinger*, 86.

22. In the 1965 Report, the stated purpose of the seminar was: "to promote international understanding and cooperation by giving its members an opportunity: (1). To increase their stature as individuals and their general competence in their various fields; (2). To study and discuss the relations of the various countries of the world and to develop and deepen the sense of community among them. (3). To acquaint themselves with the attitudes and values underlying American life and thought. (4). To bring foreign concerns and thinking to the attention of Americans." (Mazlish, *Kissinger*, 67)

23. Ibid.

24. See Kalbs, *Kissinger*, 62-63.

25. The study group included, among others, Dean (as chair), McGeorge Bundy, Thomas Finletter, General James M. Gavin, Roswell Gilpatric, Paul Nitze, David Rockefeller, and General Walter Bedell Smith.

26. Mazlish, *Kissinger*, 107.

27. Kalbs, *Kissinger*, 70.

28. Blumenfeld et al. (*Henry Kissinger*, 120) note that Kissinger remained a Rockefeller consultant until 1968, averaging $12,000 a year on retainer.

29. Kalbs, *Kissinger,* 73.

30. Blumenfeld et al., *Henry Kissinger,* 121.

31. David Landau, *Kissinger: The Uses of Power* (New York: W. W. Norton, 1973), 85.

32. Landau, *Kissinger,* 16, 80, 59.

33. See Stephen Graubard's *Kissinger, Portrait of a Mind* (New York: W. W. Norton, 1973), for an analysis of Kissinger's academic works, particularly as critical responses to American foreign policy. For example: "Written in the 1950s and 1960s, his works provide a running commentary on the foreign policy achievements and failures of three presidents —Harry Truman, Dwight Eisenhower, and John Kennedy." (p. xiii)

34. Kalbs, *Kissinger,* 94.

35. Blumenfeld et al. point out that, earlier in 1968, Walter Kissinger had retired from his business activities in electronics. At age 44, *he* had become a millionaire (*Henry Kissinger,* 167-68).

36. James David Barber, *The Presidential Character* (Englewood Cliffs, N.J.: Prentice-Hall, 1972), 7, 11.

37. Fred I. Greenstein, "Personality and Politics," Vol. 2, *Micropolitical Theory. Handbook of Political Science* (Reading, Mass.: Addison-Wesley, 1975) 41-43.

38. A similar view of psychobiography is reflected in Robert Jervis's discussion of variables that influence perception: "The four variables that influence the degree to which an event affects later perceptual dispositions are whether or not the person experienced the event firsthand, whether it occurred early in his adult life or career, whether it had important consequences for him or his nation, and whether he is familiar with a range of international events that facilitate alternative perceptions." (*Perception and Misperception in International Politics* [Princeton, N.J.: Princeton University Press, 1976], 239)

39. Greenstein, "Personality and Politics," 39.

40. Weinstein et al., "Woodrow Wilson's Political Personality," 598.

41. Ward, "Kissinger," 291-92.

42. Mazlish, *Kissinger,* 35.

43. Quoted in Blumenfeld et al., *Henry Kissinger,* 68-69.

44. Blumenfeld et al., *Henry Kissinger,* 3; Landau, *Kissinger,* 14; Mazlish, *Kissinger,* 19; Ward, "Kissinger," 290.

45. Quoted in Valeriani, *Travels with Henry,* 228-29.

46. Kissinger, *White House Years* (Boston: Little, Brown, 1979), 228-30.

47. Mazlish, *Kissinger,* 19.

48. Blumenfeld et al., *Henry Kissinger,* 6.

49. Mazlish, *Kissinger,* 50-51.

50. Ibid., 52.

51. Ward, "Kissinger," 308-10.

52. Ibid., 320.

53. Mazlish, *Kissinger,* 48.

54. Ward, "Kissinger," 329.

55. Henry Kissinger, *For the Record, Selected Statements 1977-1980* (Boston: Little, Brown, 1981), 169.

56. Barber, *The Presidential Character,* 10. Also building on Barber's material, Jervis observes: "Experiences that established the person as an autonomous and valued individual influence his general beliefs about how he can best cope with his environment." (*Perception and Misperception,* 250)

57. Mazlish, *Kissinger,* 41-42.

58. Ward, "Kissinger," 305.

59. Wills notes that Kissinger, "always knew one does not swagger one's way to real power. One creeps." (See Garry Wills, "Kissinger" [*Playboy,* 21 (December 1974):282]).

60. Albert Eldridge, "The Crisis of Authority: The President, Kissinger and Congress (1969-1974)" (Paper presented at the annual meeting of the International Studies Association, 1976, Toronto).

61. Recall that Barber (*The Presidential Character,* 7) defines style as a decision maker's "habitual way of performing his three political roles: rhetoric, personal relations, and homework." Here, 'style' focuses on the first two aspects.

62. See Ward, "Kissinger," 312-13; Mazlish, *Kissinger,* 96-98.

63. Lloyd Etheredge, "Personality Effects on American Foreign Policy, 1898-1968: A Test of Interpersonal Generalization Theory," *American Political Science Review* 72(1978):434-51. See also the discussion of Dulles and Kissinger in chapter 5.

64. Valeriani, *Travels with Henry,* 19.

65. Several interviews were conducted at the State Department in January 1977, only days before Kissinger left office. A number of officials who had interacted with Kissinger, some very intimately, were willing to be interviewed, but not to be identified. In the interview quoted here, the official provided one fascinating ancedote to illustrate his point. During a trip to China, at a large reception for the Americans, the official had noticed Nixon beckoning to Kissinger—Kissinger immediately turned from the person to whom he had been talking and strode directly to Nixon, walking between Chou En-lai and an American diplomat, interrupting their conversation and actually knocking Chou off balance.

66. Lloyd Etheredge, "Hardball Politics: A Model" (Paper presented at the annual meeting of the International Society of Political Psychology, New York, September 1978). Let us also stress a point that Ward makes about the depressive personality: "It should be emphasized that the depressive personality can range from well integrated to psychotic depression" (p. 293). Thus, this discussion, as well as the next section on character, is not implying, and need not imply, that such a characterization means an individual is psychotic or even neurotic.

67. Ward, "Kissinger," 340.

68. Mazlish, *Kissinger,* 46.

69. Ibid, 44-45. Stoessinger (*Henry Kissinger,* 137) also notes that Kissinger "has always spent more time and energy on adversaries than on friends—until the friends turned into adversaries."

70. For example, compare the above analysis to Townsend Hoopes's comments about Dulles's style and personality: "A number of colleagues and observers of Dulles' life over the years attribute the rigid, grave and graceless manner with which he moved through most of his relationships to the fact that circumstances had denied him a normal young manhood. . . . In the bosom of his family or with close and trusted associates, he could be warm . . ., in all other groups he was notable for a flat *hardness* and a *striking insensitivity* [emphasis added] to people in the large." (*The Devil and John Foster Dulles* [London Andre Deutsch, 1974], 18)

71. Mazlish, *Kissinger,* 205.

72. Ibid., 204.

73. Ibid., 93.

74. Valeriani, *Travels with Henry,* 19. The Kalbs also note that, "he was able t convince two people with opposing viewpoints that he agreed with both of them' (*Kissinger,* 22).

75. Kissinger, *White House Years,* 282.

76. Valeriani, *Travels with Henry,* 7-8.

77. Ibid., 273, 276. Again, the Kalbs support these views: "When he caught a glimpse of a potential antagonist, Kissinger's instinct was to win him over with charm and humor" (*Kissinger,* 21). For further examples, see also Kissinger's *White House Years* (732, 786, 1249).

78. Stanley Hoffmann, in *Primacy or World Order* (New York: McGraw-Hill, 1978) observes: "Even more important was Kissinger's preference for personal diplomacy, for dealing with statesman whose trust he was eager to obtain, rather than with institutions. It was a choice that flowed from a quest for flexibility but also from his psychological gifts, his talent for patient persuasion, his art of making his interlocutor share his concerns and empathize with his plight. It was particularly suited to diplomacy with dictators, ruling monarchs, or presidents untroubled by checks and balances." (p. 50)

79. The consequences of this policy came to my attention in January 1977, when I was informed that the interpreting capability of the State Department was absolutely minimal, since good people had moved out of that area. One reason for their moving was that Kissinger had consistently used interpreters supplied by other parties, rather than Americans. It was also at this time that I was surprised to learn, for the first time, that during visits to China, Kissinger and Nixon would hold talks with Chinese leaders using only Chinese interpreters.

80. An example of the latter is given by Landau (*Kissinger,* 87); the former point on Assad is covered by Valeriani (*Travels with Henry,* 272).

81. Valeriani, *Travels with Henry,* 18, 312.

82. Vincent Davis, *Henry Kissinger and Bureaucratic Politics, A Personal Appraisal* (Columbia, S.C.: University of South Carolina, Institute of International Studies Essay Series, No. 9, 1979).

83. Ward, "Kissinger," 297.

84. Barber, *The Presidential Character,* 12.

85. See Starr, "The Kissinger Years," 476-82, for an analysis of Kissinger and Nixon, including Kissinger's observations on Nixon's active-negative character.

86. Etheredge, "Hardball Politics," 1-2.

87. Alan C. Elms (in *Personality in Politics* [New York: Harcourt, Brace, Jovanovich, 1976], 139), summarized Richard Christie's set of basic characteristics exhibited by the highly Machiavellian person: "1. A relative lack of affect in interpersonal relationships; the tendency to view others as objects to be manipulated rather than as individuals with whom one has empathy. 2. A lack of concern with conventional morality; a utilitarian, rather than a moral, view. 3. A lack of gross psychopathology. 4. Low ideological commitment." See also Richard Christie and F. L. Geis, *Studies in Machiavellianism* (New York: Academic Press, 1970).

88. Etheredge, "Hardball Politics," 5.

89. Mazlish, *Kissinger,* 89-90.

90. Quoted in Elms, *Personality in Politics,* 146.

91. Mazlish, *Kissinger,* 7.

92. Valeriani, *Travels with Henry,* 6.

93. Saul Friedlander and Raymond Cohen, "The Personality Correlates of Belligerence in International Conflict," *Comparative Politics* 7(1975):155-86.

94. Motivational analysts, such as David Winter, note that origins of the power motive may be found in the individual's family experiences, such as birth order, the eldest child having the greatest probability of acquiring a high power motive. (*The Power Motive* [New York: Free Press, 1973], 18.)

95. Mazlish, *Kissinger,* 291.

CHAPTER 3

1. For example, see Peter Dickson, *Kissinger and the Meaning of History* (London: Cambridge University Press, 1978), 17.

2. Earlier versions of this chapter have appeared as: "Henry Kissinger's Belief System and World Order: Perception and Policy" (in H.H. Han, ed., *World in Transition* [Washington, D.C.: University Press of America, 1979], 239-55), "Kissinger's Operational Code" (Paper delivered at the annual meeting of the International Studies Association, Los Angeles, 1980), and "Kissinger's Operational Code" (*Korea and World Affairs,* 1980, 4(4):582-606). Other portions have been taken from "The Kissinger Years: Studying Individuals and Foreign Policy" (*International Studies Quarterly,* 24, no. 4(1980):465-96).

3. Stephen R. Graubard, *Kissinger, Portrait of a Mind* (New York: W.W. Norton, 1973), ix.

4. See Milton Rokeach, *The Open and Closed Mind* (New York: Basic Books, 1969), 33.

5. Giovanni Sartori, "Politics, Ideology, and Belief Systems," *American Political Science Review,* 63(1969):400.

6. Ole R. Holsti, "The Belief System and National Images: John Foster Dulles and the Soviet Union" (Ph.D. diss., Stanford University, 1962), 5-6.

7. Ibid.

8. Ole R. Holsti and Alexander George, "The Effects of Stress on the Performance of Foreign Policy Makers" (in C.P. Cotter, ed., *Political Science Annual* [Indianapolis: Bobbs-Merrill, 1975], 263-64).

9. Robert Jervis, *Perception and Misperception in International Politics* (Princeton, N.J.: Princeton University Press, 1976), 145-46.

10. The results of Leites's endeavors were published in *The Operational Code of the Politburo* (New York: McGraw-Hill, 1951), and *A Study of Bolshevism* (New York: Free Press of Glencoe, 1953).

11. See Alexander George, "The Operational Code: A Neglected Approach to the Study of Political Decision Making," *International Studies Quarterly,* 13(1969):190-222. The ten questions are taken from pp. 201-216. This list is similarly reproduced in other operational-code studies, such as Holsti's "The 'Operational Code' Approach to the Study of Political Leaders: John Foster Dulles' Philosophical and Instrumental Beliefs," *Canadian Journal of Political Science,* 3(1970):123-57, or Stephen G. Walker's "Cognitive Maps and International Realities: Henry A. Kissinger's Operational Code" (Paper presented at the annual meeting of the American Political Science Association, San Francisco, 1975).

12. In addition, Holsti has also provided coding rules and exercises for the training of researchers who would like to use the operational-code approach. See "The 'Operational Code' as an Approach to the Analysis of Belief Systems: Final Report to the National Science Foundation" (Duke University, 1977).

13. Holsti, "The 'Operational Code' Approach . . . John Foster Dulles," 153.

14. David McLellan, "The 'Operational Code' Approach to the Study of Political Leaders: Dean Acheson's Philosophical and Instrumental Beliefs," *Canadian Journal of Political Science,* 4(1971):74.

15. See Walker, "Cognitive Maps," and also his article, "The Interface Between Beliefs and Behavior: Henry Kissinger's Operational Code and the Vietnam War," *Journal of Conflict Resolution,* 21(1971):129-68.

16. In her introduction to *A Psychological Examination of Political Leaders,* Margaret Hermann lists fifteen operational-code studies that have been performed on U.S. senators

and secretaries of state, and on heads of government of other countries (see M. Hermann, ed., *A Psychological Examination of Political Leaders* [New York: Free Press, 1977]). Other lists have also been presented, e.g., Ole Holsti, "Foreign Policy Formation Viewed Cognitively" (in Robert Axelrod, ed., *Structure of Decision* [Princeton, N.J.: Princeton University Press, 1976], 36).

Another approach to the analysis of pre-policymaker writings, value analysis, is "designed to probe antecedents of content in the autobiographical writings of an individual. The technique gives the researcher the ability to get at the value structure underlying an individual's writing, and on a broader plane, his actions." (See Howard M. Cummins, *Mao, Hsiao, Churchill and Montgomery: Personal Values and Decision Making* [Beverly Hills: Sage, 1973].)

17. Loch Johnson, "Operational Codes and the Prediction of Leadership Behavior: Senator Frank Church at Midcareer" (in M. Hermann, ed., *A Psychological Examination of Political Leaders,* 87).

18. Dickson, *Kissinger and the Meaning of History,* 1.

19. See Walker, "Cognitive Maps," 7-8.

20. Graubard, *Kissinger, Portrait of a Mind,* 7. Mazlish (*Kissinger* [see Note 21], 159) also calls Kissinger's Ph.D. thesis, *A World Restored,* Kissinger's personal statement, supporting the view that Kissinger's academic statements were honest in the sense used here. In discussions held in January 1977, only weeks before Kissinger left office, State Department acquaintances of Kissinger made observations on his views on several subjects that tallied exactly with views Kissinger presents in *White House Years* (Boston: Little, Brown, 1979). Because Kissinger's private views matched his public recitation of those views, and the State Department officials accurately recounted these views, this further indication of the honesty of Kissinger's expressed views gives greater credence to the accuracy of their observations on Kissinger in general, and Kissinger's comments on both subjects treated in his memoirs and those omitted.

21. See Bruce Mazlish, *Kissinger, The European Mind in American Policy* (New York: Basic Books, 1976), 151. Mazlish also stresses the "coherence, continuity and unity" of Kissinger's intellectual world view (p. 153). The following section also draws on the work of Graubard, the articles by Walker and Eldridge, and Marvin and Bernard Kalb, *Kissinger* (New York: Dell, 1974), David Landau, *Kissinger: The Uses of Power* (New York: W.W. Norton, 1973), and John Stoessinger, *Henry Kissinger: The Anguish of Power* (New York: W.W. Norton, 1976).

22. Walker, "Cognitive Maps," 7.

23. From an interview in *Die Zeit* of Hamburg, West Germany, June 30, 1976 (reprinted in the *Department of State Bulletin,* 75(26 July 1976):124-32). Albert Eldridge has similarly observed: "The importance Kissinger places on 'conception' is underlined throughout his writings and tenures as Special Advisor and Secretary of State when he transforms discussion of specific issues . . . into discussions of the concepts inherent in the topics. Throughout, Kissinger displays an enduring preference for the comprehensiveness that he believes resides in the framework." (See "The Crisis of Authority: The President, Kissinger and Congress (1969-1974)." Paper presented at the Annual Meeting of the International Studies Association, Toronto, 1976.) This illustrates Kissinger's drive both to be a teacher and, as a statesman, to have a firm grasp of history and international relations before becoming an effective activist.

24. Stated during a question-and-answer session at the PBS luncheon held June 16, 1975 (see *Department of State Bulletin,* 73(7 July 1975):25-29).

25. Henry Kissinger, *A World Restored* (Boston: Houghton-Mifflin, 1957), 1.

26. Senate Foreign Relations Committee Hearings, September 19, 1974.

27. See Walker, "Cognitive Maps," 52; and Stoessinger, *Henry Kissinger,* 74.

28. Henry Kissinger, *For the Record* (Boston: Little, Brown, 1981), 115-116. In his memoirs, Kissinger refers to the Soviet Union in exactly these terms: "Absolute security for Russia has meant infinite insecurity for all its neighbors" (*White House Years,* 118).

29. "Force and Diplomacy in the Nuclear Age," *Foreign Affairs,* 34(1956):349. This example is discussed in Dickson, *Kissinger and the Meaning of History,* 81.

30. Cited in Dickson, *Kissinger and the Meaning of History,* 51.

31. *White House Years,* 70.

32. Stoessinger, *Henry Kissinger,* 7, 37. Stoessinger's observations actually hark back to the teacher-activist figure Kissinger became in the army.

33. That is, Kissinger's operational code is discussed with regard to the cognitive framework (and its categories) that Kissinger developed. The flexibility discussed in chapter 2 concerns the way Kissinger would evaluate and re-evaluate people, states, and/or situations in terms of those categories, *not* those categories themselves. The continuity discussed directly above concerns the durability of the categories over time.

34. See "The White Revolutionary: Reflections on Bismarck," *Daedalus,* Summer 1968, 888-924. A number of Kissinger scholars have identified *A World Restored* as the central work in understanding Kissinger's theory of international relations—"the book which provides the clearest indication of (Kissinger's) political thinking" (Philip Windsor, "Henry Kissinger's Scholarly Contribution" [*British Journal of International Studies,* 1(1975):28]). Writing of *A World Restored,* Dana Ward observes that, "The work describes not simply a world restored, but a self restored." (See "Kissinger: A Psychohistory," *History of Childhood Quarterly,* 2(1974-75):327.)

35. Henry Kissinger, "Central Issues of American Foreign Policy" (in Kermit Gordon, ed., *Agenda for the Nation* [New York: Doubleday, 1968], 588).

36. *A World Restored,* 1.

37. Clearly, the Germany of Kissinger's youth was a revolutionary state.

38. This view occurs frequently in discussions of the balance of power systems of eighteenth- and nineteenth-century Europe. Note that Kissinger's conception of stability is very similar to Morton Kaplan's rules for the balance of power system (described in Kaplan, *System and Process in International Politics* [New York: Wiley, 1957], Chapter 2).

39. Stoessinger, *Henry Kissinger,* 12.

40. *White House Years,* 442.

41. *A World Restored,* 316.

42. Ibid., 10-11, 326. In his memoirs, Kissinger returns explicitly to his intellectual framework. He describes the nature of his 1971 interchange with four dedicated anti-war activists: "Ours was the perpetually inconclusive dialogue between statesmen and prophets, between those who operate in time and through attainable stages and those who are concerned with truth and the eternal" (*White House Years,* 1016).

43. *White House Years,* 1223, 1352, 1422.

44. Ibid., 965.

45. Ibid., 1089.

46. Ward, "Kissinger: A Psychohistory," 320.

47. Mazlish, *Kissinger* 212.

48. Ward, "Kissinger: A Psychohistory," 320.

49. Stoessinger reports this as Kissinger's response to Stoessinger's question (*Henry Kissinger,* 14).

50. Dickson, *Kissinger and the Meaning of History*, 49. On p. 9 Dickson observes, "Indeed, Henry Kissinger embodies the conflict between ethics and power." Here again, Kissinger and "power" are linked by personality and style factors. If power is to be wielded, it is for the creation of order—even if justice must suffer. This may be the clearest indication that the search for order, derived from Kissinger's experiences in Nazi Germany, was central to both Kissinger's personality and his belief system.

51. Some observers have argued that Kissinger ignored third-world countries in single-minded pursuit of a policy toward the Soviet Union. Others have thought his policies were mistaken. Kissinger did, however, find a place for the less-developed countries in his analytic scheme. In "Central Issues of American Foreign Policy," he wrote directly of the countries of the emerging third world. He saw them as being a major challenge to international order, especially a danger to the "meaning of political legitimacy." He observed that, "Almost all of the new countries suffer from a revolutionary malaise." Kermit Gordon, ed., *Agenda for the Nation* (Washington: Brookings, 1968), 603.

52. See Stanley Hoffmann, *Primacy or World Order* (New York: McGraw-Hill, 1978), 44-45.

53. *Nuclear Weapons and Foreign Policy* (New York: Harper, 1957); *The Necessity for Choice* (New York: Harper, 1961); *The Troubled Partnership* (New York: McGraw-Hill, 1965); Graubard, *Kissinger, Portrait of a Mind*, 243, 248, 252, 253.

54. Townsend Hoopes, *The Devil and John Foster Dulles* (London: Andre Deutsch, 1974), 83.

55. Holsti, "The 'Operational Code' Approach . . . John Foster Dulles," 126. Compare Dulles's fourth belief to Kissinger's beliefs concerning statesmen and leadership, especially the idea of the statesman as educator. Here is a classic contrast between the prophet and the more moderate statesman.

56. Ibid., 129.

57. McLellan, "The 'Operational Code' Approach . . . Dean Acheson," 55-57.

58. Ibid., 74-75.

59. See George F. Kennan, *Memoirs: 1925-1950* (Boston: Little, Brown, 1967): for example, p. 54 or p. 322. See also John C. Donovan, *The Cold Warriors* (Lexington, Mass.: D.C. Heath, 1974), for a very useful overview and comparison of Kennan's positions and those taken by the more ideologically oriented cold warriors.

60. See "Central Issues of American Foreign Policy," and Graubard, *Kissinger, Portrait of a Mind*, 131.

61. See Arthur L. Gladstone, "The Conception of the Enemy," *Journal of Conflict Resolution* 3(1959):132-37.

62. *White House Years*, 161-62.

63. See Walker, "Cognitive Maps," 13.

64. "The Meaning of History," 348.

65. Stoessinger, *Henry Kissinger*, 7.

66. Interview with James Reston, *New York Times*, October 13, 1974, p. 35. Also, in discussing the North Vietnamese 1972 Spring offensive, Kissinger records this interchange with Nixon, illustrating his optimistic belief in the activist: "Nixon mused that if we failed, it was because the great forces of history had moved in another direction. Not only South Vietnam but the whole free world would be lost. 'No,' I replied, 'if it fails, we'll have to tighten our belts and *turn the forces around.*' " [emphasis added] (*White House Years*, 1117).

67. *Department of State Bulletin*, 73(October/December 1975):697.

68. Mazlish, *Kissinger*, 163.

69. Quoted in Joseph Kraft, "In Search of Kissinger" (*Harpers*, January 1971, 58).

70. Mazlish, *Kissinger*, 165.

71. Dickson, *Kissinger and the Meaning of History*, 38, 74. See also Chapter 1, "The Judgment of History," and Chapter 2, "Kant and Kissinger."

72. Stoessinger, *Henry Kissinger*, 80. Furthermore, Kissinger showed genuine admiration for another aspect of America, its opportunity and optimism, which are referred to in several moving passages in *White House Years* (e.g., p. 229).

73. Eldridge, "Pondering Intangibles," 39-40.

74. *The Necessity for Choice*, 2.

75. "The Meaning of History," 347-48. Stoessinger recalls that Kissinger once said to him, "The past is dead. I am interested in the future." (*Night Journey* [Chicago: Playboy Press, 1978], 73.)

76. Cited in Stoessinger, *Henry Kissinger*, 140.

77. See Ward, "Kissinger: A Psychohistory," 300.

78. *A World Restored*, 326.

79. Kissinger's view of the statesman as educator is presented repeatedly in *White House Years*. A student of Kissinger's operational code can recognize that his efforts to explain the Nixon administration's policies are sincere and deeply ingrained in his conception of the statesman. Discussing Vietnam policy in 1970-71, Kissinger notes: "I had not given up hope that I could bridge somewhat the chasm between the Administration and its critics. Between April 1, 1970 and April 1, 1971, *without publicity* [emphasis added] I met with groups of students and young protesters nineteen times, with academic critics of the war twenty-nine times, and Senators and other prominent critics thirty times—a total of seventy-eight occasions, or more than one a week." (p. 1015)

80. See Harvey Starr, "Alliances: Tradition and Change in American Views on Foreign Military Entanglements," in Ken Booth and Moorehead Wright, eds., *American Thinking About Peace and War* (New York: Barnes & Noble, 1978), 37-57.

81. Kalbs, *Kissinger*, 98.

82. *White House Years*, 14-15. Note that Kissinger was also acting on a lesson he had learned so painfully in the early 1960s. The principal reason that he had been "fired" by McGeorge Bundy was Kissinger's attempt to bypass Bundy and move directly to the president. Kissinger was clearly determined to follow the same bureaucratic imperatives, by gaining control of all access to the president on foreign-policy issues. This in turn would assure Kissinger of access whenever he wanted it—no Bundy would stand between Kissinger and the president.

83. "The Policymaker and the Intellectual," *The Reporter* (March 5, 1959), pp. 3-35; "Bureaucracy and Policymaking: The Effect of Insiders and Outsiders on the Policy Process," in Bernard Brodie, ed., *Bureaucracy, Politics and Strategy*, Security Studies Paper No. 17, University of California, Los Angeles, 1968, pp. 1-14.

84. "Domestic Structure and Foreign Policy," 507.

85. Ibid., 510-11.

86. Stoessinger, *Henry Kissinger*, 191-92.

87. Hoffmann, 74.

88. Stoessinger, *Henry Kissinger*, 15.

89. The following discussion draws many points from Walker, "Cognitive Maps," 13-20.

90. See also Kenneth Waltz's discussion of the "third image"—the influence of the international system on the occurrence of war—in *Man, The State and War* (New York: Columbia University Press), Chapters 6 and 7.

91. "Dr. Kissinger on World Affairs, An Interview," *Encounter*, 51(November

1978):23-24. Kissinger scholars must also take more careful note of Kissinger's comments on Bismarck for a truer reading of Kissinger's beliefs. In another 1978 interview, Kissinger noted: "The unfortunate problem for the Metternich theory is that I really wanted to write a book about Bismarck, and I only started writing about Metternich as a counterpoise to Bismarck in order to understand the context which Bismarck inherited." (*For the Record,* 117)

92. "The Meaning of History," 345-46.
93. *Necessity for Choice,* 312.
94. *White House Years,* 128.
95. Dickson, *Kissinger and the Meaning of History,* 89.
96. Mazlish, *Kissinger,* 177.
97. Walker, "Cognitive Maps," 17. Other observers have noted Kissinger's "risk aversion" (see G. Warren Nutter, *Kissinger's Grand Design* [Washington D.C.: American Enterprise Institute, 1975], 111-12), or his "distaste for high risks" (see Hoffmann, *Primacy or World Order,* 76). Eldridge (in "Pondering Intangibles") isolated four "terminal values." The most important of these is safety (which includes physical security, and the absence of war and violence). Kissinger's concern with safety (and thus order) is found throughout his works, and leads Eldridge to conclude that Kissinger was primarily defensive in his outlook. This coincides with the statesman's role—seeking stability and order and defending the status quo.
98. In Kissinger's public statements as a decision maker, investigated in Part II, he refers constantly to the ability of the Soviet Union and the United States to destroy civilization. He stresses the care that must be taken in U.S.–Soviet relations because of the nuclear capabilities the two superpowers possess.
99. See Walker, "Cognitive Maps," 18, and Kissinger's *Nuclear Weapons and Foreign Policy,* 168. At approximately the same time that Kissinger was working on *Nuclear Weapons and Foreign Policy,* Thomas Schelling was writing about the continued use of bargaining techniques during war, even during a nuclear war. See *The Strategy of Conflict* (New York: Oxford University Press, 1969), which had been copyrighted by Harvard in 1960. In addition, in *White House Years,* (see pp. 607-8, 1117-18), Kissinger indicates a penchant for the use of brinkmanship during crisis very similar to Schelling's analysis of brinkmanship in Chapter 8 of *Strategy of Conflict.*
100. Walker, "Cognitive Maps," 19.
101. *White House Years,* 1102.
102. *Department of State Bulletin,* February 23, 1976, pp. 201-12.
103. *White House Years,* 129.
104. Ibid., 818.
105. Ibid., 1143, 569, 535.
106. Some observers have argued that a lack of clarity was exactly the problem in the Soviet move into Afghanistan. For a further discussion of precision and clarity as functions of alliances, see Starr, "Alliances: Tradition and Change."
107. Stoessinger, *Henry Kissinger,* 202.
108. Walker, "Cognitive Maps," 20.
109. Mazlish, *Kissinger,* 154.
110. Ibid.

CHAPTER 4

1. See Ole R. Holsti, "The Belief System and National Images: John Foster Dulles and the Soviet Union" (Ph.D. diss., Stanford University, 1962); "Cognitive Dynamics and

Images of the Enemy: Dulles and Russia," in D.J. Finlay, O.R. Holsti, and R.R. Fagen, eds., *Enemies in Politics* (Chicago: Rand-McNally, 1967), 25-96; "Cognitive Dynamics and Images of the Enemy," *Journal of International Affairs,* 21 (1967):16-39; and "The Belief System and National Images: A Case Study," *Journal of Conflict Resolution,* 6 (1962): 244-52. See also the operational-code article, "The 'Operational Code' Approach to the Study of Political Leaders: John Foster Dulles' Philosophical and Instrumental Beliefs," *Canadian Journal of Political Science,* 3 (1970):123-57.

2. See: Arthur L. Gladstone, "The Conception of the Enemy," *Journal of Conflict Resolution,* 3 (1959):132-37; Finlay, Holsti, and Fagen, "Some Theoretical Dimensions of the Idea of the Enemy," *Enemies in Politics,* 1-24; and Ralph K. White, *Nobody Wanted War* (Garden City, N.Y.: Doubleday, 1970), especially Chapters 3, 7, & 10.

3. Holsti, "Cognitive Dynamics," 17.

4. Rudolph J. Rummel, *Understanding Conflict and War,* Vol. 1, *The Dynamic Psychological Field* (New York: Halstead Press/Sage, 1975), 157.

5. Townsend Hoopes, "Henry and Richard and John and Dwight," *New York Times,* Sunday, 10 Feb. 1974, Sec. IV, p. 15.

6. Holsti, "The Belief System and National Images," 15.

7. Ibid., 16.

8. Garry Wills, *Nixon Agonistes* (Boston: Houghton-Mifflin, 1970), Ch. 6.

9. Henry Brandon, *The Retreat of American Power* (Garden City, N.Y.: Doubleday, 1973), 64.

10. Ibid., 33.

11. Hoopes, "Henry and Richard," 15.

12. Holsti, "The Belief System and National Images" (Ph.D. diss.), 16. See also "The Belief System and National Images" *(J. Conflict Resolution),* 241.

13. Hoopes, "Henry and Richard," 15.

CHAPTER 5

1. Ole R. Holsti, "The Belief System and National Images: John Foster Dulles and the Soviet Union" (Ph.D. diss., Stanford University, 1962), 12.

2. Ibid., 13.

3. The problem of studying high-level foreign-policy decision makers is summarized by Richard Brody's famous question: "How can we give a Taylor Manifest Anxiety Scale to Khrushchev during the Hungarian revolt, a Semantic Differential to Chiang Kai-shek while Quemoy is being shelled, or simply interview Kennedy during the Cuban missile crisis?" (Richard Brody, "The Study of Politics Qua Science," in Klaus Knorr and James N. Rosenau, eds., *Contending Approaches to International Politics* [Princeton, N.J.: Princeton University Press, 1969], 116). For a discussion of access, see Ole R. Holsti, Robert North, and Richard Brody, "Perception and Action in the 1914 crisis," in J.D. Singer, ed., *Quantitative International Politics* (New York: Free Press, 1968).

4. Holsti, in *Content Analysis for the Social Sciences and Humanities* (Reading, Mass.: Addison-Wesley, 1969), begins with the observation: "Communication, the most basic form of human interaction, is necessary for any enduring human relationship, from interpersonal to international. Groups, institutions, organizations, and nations exist by virtue of communication and cease to exist once communication becomes totally disrupted. . . . It therefore follows that the study of the processes and products of communication is basic to the student of man's history, behavior, thought, art and institutions. Often the only surviving artifacts that may be used to study human activity are to be found in documents." (p. 1)

5. David Bell, *Power, Influence, Authority* (New York: Oxford University Press, 1974), 12.

6. Holsti, *Content Analysis* 3. David Winter and Abigail Stewart are more specific regarding the notion of inferences, seeing content analysis "as a technique for making psychological inferences about politically relevant aspects of the personality of political actors from the systematic, objective study of written and transcribed oral material." See "Content Analysis as a Technique for Assessing Political Leaders," in Margaret G. Hermann, ed., *A Psychological Examination of Political Leaders* (New York: Free Press, 1977), 29.

7. Holsti, *Content Analysis,* 3. The literature on the utility, application, and features of content analysis is extensive. The basic reference used throughout the present study is Holsti's *Content Analysis for the Social Sciences and Humanities,* Chapter three of which provides a useful review of the content-analysis literature and which has a lengthy bibliography on pp. 195-221. Other basic works that also provide numerous references are Ithiel De Sola Pool, ed., *Trends in Content Analysis* (Urbana, Ill.: University of Illinois Press, 1959), Robert C. North et al., *Content Analysis* (Evanston, Ill.: Northwestern University Press, 1963), and B. Berelson, *Content Analysis in Communications Research* (Glencoe: Free Press, 1952). For a more recent literature review, see Winter and Stewart, "Content Analysis as a Technique," 27-61. Issues of utility and applicability (e.g., the "representational/instrumental" debate) and critiques are especially well treated by Holsti in Chapter one, and by Alexander George, "Quantitative and Qualitative Approaches to Content Analysis," 7-32, and Ithiel De Sola Pool, "Trends in Content Analysis Today: A Summary," 189-233, both in Pool, ed., *Trends in Content Analysis.*

8. Holsti, *Content Analysis,* 16-17.

9. Paul A. Anderson, "Justifications and Precedents as Constraints in Foreign Policy Decision Making" (Carnegie-Mellon University, November 1979, Mimeographed), pages 5-6.

10. Ibid., 2.

11. Ibid., 1.

12. Henry A. Kissinger, *White House Years* (Boston: Little, Brown, 1979), 425.

13. Ole R. Holsti, "Foreign Policy Formation Viewed Cognitively," in Robert Axelrod, ed., *The Structure of Decision* (Princeton, N.J.: Princeton University Press, 1976) 44. See also Pool, ed., *Trends in Content Analysis:* Robert Osgood, "The Representational Model and Relevant Research Methods," and Pool's introduction.

14. Holsti, *Content Analysis,* 27-29. Different audiences are investigated and discussed in the Appendix.

15. For the original presentation of evaluative assertion analysis, complete with specific descriptions of stages, coding rules, reliability checks, etc., see Charles E. Osgood, Sol Saporta, and Jum C. Nunnally, "Evaluative Assertion Analysis," *Litera* 3(1956):47-102. A much briefer description of the technique is found in Charles E. Osgood, "The Representational Model and Relevant Research Methods," in Pool, ed., *Trends in Content Analysis,* 33-88. Good, short descriptions are also found in Holsti, "The Belief System and National Images," Appendix, and in North et al., *Content Analysis,* ch. six. The evaluative assertion analysis method is based heavily on Osgood's earlier work on the semantic differential, congruity theory, and mediation hypotheses. See G. Cleveland Wilhoit, "A Methodological Critique of the Application of Evaluative Assertion Analysis to Studies of Media Performance" (Bureau of Media Research, School of Journalism, Indiana University, April 1977), 2. Only the most salient aspects of evaluative assertion analysis are touched on here.

16. Winter and Stewart, "Content Analysis as a Technique," 42.

17. Specifying one or two attitude objects also provides the opportunity to skip a "Masking technique" stage.

18. Osgood et al., 47.

19. Further aspects of this stage of the analysis are found in the section on reliability in the Appendix. Also, Holsti, in "The Belief System and National Images," gives a useful example of the analysis: "The method can be illustrated by translating a statement: 'The leaders of the Soviet Union are evil men, who attack not only American interests but the finest traditions of Western civilization.' After translation, the sentence would appear as: 1. Soviet leaders / are / evil. (form 1). 2. Soviet leaders / are / men. (form 2). 3. Soviet leaders / attack / American interests. (form 2). 4. Soviet leaders / attack / the traditions of Western civilization. (form 2). 5. Western civilization / has / fine traditions. (form 1)." Sentence two, because it is non-evaluative, is discarded. While the fifth statement is not directly germane to the present analysis, which does not deal with Dulles' evaluation of Western civilization, it can be used to determine what value should be placed on the term 'Western civilization,' which is perceived to be under Soviet attack in sentence four." (p. 245)

20. Although the evaluators in Note 19 are ranked as "favorable" or "unfavorable" on a good-bad scale, the method can be employed with any scale (e.g., strong-weak, hostile-friendly, or success-failure).

21. Holsti, "The Belief System and National Images," 248. See pp. 248-49 for Holsti's explanation of why he modified Osgood's computational formula. Particularly for comparability (and because Holsti's procedure makes sense), Holsti's methods are followed in this study.

22. See Holsti, "Belief System and National Images," 246-47, for descriptions of these categories. Osgood et al., in "Evaluative Assertion Analysis," give psycholinguistic rationales for these categories. Briefly, 'hostility' refers to verbal and physical actions of the AO that seek to harm the interest of, weaken, destroy, or obstruct the achievement of the goals of the U.S. or other international actors (other AO_2s, from which the evaluation is derived). 'Capabilities' refers to the presence or absence of the various elements of military, economic, technological, and political capability. 'Success' refers to the achievement by the AO of the goals and ambitions attributed to it. This might range from limited tactical successes to the achievement of major goals or undertakings. 'General evaluation' includes all references of a good-bad nature, from the perspective of Kissinger's values. In his dissertation (see Note 1), Holsti also used a fifth category, the degree of internal Soviet liberalization. In the present study, this category has been omitted, as it was by Holsti in the most of his published research.

23. Holsti, "The Belief System and National Images," 14.

24. Other sources included the *New York Times Index,* the *Reader's Guide to Periodical Literature,* the *Public Affairs Information Service Index, Vital Speeches,* several indexes to Congressional hearings and documents, the *Weekly Compilation of Presidential Documents,* and the bibliographies and references provided in the biographical literature on Kissinger.

25. According to a high-ranking State Department colleague of Kissinger's, the prepared speeches and addresses were very much Kissinger's ideas and words, and were neither ghost written nor bureaucratic compromises. The same holds for Kissinger's Congressional presentations. According to this State Department official, Kissinger took "enormous time" in developing these speeches, engaging in extensive discussions with speechwriters before the first draft in order to make clear what the content was to be. Kissinger would then heavily edit the subsequent drafts. Margaret G. Hermann also raises

the important issue of ghost writing in the use of content analysis for studying decision makers. (see "Leader Personality and Foreign Policy Behavior," in James N. Rosenau, ed., *Comparing Foreign Policies* [New York: Halsted, 1974], 210.) In a section titled "Some Problems of Empirical Research," Holsti lists 'authorship'—"Establishing authorship may also pose difficulties for the student of cognitive processes." Holsti reviews possible strategies to avoid authorship problems (e.g., use only interviews or press conferences), and, in turn, the drawbacks of these strategies. He concludes, "By this point it should be evident that there are no easy rules of thumb by which the investigator can overcome problems of access to and inference from documentary data." See "Foreign Policy Decision Makers Viewed Psychologically: 'Cognitive Process' Approaches" (Duke University, 1975, Mimeographed), 31-32.

26. Kissinger himself notes that, "Eventually, though not for the first one and a half years, I became the principal adviser." (*White House Years,* 48)

27. Holsti, "The Belief System and National Images," 18.

28. Dulles's vague yet conspiratorial view of worldwide aggressive Communism is well illustrated by his exchange with Senator Henry Jackson before the Senate Foreign Relations Committee in January 1957:

SECRETARY DULLES: I say countries controlled by international Communism.

SENATOR JACKSON: Yes. Well, they are synonymous (with "Soviet") but for the purpose—

SECRETARY DULLES: No, it is much broader. . . . International Communism is a conspiracy composed of a certain number of people, all of whose names I do not know, and many of whom I suppose are secret. They have gotten control of one government after another. They first got control of Russia after the First World War. They have gone on getting control of one country after another until finally they were stopped. But they have not gone out of existence.

SENATOR JACKSON: Would you not agree on this: that international Communism has been used as an instrument of Russian foreign policy since 1918?

SECRETARY DULLES: I would put it the other way around. Russian foreign policy is an instrument of international Communism.

Quoted by Holsti in "Cognitive Dynamics and Images of the Enemy," 51.

29. The external threat-internal cohesiveness relationship has been developed and discussed in sociology, psychology, and political science. For two introductory treatments, see Lewis Coser, *The Functions of Social Conflict* (New York: Free Press, 1956), and Arthur Stein, "Conflict and Cohesion, A Review of the Literature," *Journal of Conflict Resolution,* 20, no. 1(1976):143-72.

30. For example, taking all of Kissinger's hostility assertions about the Soviet Union, the DS hostility assertions provide an overall evaluation score of $-.059$. The non-DS hostility assertions give $-.563$: a somewhat more hostile score, but still on the low side of neutral. The same can be seen for DS general evaluation, which is $+.062$, while non-DS general evaluation is $-.238$. Similar patterns hold for China: DS hostility $= +1.484$, non-DS hostility $= +1.354$; DS general evaluation $= +1.254$, non-DS general evaluation $= +1.051$.

31. Following Holsti, the analysis here will use trimonthly, half-year, and yearly aggregations of assertions (with the occasional use of bimonthly aggregations). Spearman rank-order correlations, as Holsti used, will be calculated along with Pearson product moment correlations. These procedures produce a set of eight correlations—two for each

of the four time-period aggregations. Of the eight correlations between DS general evaluation and non-DS general evaluation for the Soviet Union, the lowest is .83 and the highest
is .94 (all significant). For Soviet DS hostility and non-DS hostility, the lowest correlation
is .77 and the highest is .99 (all significant). The China correlations are somewhat lower.
From another perspective, if we use the *document* as the unit of analysis (correlating the
evaluation scores that emerge from each individual document, and not aggregating all
the assertions that occur during some period of time), the correlations are all very high,
the lowest being .89 for China DS hostility and non-DS hostility. Thus, the two data sets
are very similar.

32. Holsti also located 346 assertions for the internal governmental support category,
which has been omitted from the present study.

33. See Richard Neustadt, *Alliance Politics* (New York: Columbia University Press,
1970).

CHAPTER 6

1. *Journal of International Affairs,* 21(1967):16.

2. In a January 1977 interview.

3. Henry Kissinger, *White House Years* (Boston: Little, Brown, 1979), 413. See also
p. 522.

4. "Dr. Kissinger on World Affairs: An Interview," *Encounter,* 51(November 1979):
15.

5. Ted R. Gurr, *Politimetrics* (Englewood Cliffs, N.J.: Prentice-Hall, 1971), 45.

6. One would also want to review the biographical and analytic work, and perhaps
rework the operational-code analyses to make certain that the conclusions drawn from the
work were not erroneous.

7. Alternatively, this could simply mean that the coders were poorly trained.

8. Inasmuch as Holsti presents much of his data in half-year aggregations (see especially "The Belief System and National Images: A Case Study," *Journal of Conflict Resolution,* 6(1962):244-52), the present discussion also uses this level of data aggregation. At
several points in the discussions it is demonstrated that aggregation of the data into
six-month periods produces no distortion in the analyses. For a more complete set of
Holsti's data, see "The Belief System and National Images." The complete set of Kissinger
data—also broken down into two-month, three-month, and yearly aggregations—is presented in chapter 6. Furthermore, as noted, in the present study, the sign for Dulles'
hostility scores has been reversed, to match the Kissinger coding.

9. The t-test indicating that the means are statistically different is significant at the
.0001 level, with $t = 28.34$.

10. Significant at the .0001 level, with $t = 11.89$. Also, another comparison can be
made. The general evaluation scores above were based on the total number of assertions
located and aggregated for six-month periods. While data are unavailable for Dulles, for
Kissinger it is possible to calculate a single general evaluation score for *all the assertions*
identified over the entire five-year period: general evaluation $= -.238$; DS general evaluation $= +0.062$. These scores are very close to the means taken from the ten six-month
periods, and are exactly the same substantively. These scores assure us that there is no
distortion through aggregating the data into time periods of specific (and, of course,
arbitrary) length.

11. For hostility, $t = 6.00$; for DS hostility, t 8.04. Both are significant at the .0005
level.

12. Douglas Stuart and Harvey Starr, "Inherent Bad Faith Reconsidered: Dulles, Kennedy and Kissinger", *Political Psychology* 3, 1981-82, pp. 1-33.

13. See Holsti, "The Belief System and National Images," 246.

14. Whether Dulles's assertions were aggregated in three-, six-, or twelve-month periods, these two relationships are statistically significant at the .001 level.

15. While well within the range of the other DS hostility and DS success correlations, due to the larger value of *N*, the correlation between DS hostility and DS success is significant at the .05 level. This should not be surprising, since DS means dual subject, and Kissinger would be associating joint friendliness with references to joint successes. Again, we see that the time-period aggregations are a reasonable way to arrange and analyze the data.

16. Holsti, "The Belief System and National Images," 140.

17. The sign for hostility is *not* reversed on this graph, nor is it reversed for Figure 3, which graphs Kissinger's evaluations.

18. Kissinger, *The Necessity for Choice* (New York: Doubleday, 1962), 201.

19. See Holsti, "Cognitive Dynamics and Images of the Enemy," especially pp. 47-56.

20. Ibid., 52.

21. Possible explanations for the existence of such patterns do exist, however. If Kissinger intended to send clear verbal signals to the Soviet leaders he might have, early on, decided to use certain labels with negative comments and stayed with those labels to let the Kremlin know when he was displeased. And Kissinger did understand the value of the manipulation of labels. In his memoirs, he recalls a Nixon toast at a state dinner for Romanian President Ceausescu in October 1970: "At the state dinner, Nixon toasted the many common interests of the United States and Romania, listing prominently that of good relations, such as Romania had, with the United States, the Soviet Union, and the 'People's Republic of China.' It was the first use of China's official name by an American President." (*White House Years,* 699).

22. A close State Department colleague of Kissinger's, asked about this point several months before the content analysis was undertaken, was emphatic that these labels held no special meaning for Kissinger.

23. Mr. John Main, formerly of the Foreign Office, and currently lecturer in International Politics at the University of Aberdeen, Scotland, brought this point to my attention.

CHAPTER 7

1. For examples, see: Alan M. Jones, Jr., "Nixon and the World," in Jones, ed., *U.S. Foreign Policy in a Changing World* (New York: David McKay, 1973), 1-66, especially p. 22; Wayne Wilcox, "American Foreign Policy: A Year of Mixed Fortunes," in Peter Jones, ed., *The International Yearbook of Foreign Policy Analysis* (London: Croom Helm, 1975), 8-29, especially pp. 12-13; Robert E. Osgood, "Introduction: The Nixon Doctrine and Strategy," in Osgood et al., *Retreat from Empire?* (Baltimore: Johns Hopkins University Press, 1973), 1-27, especially pp. 4-5.

Kissinger, whose ideas were and are similar to many espoused by George Kennan, often reflected Kennan's view of the central importance of the Soviet Union. Kennan has reiterated this view himself. Referring to the Soviet Union, he noted: "Now, finally with these various other elements of the world scene in mind, it is time to turn to the central problem of American foreign policy—a problem which exceeds all the others importance and complexity, and on the approach to which many other facets of American policy depend." (*The Cloud of Danger, Some Current Problems of American Foreign Policy* [London: Hutchison, 1978], 150).

2. See A. Hartley, "American Foreign Policy in the Nixon Era," *Adelphi Papers,* no. 110(Winter 1974/75):20.

3. Stanley Hoffman, *Primacy or World Order* (New York: McGraw-Hill, 1978), 66.

4. George Ball, *Diplomacy for a Crowded World* (Boston: Little, Brown, 1976), 9.

5. Interview with James Reston, "Kissinger Sees the World on Verge of Historic Era," *New York Times,* 13 October 1974.

6. *U.S. News and World Report,* 15 March 1976, 24-30.

7. See "Dr. Kissinger on World Affairs, An Interview," *Encounter,* 51, no. 5(November 1978):21-22.

8. Henry Kissinger, *White House Years* (Boston: Little, Brown, 1979), 763.

9. In the non-DS data for 1972, the Soviet Union was the attitude object of 172 assertions, against 10 for China; in 1973 it was 219 to 109; in 1974 it was 483 to 81; in 1975 it was 452 to 134; and in 1976 it was 1030 to 134.

10. The dashes in Tables 9 and 10 indicate periods during which *no* assertions were made about the attitude object, and thus no score could be calculated. These periods should not be represented by zeros. To do so would equate a period of no assertions with one where assertions were made, but their calculated aggregate score equalled zero, as is true for PRC capabilities for October–December 1973.

11. Quoted from a Kissinger press conference, 22 April 1976, *Department of State Bulletin,* 74(17 May 1976):617-27.

12. This quote is a Kissinger retrospective, expressed in a 1978 interview published in *Encounter.* For a good overview of Kissinger's feelings on Angola, Soviet and Cuban activity there, and Congress's obstruction of the Kissinger-Ford policy, see pp. 12-14 of that interview (which is reprinted in Kissinger's *For the Record* [Boston: Little, Brown, 1981] 127-69).

13. Both increase absolutely—the Soviet mean rises to +1.26, the Chinese mean rises to +0.66—as would be expected for dual subject assertions. However, the difference of means test indicates that the overall relationship has not been altered, and there is still no statistically significant difference ($t = 1.17$).

14. On the subjects of perceptions and evaluations of Chou and Mao, and comparisons of the Soviet and Chinese bargaining styles, the officials' comments were right on the mark. Kissinger's observations, in *White House Years,* on Soviet and Chinese style, and his preferences, match almost perfectly the descriptions given me in January 1977. See, for example, Kissinger's comments on China on pp. 686-60 and 745-49, or his comments on the Soviets on pp. 818 and 1137-42.

15. It was said that Kissinger thought he had finally found people on or above his own intellectual plane. One official paraphrased a comment by Kissinger after Kissinger had held a long session with the Chinese: "These are the only people who see the world realistically. We're very fortunate they have no resources or they'd bury us." Kissinger admired the realism and cynicism of the Chinese. Kissinger's admiration of the Chinese style, and individual Chinese leaders, is reflected throughout his memoirs. This could not be said for the Soviets. In *White House Years,* Kissinger notes, "Gromyko's method of negotiation approached a stereotype. . . . There were no minor issues; every point was pressed with impartial tenacity, eroding all dividing lines and permitting him to trade what should never have been raised into something essential" (p. 789). Kissinger was exasperated by the "petty chiseling by which the run-of-the-mill Soviet diplomat demonstrates his vigilance to his superiors" (p. 140). On the other hand, "Chou never bargained to score petty points" (p. 747).

16. Both nations' scores improve for the DS data set, with the Chinese mean general evaluation score rising somewhat more than the Soviet mean score: Soviet DS general evaluation mean = +0.14; Chinese DS general evaluation mean = +0.94.

17. Note, this is not an average, but simply a single evaluative assertion analysis score for all assertions that appeared in all the documents (here, for general evaluation). Thus it is not possible to indicate differences through the use of statistical tests.

18. Soviet DS Hostility = + 0.53; Chinese DS hostility = +1.54.

19. It is also possible that positive statements about one would be accompanied by positive statements about the other, if Kissinger wished to stay on the good side of both Communist powers at the same time.

20. As is discussed in the Appendix, an analysis was performed concerning the "audience," or the location, of Kissinger's public statements. This analysis only very weakly supports the point made above. While in the Soviet Union, Kissinger made no evaluative assertions about the Chinese in any of his public statements. While in China, Kissinger did make some, although not very many, references to the Soviet Union in his public remarks. Some supporting evidence for general evaluation comes from these assertions. The average general evaluation score for the Soviet Union, from assertions made *while in the Soviet Union*, was +1.79. The average general evaluation score for the Soviet Union, from assertions made *while in China*, was +1.00 (a difference significant at the .01 level). However, the difference for hostility is not statistically significant—the average hostility score for the Soviet Union, from assertions made in the Soviet Union, was +1.84, the average for hostility assertions made while in China was +1.25.

21. Table 7, paralleling Holsti's presentation of data on Dulles, does not include correlations between Kissinger's general evaluation of the Soviet Union and Soviet capabilities and Soviet success. Of the twelve correlations (for three-month, six-month, and yearly aggregations, for DS and non-DS data, and using Spearman and Pearson techniques), eight are *negative*. None of the positive correlations is significant. The correlations between general evaluation and capabilities for the three-month aggregations are: Pearson, $r = -.35$; Spearman, $rs = -.40$. Both are significant at the 0.5 level.

In comparison to the Chinese correlations in Table 14 (non-DS), the twelve correlations with DS data are all *positive* for DS general evaluation, and all are significant at least at the .10 level. On the whole, the correlations are somewhat lower than for the non-DS data. The same holds true for DS hostility, with only half the correlations being statistically significant.

CHAPTER 8

1. Another version of this chapter, looking only at U.S.–Soviet–Chinese behavior and omitting the perceptual data completely, has appeared as Harvey Starr, " 'Detente' or 'Two Against One'?: The China Factor" in Pat McGowan and Charles Kegley, eds., *Sage International Yearbook of Foreign Policy Studies*, Vol. VIII, *USA/USSR* (Beverly Hills: Sage, 1982), pp. 213-239. The analysis and results reported in the present chapter are supported by a more complete investigation of events interaction that spans the Nixon, Ford, and Carter years and uses slightly different COPDAB measures, modified models of détente, and modified theories of the triad.

2. Theodore Caplow, *Two Against One: Coalitions in Triads* (Englewood Cliffs, N.J.: Prentice-Hall, 1968), 1.

3. Ibid., 2-3. David Wilkinson, in *Cohesion and Conflict* (London: Frances Pinter, 1976), discusses the 2-1 coalition in terms of stability—"Most theory indicated that the triad was unstable, the 2-1 split always tending to occur" (p. 236). He notes repeatedly (e.g.,

p. 239) that "strong forces" are at work, making for the two-against-one split.

4. Caplow, *Two Against One,* 4. Wilkinson observes that "what usually happens is that two members become more intimate with each other than the third, who then becomes isolated" (p. 65).

5. Wilkinson, *Cohesion and Conflict,* 35.

6. See Michael Pillsbury, "Salt on the Dragon: Chinese Views of the Soviet-American Strategic Balance," RAND Paper P-5457, April 1975, 5.

7. Wilkinson, *Cohesion and Conflict,* 89. In terms of U.S. policy, Theodore H. White quotes Kissinger's reflection on the international needs of 1969: "What the world needed was a self-regulating mechanism . . .," the key to this being China. See *The Making of the President 1972* (New York: Atheneum, 1973), xii. For a review of the coalition models, see Barbara Hinckley, *Coalitions and Politics* (New York: Harcourt, Brace, 1981), parts I and II.

8. For detailed descriptions of data collection and coding procedures and a presentation of the data, see: Edward E. Azar and Thomas J. Sloan, *Dimensions of Interaction: A Source Book for the Study of Behavior of 31 Nations from 1948 Through 1973* (Pittsburgh: International Studies Association, Occasional Paper Number 8, 1975), and Thomas J. Sloan, *International Interactions: Events Data Analysis Applied to the Middle East* (New York: Learning Resources in International Studies/CISE, Learning Package Number 12, 1975).

9. Information on inter-nation and intra-nation behavior is coded in a form that retains the maximum informational content of the event: a) the date (year, month, and day) of the event; b) the actor (who initiated the event); c) the target (to whom the event was directed); d) the source (where the event was gathered); e) the activity (the verbal or physical act that an actor initiated); f) the issue area (information about the substance of the event). The COPDAB data also benefit from over thirty data sources, for as complete data-source coverage as possible. The sources are: *New York Times, Middle East Journal, New Times, Swiss Review of World Affairs, Middle Eastern Affairs, Deadline Data, Facts on File, World Almanac and Book Facts, Keesing's Contemporary Archives, London Times Index, Annual Register of World Events, Asian Recorder, Al-Ahram* (Egypt), *Jerusalem Post* (Israel), *Al-Nahhar* (Lebanon), *Arab Political Documents, Arab States and Arab League, China Mainland Review, Hsinau News Agency Release, The China Quarterly, Current Scene, China Report, Mizan, Mideast Mirror, Washington Post, Christian Science Monitor, Asian Almanac, Far Eastern Survey, Far Eastern Economic Review, Chronology of Events, El Mercurio* (Chile), and *La Prensa* (Argentina).

10. See Theodore J. Rubin, "International Affairs Indicators for Defense Decision-Making" (Arlington, Va.: Consolidated Analysis Centers, Inc., January 1973), 25-26.

11. Ibid., 22. Policy style indicates the quality of the actions of one nation directed toward another:

$$S = \frac{p - n}{p + n + (ne/2)}$$

S = policy style
p = total positive actions
n = total negative actions
ne = total neutral actions

Rubin notes: "The values of this policy style function range from $+1.0$ to -1.0. A plus value of S indicates that positive actions exceed negative actions; a minus value of S indicates the opposite. The magnitude of the value of S indicates the degree to which the policy style of a country toward another is positive or negative. High plus values imply a friendly or supportive style. High minus values imply a hostile style. Values near zero imply a neutral style" (p. 26).

12. The aggregation of Kissinger's statements into two-month period permits the use of eighteen periods, or units of analysis. See also Note 19.

13. Holsti, *Content Analysis for the Social Sciences and Humanities* (Reading, Mass: Addison-Wesley, 1969), 32.

14. The null hypothesis, however, is also plausible, reflecting the "puzzle" of *non-interaction* presented by Dina A. Zinnes in her review of findings from arms race and other action-reaction studies. (See Dina A. Zinnes, "Three Puzzles in Search of a Researcher," *International Studies Quarterly*, 24[1980]:215-42.)

15. Evidence from another content-analysis study of the European decision makers in the period immediately preceding World War I supports this reactive relationship. It was found that as decision makers perceived themselves as the objects of hostility from other nations, they in turn expressed hostility that was directed toward the perceived sources of external hostility. See Dina A. Zinnes, "The Expression and Perception of Hostility in Prewar Crisis: 1914," in J. David Singer, ed., *Quantitative International Politics* (New York: Free Press, 1968), 85-119. See also, "Hostility in International Decision-Making," *Journal of Conflict Resolution*, 9, no. 3(1962):236-43.

16. Robert E. Osgood et al., *Retreat from Empire?* (Baltimore: Johns Hopkins University Press, 1973), 5.

17. Although only the correlation coefficients are reported, the SPSS regression program was employed for these analyses. In the programming of the regression analyses when no lags were used, the appropriate perceptual or behavioral variables were programmed as the dependent variables.

18. There is also some support in the US to PRC/A-SINE and US to PRC/PS variables.

19. Although the analyses in the present chapter exclude 1975-76, Angola is the clearest evidence that Kissinger's evaluations are based on perceptions of global activity. The analyses in this chapter are designed so that they are *not* affected by the Angola situation, in order to indicate that other, less prominent events may affect the perception-behavior relationship. Omission of 1975-76 also permits discussion of the results without their being dominated by a single, very important foreign-policy situation.

20. *White House Years,* 712.

CHAPTER 9

1. Note also that, of the eight correlations of USSR to US/A-SINE and USSR to US/PS with U.S. events-data variables, seven are in the predicted direction.

2. See Maurice A. East and Philip M. Gregg, "Factors Influencing Cooperation and Conflict in the International System," *International Studies Quarterly*, 11, no. 3(1967): 244-69, and Charles A. McClelland and Gary D. Hoggard, "Conflict Patterns in the Interactions Among Nations," in James N. Rosenau, ed., *International Politics and Foreign Policy* (New York: Free Press, 1969).

3. See Henry Kissinger, *White House Years* (Boston: Little, Brown 1979), 128-29. See also Charles E. Osgood, *An Alternative to War or Surrender* (Urbana: University of Illinois Press, 1962).

4. Kjell Goldmann and Johan Lagerkranz, "Neither Tension Nor Detente: East-West Relations in Europe, 1971-75," *Cooperation and Conflict,* 12(1977):251-264. For a more complete description of the methodology used, see Goldmann, *Tension and Detente in*

Bipolar Europe (Stockholm: Esselte Studium, 1974), and "East-West Tension in Europe, 1947-1970: A Conceptual Analysis and a Quantitative Description," *World Politics,* 26(1973):106-25. The analyses discussed here were presented by Goldmann at the conference "Research Agendas for the Study of International Conflict," the annual meeting of the Midwest Section of the Peace Science Society (International), Ann Arbor, Michigan, April 1978.

5. For a brief but useful overview of Soviet-Chinese relations during the time under consideration here, see Harold Hinton, *The Sino-Soviet Confrontation: Implications for the Future* (New York: Crane, Russak, 1976), especially Chapters 4 and 8.

6. The data available made analysis up to 1973 the most convenient. The last year of the Nixon presidency is omitted.

7. As he waited for the Senate to confirm him as secretary of state, Kissinger was asked at a press conference. "Do you prefer to be called Mr. Secretary or Dr. Secretary?" Kissinger's answer, couched in his usual self-deprecating humor, was: "I don't stand on protocol. If you just call me Excellency it will be okay." (Marvin and Bernard Kalb, *Kissinger* [New York: Dell, 1974], 506.)

8. See Morton Halperin, *Bureaucratic Politics and Foreign Policy* (Washington, D.C.: Brookings Institution, 1974), Chapters 3 and 5.

9. The formula is presented in John Johnston, *Econometric Methods,* Second Edition (New York: McGraw-Hill, 1972), 207.

10. For the other significant Chow F statistic, the Durbin-Watson indicated autocorrelation.

11. For example, see the interview in *Encounter,* November 1978, especially pp. 9-10.

CHAPTER 10

1. George Liska, *Beyond Kissinger: Ways of Conservative Statecraft* (Baltimore: Johns Hopkins University Press, 1975).

2. William Pfaff, "Kissinger and Nixon," *New Yorker,* 13 September 1982, 156-71.

3. In *White House Years,* Kissinger comments on the relationship between crisis and the operation of idiosyncratic influences: "During the period of crisis the elements from which policy is shaped suddenly become fluid. In the resulting upheaval the statesman must act under constant pressure. Paradoxically, this confers an unusual capacity for creative action; everything suddenly depends on the ability to dominate and impose coherence on confused and seemingly random occurrences." (p. 597).

4. Graham T. Allison, *Essence of Decision* (Boston: Little, Brown, 1971).

APPENDIX

1. Holsti, *Content Analysis for the Social Sciences and Humanities* (Reading, Mass.: Addison-Wesley, 1969), 64.

2. Holsti, in "The Belief System and National Images: John Foster Dulles and the Soviet Union" (Ph.D. diss., Stanford University, 1962), notes that, "Because this method first reduces the theme to its parts and specifies which elements of the theme are to be scored, it can be used with a high degree of reliability. Coders can be trained rapidly" (126).

3. These documents were: "Moral Purposes and Public Choices" (Address to the third Pacem in Terris conference, Washington, D.C., October 8, 1973), *Department of State Bulletin* 69, no. 1792 (October 1973):525-31; "Secretary Kissinger Holds Meeting with UN Secretary General," *Department of State Bulletin* 73, no. 1893(September 1975):479-80;

"America's Destiny: the Global Context" (Address at the University of Wyoming, 4 February 1976, question and answer session), *Department of State Bulletin* 74, no. 1914(March 1976):257-61; "Secretary Kissinger Interviewed by Sigma Delta Chi Panel at Atlanta," *Department of State Bulletin* 74, no. 1918(March 1976):385-93; "Secretary Kissinger Interviewed for Hearst Newspapers," *Department of State Bulletin* 74, no. 1928(June 1976):726-31; "America and Asia" (Address to the Seattle Rotary, 22 July 1976, question and answer session), *Department of State Bulletin* 75, no. 1938(August 1976): 226-31.

4. Rules for coding are given in detail in Charles E. Osgood, Sol Saporta, and J. C. Nunnally, "Evaluative Assertion Analysis," *Litera,* 3(1956), and in Ole R. Holsti, "The Belief System and National Images," Appendix.

5. Osgood et al., "Evaluative Assertion Analysis," 57.

6. Ibid. 47.

7. See also G. Cleveland Wilhoit, "A Methodological Critique of the Application of Evaluative Assertions Analysis to Studies of Media Performance," Bureau of Media Research, School of Journalism, Indiana University, April, 1977.

8. Holsti, "The Belief System and National Images" (Ph.D. diss.), 151.

9. Henry Kissinger, *A World Restored* (Boston: Houghton-Mifflin, 1957), 325-30.

10. The same trend occurs in the comparison of In U.S.S.R. to In China, but, due to the very low number of public statements about the Soviet Union made in China, the differences cannot be discussed with the same confidence.

Index

access, 3, 158
Acheson, Dean, 47, 58-59
Alexander I (czar), 53
Allison, Graham T., 6, 9, 161
Allon, Yigal, 23
Anderson, Paul, 84
Angola: and detente, 69, 71, 107, 159; Soviet-Cuban activity in, 155; as a case study, 197 n. 19
Arafat, Yasir, 72
Army Special Training Program (ASTP), 19-20, 34
Assad, Hafez al-, 38
attributional behavior. *See* evaluative assertion analysis; Kissinger, Henry A.: Soviet Union, images of; China, images of
Axelrod, Robert, 175 n. 17
Azar, Edward E., 126
Azar-Sloan scale for international events, 126, 127

backchannels, 65
balance of power systems, 184 n. 38
Ball, George, 66, 107
Barber, James David, 29, 33, 39-40, 180 n. 61
Bay of Pigs, 70
belief system, 3-4, 45, 176 n. 27
Bell, David, 83
Bensheim, Germany, 21
Berelson, Bernard, 83
Berlin Wall, 27
biased triad, 130-31, 146-47, 160
biographical method, 16-17
Bismarck, Prince Otto von, 52, 67, 187 n. 91
Bismarckian policy, 160-61

Blumenfeld, Ralph, 3, 16, 20, 178 n. 8
Bowie, Robert, 26
Bowles, Chester, 26
Brandon, Henry, 5, 80
Brandt, Willy, 48
brinksmanship, 187 n. 99
Brody, Richard, 188 n. 3
Brzezinski, Zbigniew, 178 n. 20
Bundy, McGeorge, 25, 26, 27, 178 n. 25, 186 n. 82
"Bureaucracy and Policy Making" (Kissinger), 64
bureaucratic politics: during Nixon administration, 5-6, 159; and role, 152, 161; and Kennedy administration, 186 n. 82

Caplow, Theodore, 124-25, 160
Carter, Jimmy, 17
Carter administration, 73, 159
Castlereagh, Robert Stewart, Lord, 53, 69, 172
Ceausescu, Nicolae, 193 n. 21
Center for International Affairs, 26
"Central Issues of American Foreign Policy" (Kissinger), 185 n. 51
Chiang Kai-shek, 188 n. 3
Chou En-lai: as a statesman, 32, 55, 115, 187 n. 97; style, 194 nn. 14, 15
Christie, Richard, 41, 181 n. 87
Church, Frank, 48
City College of New York, 19, 22
Clay, Lucius, 26
cognitive approach to study of foreign policy. *See* psychological approach to study of foreign policy
Cohen, Raymond, 42
Cold War, 147-48, 152